MUZZLED

JUAN WILLIAMS
MUZZLED

THE ASSAULT ON HONEST DEBATE

CROWN PUBLISHERS
NEW YORK

CROWN and the Crown colophon are registered trademarks
of Random House, Inc.

Library of Congress Cataloging-in-Publication Data
Williams, Juan.
Muzzled : the assault on honest debate / Juan Williams.
p. cm.
Includes index.
1. Freedom of speech—United States. 2. Political correctness—
United States. 3. Williams, Juan—Political and social views. I. Title.
JC591.W55 2011
323.44'30973—dc22
2011016800

ISBN 978-0-307-95201-1
eISBN 978-0-307-95203-5

PRINTED IN THE UNITED STATES OF AMERICA

Jacket design by Ben Gibson

1   3   5   7   9   10   8   6   4   2

First Edition

This book is dedicated to Crown Books, Fox News, FoxNews.com, *The Hill* newspaper, thehill.com, and the American Program Bureau—Guiding Lights in the storm—standing tall in the faith that speaking the truth is the heart of great journalism.

"For why should my freedom be judged by another's conscience?"

—1 CORINTHIANS 10:29

CONTENTS

CHAPTER 1

I SAID WHAT I MEANT

I AM A BIGOT. I hate Muslims. I am a fomenter of hate and intolerance. I am a black guy who makes fun of Muslims for the entertainment of white racists. I am brazen enough to do it on TV before the largest cable news audience in America. And I am such a fraud that while I was spreading hate to a conservative audience at night I delivered a totally different message to a large liberal morning-radio audience. I fooled the radio folks into thinking of me as a veteran Washington correspondent and the author of several acclaimed books celebrating America's battles against racism.

My animus toward Muslims may be connected to my desire for publicity and the fact that I am mentally unstable. And I am also a fundamentally bad person. I repeatedly ignored warnings to stop violating my company's standards for news analysis. And I did this after repeated warnings from my patient employer. Therefore, my former employers made the right decision when they fired me. In fact, they should be praised for doing it, and rewarded with taxpayer money. Their only sin was that they didn't fire me sooner.

This is just a sampling of some of the reaction to National Public Radio's decision to fire me last year after a ten-year career as a national talk show host, senior correspondent, and senior news analyst. They were not taken from the anonymous comments section of a YouTube page or the reams of hate mail that flooded my in-box in the days before the firing. No, this is the response from the NPR management whom I had served with great success for nearly a decade. It is also the reaction from national advocacy groups like the Council for American Islamic Relations (CAIR), whose work I had generally admired and occasionally defended over the years. Joining them was a small, knee-jerk mob of liberal commentators, including a *New York Times* editorial writer, who defended NPR as an important news source deserving federal funding even if it meant defaming me—"he made foolish and hurtful remarks about Muslims." Cable TV star Rachel Maddow, a fervent champion of free speech, agreed that I had a right to say what was on my mind, but in her opinion the comments amounted to bigotry. I had a right to speak but no right to "keep [my] job." NPR also found support among leftist intellectuals who regularly brag about defending the rights of the little guy but had no problem siding with a big institution over an individual journalist when the journalist was me. One writer said I had long ingratiated myself with conservatives and I had gotten what was coming to me. His conclusion about me: "Sleep with dogs, get fleas."

What did I do that warranted the firing and the ad hominem attacks that preceded and followed?

I simply told the truth.

Looking back on the torrential media coverage surrounding my dismissal, I am struck by how little of it tells the full story of what actually happened. Basic facts were distorted, important context was not provided, and personal attacks were treated as truth. The lack of honest reporting about the firing and the events that led up to it was not just unfair— most of it was flat-out lies.

In this first chapter, I will tell you the full story of what happened to me. My purpose in doing this is not to get people to feel sorry for me. The goal of this book is to set the record straight and to use my experience in what amounts to a political and media whacking as the starting point for a much-needed discussion about the current, sad state of political discourse in this country. It is time to end the ongoing assault against honest debate in America.

This story begins with a typical Monday night for me. I went to the Fox News Channel's bureau in Washington, DC, to do a satellite interview for Bill O'Reilly's prime-time show, *The O'Reilly Factor*. I have appeared on Bill's show hundreds of times since I joined Fox in 1997. The drama here is watching me, a veteran Washington journalist with centrist liberal credentials, enter the lion's den to debate the fiery, domineering, right-of-center O'Reilly. When I do the show I am almost always paired with a conservative or Republican guest. My usual jousting partner is Mary Katharine Ham, a conservative writer. This strikes some critics as stacking the deck by having two conservatives take me on. In reality the combination offers viewers a range of opinions, because O'Reilly is unpredictable. He listens and admits when he is wrong. Ham is an honest debate partner who is willing to call them as she sees them and to veer off any conservative party line. If the deck is stacked, it's because there can be no doubt that this is Bill's party and he runs the show. The audience tunes in to see him, and they keep tuning in because they love his cranky but vulnerable personality. He is a star and he can be intimidating, but I see no need to back down in a debate and I genuinely respect him. I think he respects me too. Along with Mary Katharine, Bill and I share a sense that we can disagree without the personal attacks and put-downs. I hear from viewers that the segment is a hit because they learn something from watching people with different political convictions and viewpoints—but also with affection for each other—try to make sense of emotional, political issues. We don't play the cheap TV debate trick—often used to stoke TV political debate shows and soap operas—of creating false tensions by shouting over each other and calling each other liars. We treat each other as sincere people with integrity and the courage of our convictions. But make no mistake, we are painfully direct with each other. To survive on the show, you'd better know how to think quickly and counterpunch with a fast, pithy point or you'll be left behind with less time to talk, reduced to what Bill calls a "pinhead."

The intensity and the variety of views and insights that come from such debate is one of the reasons I enjoy my job at Fox. The news channel looks for the conservative slant in the stories it selects to tell, and its leading personalities in prime time are right-wingers. But you can hear all sides of the debate on Fox.

Our segment led the O'Reilly show that Monday night in late October. The topic for debate was the effect of political correctness on the country's ability to talk about the threat posed by radical Muslims.

O'Reilly set up the segment by talking about his recent experience on ABC's daytime program *The View*, where he had discussed the proposal to build an Islamic community center near the site of the September 11 attacks in downtown Manhattan. O'Reilly expressed his agreement with the millions of Americans who felt it was inappropriate. When asked by cohost Whoopi Goldberg why it was inappropriate, O'Reilly said, "Because Muslims killed us on 9/11." This prompted Goldberg and Joy Behar to walk off the set in protest. Barbara Walters criticized her cohosts, saying they should not have done that—we should be able to have discussions "without washing our hands, screaming and walking off stage." They did return after O'Reilly apologized for not being clear that he meant the country was attacked not by all Muslims but by extremist radical Muslims.

The episode got national attention as a celebrity TV mashup between the conservative, brash, male O'Reilly and two furious, liberal women. But a serious analysis of the heart of the exchange—the truth and the lies—never took place. So O'Reilly took it to the very top of his next show, with me as his guest. At the start of the debate, Bill invited me, indeed challenged me, to tell him where he went wrong in stating the fact that "Muslims killed us there," in the 9/11 attacks. I accepted Bill's challenge and began by crafting my argument with a point of agreement—an approach intended to get Bill and Bill's audience to listen to my concerns about what he had said on *The View*. First, I said he was right on the facts; political correctness can cause people to ignore the facts and become so paralyzed that they don't deal with reality. And the reality, I said, is that the people who attacked us on 9/11 proudly identified themselves as devout Muslims and said that they attacked in the name of Allah.

To illustrate my appreciation of the underlying truth of his statement, I then made an admission about my feelings. I said that I worry when I'm getting on an airplane and see people dressed in garb that identifies them first and foremost as Muslims. This was not a bigoted statement or a policy position. It was not reasoned opinion. It was simply an honest statement of my fears after the terrorist attacks of 9/11 by radical Muslims who professed that killing Americans was part of their religious duty and would earn them the company of virgins in heaven. I don't think that I'm the only American who feels this way. Anyone who has lived through the last few years of attacks and attempted attacks knows that radical Islam continues to pose a threat to the United States and to much of the world. That threat had been expressed in federal court the very week before the O'Reilly show, when the unsuccessful Times Square bomber, Faisal Shahzad, bragged in court that he was just one of the first to come in a Muslim-inspired fight against the United States. "Brace yourselves," he said defiantly, "because the war with Muslims has just begun."

So there is no doubt that there's a real war being waged and that people are trying to kill us.

Intelligence agencies worldwide, even in countries with a majority of Muslims, agree that Muslim extremists with a murderous jihadist mind-set are recruiting others to carry out the bloodletting against the United States, Western Europe, and their global allies. I wanted Bill and his audience to know that I was not there to play a game of pretending that everyone in the world is a good soul deserving of a hug and a Coke.

Having established agreement with Bill on the underlying facts, I began the next line of reasoning in my argument. I challenged O'Reilly not to make rash judgments about people of any faith. I took the fight to O'Reilly because I felt that he had done exactly that in his comments about Muslims on *The View*. I urged him to choose his words carefully when he talks about the 9/11 attacks, so as not to provoke bigotry against all Muslims, the vast majority of whom are peaceful people with no connection to terrorism. I pointed out that Timothy McVeigh—along with the Atlanta Olympic Park bomber and the people who protest against gay rights at military funerals—are Christians, but we journalists rarely identify them by their religion. I made it clear that all Americans have to be careful not to let fears—such as my own when I see people in Muslim clothes getting on a plane—color our judgment or lead to the violation of another person's constitutional rights, whether to fly on a plane, to build a mosque, to carry the Koran, or to drive a New York cab without the fear of having their throat slashed—which had happened earlier in 2010.

Mary Katharine joined the debate to say that it is important for everyone to make the distinction between moderate and extreme Islam. She said conservative support for the wars in Afghanistan and Iraq is predicated on the idea that the United States can help build up moderate Islamic elements in those countries and push out the extremists. I agreed with her and later added that we don't want anyone attacked on American streets because "they heard rhetoric from Bill O'Reilly and they act crazy." Bill complained that he was tired of "being careful" in talking about radical Muslim terrorists but agreed that the man who slashed the cabby was a "nut" and said the same about the Florida pastor who wanted to burn the Koran.

My point in recounting the on-air debate blow by blow is to show that it was in keeping with the great American tradition of argument. It was a fair, full-throated, and honest discourse about an important issue facing the country. There was no bigotry expressed, no crude provocation, and no support for anti-Muslim sentiments of any kind. Just the opposite was true. I left the studio thinking I'd helped to dispel some of the prejudice toward Muslims and moved an important national conversation forward in some modest way.

The next day I flew to Chicago to give a speech to the leaders of a Catholic health-care system. It was a 7:00 a.m. flight, so the terminal at Reagan National Airport in DC was fairly empty when I arrived at around 6:00 a.m. It was easy for other travelers to pick me out as I waited at the newsstand and while I was in line to buy coffee. Several said they had seen the segment and told me their stories of being nervous on planes and trains when encountering people in Muslim garb. One young woman, who worked for a liberal senator, also thanked me for "manning up"—a hot political term at the end of the midterm campaign that year—about the danger of letting our fears lead us to become "haters." When I got to Chicago, I heard similar comments from people at the hotel and even during the question-and-answer period following my speech.

While I was waiting to fly out of Chicago's jam-packed O'Hare International Airport that evening, a middle-aged man in a business suit made his way through the crowd to get to me. He looked to be of Arab descent and asked, "Are you Juan Williams?" I told him that I was, and we shook hands.

He told me that he was a Muslim. He'd apparently watched O'Reilly the previous night. I didn't know where this was going—what he would say next. Speaking with pride, he confided that he had recently decided to get involved with Muslim political organizations in Washington because he could no longer tolerate negative stereotypes of Muslims as violent and unpatriotic. Then he told me a moving story. He said his son had recently seen him put a letter with Arabic writing in his home office's paper shredder. The twelve-year-old asked his dad if he was shredding the letter because he didn't want to put it in the trash and risk having neighbors see it and realize that the family is Muslim. The father explained to his son that he was shredding the letter because it included the name of Allah and it was wrong to throw something sacred in with the garbage.

What struck him, he said, was that his little boy thought it was shameful to be a Muslim. He said his son's embarrassment had made him realize he was making a mistake by thinking that just by being a normal suburban businessman he was creating a positive image of Muslims in America. He said that in light of ongoing controversies, he realized he had to speak out against people who miscast all Muslims as terrorists and to take a stand against Muslim extremists who feed the negative images of Islam.

The man thanked me for comments made on the O'Reilly show because he feared the kind of anti-Muslim sentiment I was speaking out against.

One of the nicest things about being a television personality is the fans who approach you in airports and restaurants. Even the most strident conservatives who watch Fox will come up to me and say that while they may disagree with almost everything I say, they enjoy listening to me. Sometimes they will ask me to sign an autograph or pose for a picture, and I'm happy to oblige because I appreciate intellectual honesty. But there are also those rare moments—like when that man came up to me at O'Hare—when people compliment a point you made publicly and appreciate the reasoning behind it. This was one of those moments.

Little did I know that as I was talking to this man, a well-organized campaign was being waged against me by CAIR and other organizations that claimed to represent him. They set up a Facebook group and circulated a sample letter to be filled out by their members and sent to NPR. Apparently upset that I had offered O'Reilly support for any part of his comments about Muslims on *The View*, CAIR's letter quoted only the first part of my comments. This was an unfair distortion, with no hint of the full context. The author attacked me for "irresponsible and inflammatory comments [that] would not be tolerated if they targeted any other racial, ethnic or religious minority" and went on to say that "they should not pass without action by NPR. I respectfully request that your network take appropriate action in response to Mr. Williams' intolerant comments."

Media Matters, the far-left Web site that purports to show daily, if not hourly, instances of conservative bias on Fox, accused me of bigotry and called for me to be fired. Of course, it had been urging NPR to fire me for years because I appear on Fox. Some of my colleagues at Fox have likened Media Matters to a determined stalker and sarcastically thank it on air for contributing to Fox's high ratings.

I didn't take any of this too seriously. To speak and write about politics, people, and culture on a national platform— at Fox and NPR or in books and the *Washington Post*—is to quickly realize that the blogs, the phones, and the mailbag are going to be filled with criticism. My judgments are constantly questioned, my word choices are scrutinized, and alarms are raised even when things go unsaid. As far as I could tell, the criticism of what I had said on the O'Reilly show had little substance. These attacks amounted to weak, baseless distortions of a fast-paced debate on a difficult subject. Any fair-minded person taking a look at the entire conversation could easily see that my comments had been twisted to serve the political agendas of CAIR and Media Matters. And my conversations with viewers about the show revealed no such confusion, no backlash against my stand in opposition to anti-Muslim bigotry. So I dismissed the whole thing as a minor snit. I'd seen much worse when a powerful politician didn't like some comment I'd made or when I'd actually misstated a fact of substance in offering an opinion. A lot of that comes with the job, and in some ways it reassures me that people are listening and believe I have influence.

The next day I took the shuttle to New York. A few minutes after I landed in New York, my cell phone rang. A friend at a Washington advocacy group said she wanted to see how I was doing because of the e-mail going around her office calling for me to be fired from NPR for my comments about Muslims on Fox. I thanked her for the support but told her that people with vested interests in any hot-button debate always take shots at me—Republicans and Democrats, blacks and whites, Israelis and Palestinians, pro-life and pro-choice.

I went about my work at Fox that day, talking politics as the midterm elections heated up. Shortly after 5:00 p.m., I checked my cell phone and saw that I had a missed call from Ellen Weiss, the vice president of the news division at NPR. When I got her on the phone, she told me she had been inundated with complaints about my comments to O'Reilly on Monday night. Ellen said I had crossed the line and essentially accused me of bigotry. She gave me no chance to tell her my side of the story. She focused on the admission of my fear of people dressed in Muslim garb at the airport as prima facie evidence of my bigotry. She said there are people who wear Muslim garb to work at NPR and they were offended by my comments. She never suggested that I had discriminated against anyone. Instead, Ellen continued to ask me what I had really meant. I told her I had meant exactly what I said. She retorted that she did not sense remorse from me. I said I had nothing to apologize for. I had made an honest statement about my feelings. I urged her to go back and look at the full transcript. Had she done that, she would have seen that I was arguing against exactly the kind of prejudicial snap judgments she was now accusing me of making. But Ellen would hear none of it. She claimed she had reviewed the segment. She informed me that I had violated NPR's values for editorial commentary and my contract as a news analyst was being terminated.

I was stunned. I said that this was an outrage, that it made no sense. I appealed to her to reconsider before firing me. I asked if she had some personal animus toward me. I pointed out that I had not made my comments on NPR. When she asked if I would have said the same thing on NPR, I said yes, because I believe in telling people the truth about my feelings and opinions, regardless of the venue. I asked why she would fire me without speaking to me face to face and reviewing the entire episode. At that point she bluntly told me there was nothing I could say or do to change her mind. She added that the decision had been confirmed above her and that there was no point in meeting in person. The decision had already been made, and there was nothing I could do about it.

Years earlier, NPR had tried to stop me from appearing on Fox. Some NPR listeners had written to ask why a top NPR personality was showing up on a conservative cable channel. I reminded the management back then that I was working for Fox before NPR signed me to host its afternoon talk show. And I pointed out that other NPR staff appeared on CNN, as well as news discussion shows where they expressed opinions, without any pressure to shut them down. I was told that Fox had grown into the number one cable news network and was a loud, controversial, conservative network at that. My response was that debate on Fox was first rate—that was why the audience was growing—and no one at Fox tried to tell me what to say. I also pointed out that I was advertising the NPR brand with every appearance before Fox's large audience. Then it was suggested that I not express my opinions on Fox. I said I expressed my opinions every day as an NPR host and I did not say anything on Fox or in my books or newspaper columns that was different from what I said on NPR. Different NPR ombudsmen wrote about the issue over the years and concluded that while having my face on Fox bothered a few at NPR who hated Fox's conservative approach to the news, it did not amount to a sin against NPR's standards of journalism.

When Ellen Weiss became NPR's top news executive, she

renewed the discussion about my work for Fox, telling me that she didn't like Fox's format. She said its fast-paced debates provoked pointed expression of opinions. On Fox, she observed, liberals are outnumbered by conservatives. I replied that NPR often edited interviews and even debate segments to make them move faster and sharpen contrasting viewpoints. As for the political imbalance she saw on Fox, I asked if she realized that liberals outnumbered conservatives at NPR. She responded that any controversial stand I took on Fox compromised my role as a journalist at NPR. I disagreed. But she outranked me. She insisted that I not identify myself as an NPR employee when I appeared on O'Reilly or any other Fox prime-time show.

To me this was absurd. I thought she was condescending to NPR listeners by suggesting they could not distinguish between my roles at NPR—as a talk show host, correspondent, and analyst—and my role as an occasional debating partner for conservative TV personalities on Fox.

It was the latest in a troubling history of high-ranking NPR editors and producers expressing concern about my journalistic independence because of my role at Fox. Years before that incident, NPR officials asked me to help them get an interview with President George W. Bush. Bush's top aides felt NPR had been unfair to Bush during the 2000 campaign, and they kept NPR at a distance once Bush was in the White House. But some NPR officials noted that I had long-standing relationships with some of the key players in the Bush White House due to my years as a political writer at the *Washington Post*. They asked me to take the lead for NPR in trying to get an interview with the president. Later, when other anchors and political reporters asked why I was leading the effort, I heard that some NPR managers suggested that the Bush White House was more likely to grant the interview because of my appearances on Fox. There was an element of petty jealousy that irritated me, but it was also true that the Bush White House had a good relationship with Fox. Over several years I held meetings and set up dinners to try to ease the tensions, and I got several Bush officials to appear on NPR for interviews with me and with others. When it served their purposes, NPR officials were all too happy to use my connection to Fox.

When the president finally agreed to an NPR interview, the offer was for me to interview him. After I did the interview, NPR played it in its entirety that evening on *All Things Considered*. The next day they devoted an entire segment to it on *Morning Edition*. The political editors and Weiss, who had helped me script the questions for the president, called and sent e-mails telling me they were thrilled with the interview. But the next day, Weiss phoned me to express anger that in the course of the interview I had prefaced a difficult question about the wars by saying to the president that Americans pray for him but don't understand some of his actions or policies. Weiss said some NPR staff felt it was wrong to say that Americans pray for him. I reminded her that in many churches it is customary to pray for the well-being of the president, governors, mayors, ministers, and other leaders. She claimed my words amounted to evidence that I was a bad journalist who was soft on Bush.

More than six months later, on the fiftieth anniversary of the Little Rock crisis, President Bush offered to do an NPR interview with me about race relations in America. NPR management, led by Weiss, refused the interview on the grounds that the White House had offered it to me and not to NPR's other correspondents and hosts. The implication was that I was in the administration's pocket. Had the NPR executives never heard my criticism of President Bush's handling of the war in Iraq or his curtailment of civil liberties in the war on terror? Was Weiss unaware that in looking for someone to discuss race relations with the president, the White House might have considered my expertise on the civil rights movement? I am the author of a best-selling history of the civil rights movement, *Eyes on the Prize—America's Civil Rights Years*, as well as an acclaimed biography of America's first black Supreme Court justice, *Thurgood Marshall—American Revolutionary*. My latest book, *Enough*, was about the state of black leadership in America and had found a place on the *New York Times* best-seller list. Weiss found it was easier to see me as a shill for the Bush administration. So I did the interview for Fox instead. While it made national headlines, it was never mentioned on NPR.

The shunning got worse when I wrote an editorial column for the *New York Times* that included criticism of the nation's teachers' unions for blocking school reform efforts. Weiss called me to her office to ask how NPR listeners could now trust my reporting on education. I reminded her that I was not the education beat reporter but a news analyst. Weiss was not persuaded. She wanted to review anything I wrote for newspapers, magazines, and even book proposals. When I said absolutely not, she insisted that I leave the staff and sign a new contract that limited my role at NPR to that of a news analyst. She said she wanted to insulate NPR against anything I said or wrote outside NPR. With the new contractual arrangement, she argued, management could claim I was not a staff member.

NPR is an important news outlet with a large, influential audience, and I enjoyed working there. And the NPR audience seemed to appreciate me. I was constantly being asked to visit local NPR stations and meet with listeners as well as staff. The volume of my e-mail, phone calls, letters, and requests for pledge week announcements suggested my pieces got tremendous reaction. The ombudsman said she got more response to my work than to any other voice on the network. I enjoyed my relationship with the audience, so I swallowed hard and accepted Weiss's deal. I thought my willingness to be a team player and the compromise I'd agreed to would be the end of it. But she immediately began to cut my salary and diminish my on-air appearances. Her management team began to treat me like a leper. I was prohibited from joining a panel of journalists questioning GOP presidential primary candidates in a debate. Senior editors, producers, and hosts told me that Weiss and her circle of other longtime NPR personalities—I worked there ten years and was still considered an outsider—hated Fox and hated me for appearing there. One NPR news executive told me directly that having on staff a black man with conservative social views who was personal friends with conservatives infuriated NPR's old guard. They were unhappy with *Enough*, in which I had praised Bill Cosby for his critique of black leaders. It was clear they wanted me out the door, the same executive said, because I did not fit their view of how a black person thinks—my independence of thought, my willingness to listen to a range of views, and my strong journalistic credentials be damned.

This effort to censor, control, and belittle me got so bad I was often ignored even when I gave NPR news tips. Anytime I gave them a scoop, NPR management wanted to know why Bush officials had conversations with me on background—meaning they could not be quoted by name—or with the promise that I would refer to them only generically as senior administration officials. When I replied that this was the way senior officials in Republican and Democratic administrations leaked sensitive information to journalists, Weiss and her team questioned my journalistic standards. The same dismissive attitude came into play as the Obama campaign came into the news. I had better sources among Obama's aides than anyone else at NPR. When other news organizations broke news of cabinet appointments for the Obama White House, it was often left to me to confirm the news, because no one else at NPR could do it. Yet even then I was treated as a suspect source and asked to reveal the names of sources I used to confirm the nominations. And when I took exclusive stories to NPR, I was told management was not comfortable with my getting exclusive interviews or breaking stories. They preferred that those stories come from other reporters, even if it meant that NPR did not get the stories first.

Yet when Fox let me talk about news from my inside sources, that made NPR leadership boil. After President Obama was elected, there was a lot of conversation in his camp about the upcoming role of his wife, Michelle Obama. Appearing on *The O'Reilly Factor*, I said I had been told by insiders that she would not be a policy adviser to the president but would focus on being an exemplary mom to her daughters. Obama's staff also said she planned to reach out to military families and to call attention to nutrition and obesity issues among children. I explained that this low-key approach had been planned for the First Lady, a highly opinionated Princeton- and Harvard-educated lawyer, because the new administration did not want a reprise of the moment during the campaign when Mrs. Obama had become a polarizing, racially charged figure. That episode had been triggered when she said her husband's success in the primaries made her proud of the United States "for the first time in my adult life."

Mary Katharine Ham, who was on the O'Reilly show with me that night, referring to Mrs. Obama's campaign controversy, said the future First Lady had to avoid dropping "sound bites like she did during the campaign." I added that Mrs. Obama was a potential liability for the president if she stirred racial tensions by getting her "Stokely Carmichael in a designer dress thing going." It was a catchy phrase that first came to me during conversations with Obama officials, who laughed at it. But it was reported all over left-wing blogs as an insult to Mrs. Obama. Weiss jumped on the overreaction and told me it was an inappropriate comment for an NPR journalist to make. I was called to the office of Ken Stern, then the acting president of NPR. He listened as I explained what had taken place and decided against censuring me.

But the chilly treatment persisted. When an Obama White House source mentioned that Vice President Biden was the leading critic of continuing the war in Afghanistan, despite growing calls for a "surge" from the military, I tried repeatedly to get NPR interested in the story. Several weeks later, when the same story became page-one news in the *New York Times* and *Washington Post*, NPR reported the story but claimed it had no time to air my analysis of this critical debate inside the administration. Similarly, when Elena Kagan was nominated to the Supreme Court by President Obama, my phone started ringing. Kagan had been a clerk at the Supreme Court for liberal icon Justice Thurgood Marshall, and both liberals and conservatives saw political dynamite in that relationship. The Right wanted to paint Kagan as another left-wing activist, while the Obama administration wanted to use her ties to Marshall to reassure its liberal base that Kagan was not a weak moderate about to be steamrolled by conservatives on the court. As a result of my biography of Justice Marshall, requests for interviews poured in to me personally, as well as through the communications department at NPR. Reporters as well as senate staffers, both Democrats and Republicans, wanted to talk to me. But when I pitched NPR's news division on a news analysis of the story based on my knowledge of the relationship, I was turned down. A week later, an NPR editor called to ask me to do the piece. I was elated. But only hours later she called back to say she had been told there was no room for "a Juan Williams piece."

At that point I became convinced Weiss and NPR were looking for a reason to fire me. The problem with just getting rid of me was that other NPR staff, including people who worked as straight news reporters, also appeared on opinion and debate TV shows. One news reporter even worked alongside me at Fox—national political correspondent Mara Liasson. Next, NPR management tried to get Liasson to quit Fox and leave me dangling as an aberrant journalist. NPR's management asked Liasson to spend a month watching Fox to decide whether it was a legitimate news organization worthy of her time and presence. This request from NPR came at the same time as an Obama White House effort to get other news organizations and the public to view Fox as a propaganda machine rather than a news operation. One news report described the administration's campaign as an effort to "delegitimize the [conservative] network" and pull the plug on its constant critiques of the president. Liberal columnist Jacob Weisberg wrote in *Newsweek* that any "respectable journalist—I'm talking to you, Mara Liasson—should stop appearing on [Fox] programs." A Politico story quoted one NPR executive as saying that "Fox uses Mara and Juan as cover" to counter claims that the network is right-wing and to gain journalistic legitimacy that gives it credibility.

That faulty logic is just a step away from saying that Americans are too stupid to independently judge the slant of news and talk shows and enjoy them for what they are—part of a range of views available in a robust American media. But the most dangerous idea behind the NPR effort to bully Liasson into quitting Fox was that journalists should not talk across the political divide, much less acknowledge that anyone on the other side of that divide might have something interesting or important to say.

Liasson eventually told NPR she saw nothing wrong with Fox and intended to continue working there.

This orthodoxy being applied like a straitjacket to journalists is a chilling attack on the free flow of ideas and debate. No one at Fox has ever told me what to say. The same, sadly, cannot be said of NPR.

As Weiss's long-standing antagonism toward my appearances on Fox continued to grow, the table was set, waiting for one misguided viewpoint to create a pretext for firing me. When CAIR and Media Matters distorted my comments on the Muslim terror threat, Weiss went to NPR's new president and CEO, Vivian Schiller, to make the case for getting rid of me.

After her dismissive late-afternoon call informing me that I was fired, Weiss and NPR released a statement announcing my termination that Wednesday night. I was working that same night on the panel for Sean Hannity's Fox program. I didn't mention anything about my firing on the show. When I got off the air, an NPR reporter called to ask me for a comment on it. I said I had to talk to my wife first. Sensing I was upset about something, Sean Hannity led me into a studio makeup room and—far away from our political arguments, just two friends talking—asked me what was wrong. I told him NPR had fired me; I feared for my career. NPR had the clout to tell one-sided stories disparaging me as a way to justify its action. I planned to call my agent to figure out how to tell people that I had been fired, but NPR was already putting the story out with its spin. I didn't know if I could compete with its megaphone and the admiration and loyalty of NPR's listeners. NPR's ties to other news organizations meant its attacks on me were going to get a lot of attention. And I didn't know if Fox, reacting to NPR's action, might view me as damaged goods, as a bigot who had no credibility. It was close to 11:00 p.m. when Hannity put a hand on my shoulder and told me not to worry. He picked up the wall phone and woke up Bill Shine, Fox's executive vice president for programming, who told him to tell me not to say anything about the firing until I met with Fox executives in the morning.

At 7:00 the next morning I appeared on *Fox and Friends*; I again said nothing about the firing. The hosts protected me by staying away from the controversy. But my face and story appeared all over the Internet, newspapers, and other cable networks. The story had gone viral. I was the center of a national media storm by the end of breakfast. Just after 8:00 a.m. I got a call from Bill Shine. He told me that Fox CEO Roger Ailes wanted to see me in his office at 10:00 a.m. Since I had talked with Hannity the night before, anxiety and pent-up anger and depression had all pulled at my emotions. I had not slept. At times I had cried over what had happened and over the potential destruction of my career—all because I had spoken my mind.

When I walked into Roger Ailes's office, accompanied by Shine and Michael Clemente, the senior vice president for news, Ailes greeted me with a smile and said, "Well, we can't have you working here." As my jaw dropped, he broke into a laugh. He waved his hand and said he was offering me a new three-year contract with an increased role at the network. Ailes asked me how much I made at NPR and said he'd make up every dime so I wouldn't have to go home and tell my wife and family we'd lost money because of NPR's actions. He also said he wanted to see how America's left-wing media and politicians reacted to a serious journalist being silenced this way. Ailes then released a statement that read, "Juan has been a staunch defender of liberal viewpoints since his tenure began at Fox News in 1997. . . . He's an honest man whose freedom of speech is protected by Fox News on a daily basis." I appeared on *The O'Reilly Factor* that night and guest-hosted it the following night. Bill really went to bat for me, for which

I am grateful. He called for an immediate suspension of all public money to NPR and correctly pointed out that liberal billionaire George Soros had donated $1.8 million to NPR the week before. Soros had also given money to Media Matters in the past.

Conservatives like Brit Hume and Bill Kristol, whom I had debated ferociously over the years on *Fox News Sunday,* stuck up for me and blasted NPR. Even more heartening was the support I received from fellow Fox commentators whom I had criticized when they were in positions of political power. Sarah Palin, Newt Gingrich, Karl Rove, and Rick Santorum all defended my right to free speech and called out NPR for its hypocrisy.

Sarah Palin surprised me most of all. Ever since she was picked by John McCain to be his vice presidential running mate in the 2008 campaign, I have questioned her qualifications and her command of the issues facing the country. I was especially tough on her for quitting her job as governor of Alaska less than two years into her term. Yet Palin wrote on her Facebook page: "I don't expect Juan Williams to support me (he's said some tough things about me in the past)—but I will always support his right and the right of all Americans to speak honestly about the threats this country faces. And for Juan, speaking honestly about these issues isn't just his right, it's his job. Up until yesterday, he was doing that job at NPR. Firing him is their loss."

A wave of phone calls and e-mails to NPR complained about my firing. The ombudsman, Alicia Shepard, said the day after my firing was "a day like none I've experienced since coming to NPR" three years earlier. I was told the phones "rang like an alarm bell with no off button." NPR got "more than 8,000 e-mails, a record with nothing a close second." She said most of the callers wanted NPR to hire me back immediately. So many people tried to use the "Contact Us" form on NPR's Web site that it crashed. One posting on the Web site, described as typical by the *Los Angeles Times*, read: "In one arrogant move the NPR exposed itself for the leftist thought police they really are."

Apparently NPR did not agree. The day after my firing, NPR CEO Vivian Schiller told an audience at the Atlanta Press Club that I should have kept my feelings about Muslims between me and my "psychiatrist or [my] publicist—take your pick." The videotape of her comment, complete with the look of pure contempt on her face as she spoke, appeared across the country on news shows throughout the day. She was criticized for her personal attacks on me by NPR's own ombudsman. Schiller later issued a statement of public apology for her words on the NPR Web site, although she never gave me the courtesy of a personal call. A week later she sent a FedEx envelope to my house with a letter saying she was very busy, she did not know how to reach me, and I needed to contact her secretary to set up a time to talk with her. I wrote back that since she had had no time to talk to me before firing me I saw no need to talk to her now.

In the media, Schiller tried to justify the firing by saying that my defenders failed to appreciate that "news analysts may not take personal public positions on controversial issues; doing so undermines their credibility as analysts, and that is what's happened in this situation."

Some leading liberals rallied to Schiller's side. Andrew

Sullivan said my admission of nervousness around people in Muslim garb at airports amounted to a "working definition of bigotry." Playing on the fact that I am black, Sullivan asked if a white person who feared being mugged by a black man dressed in "classic thug get-up" wouldn't be guilty of bigotry. Glenn Greenwald at Salon.com wrote that my comments amounted to "giving cover to incendiary right-wing attacks" on Muslims. Keith Olbermann, on MSNBC, claimed I was a bigot and "obtuse" and said NPR's decision to end my contract was "anything but a First Amendment issue." He added, with disdain for the people who voiced support for me: "We have to stamp it on people's foreheads so they can read it backwards in the mirror." Rachel Maddow at MSNBC said my words reminded her of appeals to white racism by Republicans in the South during the 1960s. And Michael Tomasky, a writer for London's *The Guardian*, wrote of me, "[He chose] to ingratiate himself with O'Reilly and his viewers with that Foxy rhetoric. In a sense, Williams got what was coming to him." He was the journalist who said, "Sleep with dogs, get fleas."

To be candid, the attacks from these liberal intellectuals stung me. I grew up as a liberal in New York City. As a black child during the height of the civil rights movement, Republicans seemed to me to be a bunch of Archie Bunkers, the TV character who called his son-in-law a "meathead" for welcoming black people into his neighborhood and protesting the Vietnam War. This all led me to believe the right wing had a monopoly on cruelty, intolerance, and ideological rigidity. Now, at fifty-five, it was painfully clear to me that the left wing, represented by NPR and liberal lobbying groups, had become likewise intolerant of people who did not agree with them. In demonizing Fox News and the right wing as a powerful conspiracy of wealthy, militaristic bigots—antiblack, antifeminist, and antigay—they hid their own prejudice against different points of view. They do not believe in tolerance. They do not care about open-minded debate. They care first and foremost about liberal orthodoxy. If you dare to challenge it or deviate from it even slightly, you will be punished.

My point is that what happened to me was not about me alone. It was an assault on journalism and honest debate. We need to protect a free-flowing, respectful national conversation in our country. Today, such honest debate about the issues becomes collateral damage in an undeclared war by those who make accusations of racism and bigotry whenever their political positions are challenged.

I use the emotionally charged word "war" very deliberately. My comments about Muslims on Fox were twisted and deliberately taken out of context by Weiss. She was able to use that distortion, along with a general view of Fox News as bad guys, to engage in a vigilante-style attack on me. NPR's standards for its journalistic ethics, which I supposedly broke, seemed to apply only to me. When Nina Totenberg, NPR's reporter on legal issues, famously said that a conservative U.S. senator and his children ought to "get AIDS from a transfusion," she was not fired. Nor was NPR news analyst Cokie Roberts when she said that Fox's Glenn Beck was un-American and called him a terrorist.

In their hubris and fury at me, Vivian Schiller and Weiss accepted the wacky idea that I legitimize Bill O'Reilly and Sean Hannity because I *talk* with them. Did they not notice that I was almost always challenging Bill and trading ideas with Sean? Bill and Sean are major forces in American culture, media, and politics, whether or not I appear on their shows. And I believe it is important that they remain open to having their audiences hear different points of view. I continue to go on their shows and debate their ideas because I believe Americans of all political stripes are better off when they hear an experienced political observer offer an honest appraisal of the issues and the other side's point of view.

Of course, condoning political polarization goes well beyond just NPR. One-party dominance and one-sided thinking have become the rule rather than the exception in much of the media. We are creating a culture in the newsroom where facts, context, and insight take a backseat to fear of complaints of insensitivity, accusations of racism, and all sorts of phony charges of bigotry. On the Left, the politically correct police are increasingly out in force. This leads people in public life to be sent to the media equivalent of the gulag—fired, shunned, silenced—for raising the wrong questions and displaying independent thought. When I see charlatans and prevaricators sacrificing the standards of journalism and free speech on the altar of political correctness, I am compelled to speak out.

Daniel Schorr, my fellow NPR commentator, who died last year, used to talk about the initial shock of finding himself on President Nixon's enemies list. I can only imagine Dan's disgust if he saw that NPR today has created one of its own.

A lot of people in this country are tired of being afraid to speak out. I think that's part of why so many came out so strongly in support of me. Whoopi Goldberg, for example, who walked off the set when Bill O'Reilly made his initial comment about Muslims being responsible for 9/11, came to my defense after I was fired. She said NPR sent the "wrong message" about the need for people to speak up about their feelings and have an honest, respectful discussion of tough issues. "NPR, get yourself together," she said. Jon Stewart dedicated a segment of *The Daily Show* to defending the importance of giving people room to speak their minds. At his rally on the national mall, Stewart offered support for me, saying, "The press is our immune system—if we overreact to everything, we actually get sicker—and perhaps eczema." James Rainey, writing a column in the *Los Angeles Times,* said Schiller and Weiss "treated a moment of candor like it was a capital crime," while ignoring the rest of what I had to say in opposition to anti-Muslim rhetoric. "I thought this was the sort of candid conversation about race and ethnicity we were supposed to have," he wrote. "Didn't President Obama suggest that only open dialogue would chip away hardened misconceptions?"

The *Washington Post* editorial page made a similar point: "In a democracy the media must foster a free and robust political debate, even if such debate may, at times, offend some people." The *Post* concluded that in debating O'Reilly I "was attempting to do exactly what a responsible commentator should do: speak honestly without being inflammatory."

I believe I've been vindicated in the months since my firing. Ellen Weiss resigned in January 2011 in the wake of the public's response to my termination and NPR's investigation into how it was handled. A few months later, in March 2011, Vivian Schiller resigned following a scandal in which a former NPR executive was recorded on video making disparaging remarks about the conservative and Tea Party movements and constituents. I believe the compounding controversies became too much for the NPR board and alerted it to the fact that the institution needed to be reclaimed and reoriented in a manner that would allow it to live up to its virtues and purpose. I hope it does.

As for me, this episode has proven to be an inspiring reminder of what we cherish most in this country—our ability to freely engage one another in honest debate over the issues and ideas that determine our lives. I am a proud American, a registered Democrat, a Christian, a straight male, a black immigrant, a father of three, and a grandfather. This country is interested in, and built on, the insight, opinion, humor, and racial and ethnic diversity—the wide range of human experience—that I and others bring to our work. Closing ourselves off from one another and one another's honest opinions—especially at this crucial juncture in the nation's history—is the last thing we should do, encourage, or accept.

My goal in writing this book is to help advance the national conversation beyond the familiar litany of anecdotes of who got in trouble for saying what. I want to look more deeply at the problems of censorship and political correctness in our society and show how they are undermining our ability to have meaningful discussions about important issues. I cast a critical eye toward the role of money and institutions, and the changing nature of the media, in our society. I want to explain how our national discourse fell into such poor health and what we can do to rehabilitate it. You may agree or disagree with my premise or my conclusions or both. What is important is that we have the debate and speak honestly. If people won't tell one another what they think, we run the risk that bad ideas will never be refuted and many good ideas will never be expressed. When our biggest concern is not whether our words are true but whether our words will result in punishment, then we are giving away our most precious freedom. It is not just our right under the Constitution. It is our duty as citizens of the greatest country in the world.

CHAPTER 2

DEFYING THE PC POLICE

BARTENDERS ARE TOLD to avoid discussing two subjects with drinkers: religion and politics. The reason is pretty obvious. If the bartender offends a customer's religious or political beliefs, the bartender might lose a tip. Even worse, the customer might stop drinking and walk out. The very worst case is if the customer keeps drinking, stays, and begins an argument that drags everyone in the place into a fight and ruins the night for the bar. A bunch of drunks arguing and then punching one another is bad news. It's easy to see how the situation could get out of control. Given the potential for conflict and the incentive of getting money in the tip jar, it's in the interest of the bartender to limit talk to sports and celebrity gossip.

I, however, am not a bartender.

My job is to be better informed than the average citizen and tell you directly what a professional analyst and newsman thinks is really going on behind the headlines. That is what I try to do. The best news analysts describe for their audience the motivations, the desires, the inside baseball behind the basics of a daily news story—the who, what, where, when, and why. My views must be based on good reporting about current events, inside and sometimes off-the-record conversations with sources, and my past experiences. The goal is a strong presentation of all those elements in a logical manner that allows the viewer to understand how I am putting puzzling events together and why I'm thinking that way. To do my job at the highest level, I tell audiences what I know, what I think, and, yes, what I feel about people looking for advantage in power struggles, military engagements, and racial and cultural wars (the very thing NPR's Vivian Schiller and Ellen Weiss criticized me for). The only reason to listen to a professional news analyst is to get into the edgy flow of the political debate about the story—a sense of where the story is going, the insights, the ideas, and the spin, as well as the charges of sham, deceit, and corruption. Audiences dialing up news programs in search of in-depth understanding of the news don't want bartenders.

When Schiller, Weiss, and like-minded news executives claim they are upholding high standards of journalism, they are actually forcing all reporters, commentators, and analysts to tell stories from one approved perspective. It is a perspective that amounts to liberal orthodoxy. They are being politically correct.

It begins with the journalists being forced to act like bartenders. They write and speak in such a way that they avoid having anyone complain—especially powerful people with a constituency. Journalists do this because of weak knees among their bosses, the news executives and managers, who live in fear that some power player will call or write to complain that they didn't like what they read, saw, or heard on the news. So the power players' hypocrisy and lies are allowed to go unchallenged.

The power player might be a big bank or a brokerage house on Wall Street claiming to look out for America while making money by closing down American industry and shipping jobs overseas. The powerful might also be an activist, say, Al Sharpton; a politician, such as Sarah Palin; or the White House press secretary. But there are other examples that can be more difficult to see. For example, what do you do with the story of a big-city summer jobs program for poor kids in which the young people sit around all day doing nothing and still collect a check at the end of the week? Do you report on the scam or keep a politically correct silence about how the city keeps young people from stirring up trouble during the hot summer months? Here is another example of stories that go untold while journalists pretend to be bartenders. People stand to applaud the tremendous sacrifice of American soldiers even as polls show an overwhelming majority in opposition to any talk about renewing a universal draft or even a two-year national service commitment for young people. Few point out the inconsistency. No one wants to be the skunk at the garden party. No one wants to say the emperor has no clothes. No one wants to lose a tip. Similarly, our representatives in Congress refuse to deal with immigration reform. Yet it is commonplace for them to hire illegal immigrants as babysitters, contractors, and housecleaners (as well as to allow them to pick lettuce or work in factories in their districts or states). And politicians condemn drug dealers while the nation refuses to discuss why the United States is the top market in the world for consumption of illegal drugs.

The acceptance of hypocrisy and outright fabrication in journalism is a threat to the nation. It marks the end of free expression and the flow of information and ideas that are the basis for the informed debate that is essential to democracy. Much of the media plays along as baseball players, their heads as big as pumpkins, pretend not to use steroids, as bankers get rich even as they wreck the economy by giving mortgages to people who can't afford the monthly payments, as pornographic movies outsell Hollywood movies, without a word about the impact on culture, children, and families. Everyone becomes complicit in the silence.

"Politically correct" is a major theme of our times that extends far beyond journalism. Over the past few decades, the rules of bartender etiquette have been applied to the national conversation in bizarre and dangerous ways. The pernicious rule governing all conversation and debate is that even if the person you are talking to is not directly offended by your opinions, someone else within earshot might be. And if the two people are alone, their comments might be repeated or relayed at some later time in some other place and might offend someone somewhere else. In this PC environment, the preferred course of action is to not voice opinions on any controversial topic unless you know you are in the company of people with similar opinions. Always play the bartender. Americans are constantly walking on eggshells under these rules. Like the bartender, they reasonably conclude that it is better to go along to get along. Honest and constructive discussion is not worth the price they might pay if their opinions are deemed politically incorrect.

So how did we get to this point? What happened to the

American ideal of being free to speak truth to the power-ful? How did we become so damn politically correct that we stopped having honest conversations and debate?

"Political correctness" is one of the most controversial terms in the lexicon of today's public discourse. As politics have become more bitterly polarized in recent years, even the meaning of the term "politically correct" seems to change de-pending on who is speaking and who is listening. In recent years, the Right and the Left seem to have their own stable of historians, sociologists, and even linguists that they trot out to deliver expertise that supports their views on who is guilty of being politically incorrect.

Both the left wing and the right wing are heavily invested in the fight over what it means to be "politically correct." That is because the winner of that fight earns the right to decide the vocabulary of acceptable terms and labels. It allows one side or the other to own the debate, control the airwaves, and stir a base of funders and grassroots fans. This fight is the backdrop to nearly every debate in America today. As for the middle ground, it is shunned as a kind of no-man's-land.

Every issue is loaded with a set of "with us or against us" terms. Even within groups of like-minded people, we are told what we can say and can't say. I sometimes feel out of place say-ing "happy holidays" to my colleagues at Fox because in con-servative circles that term can be taken as evidence that you are part of the effort to undermine Christmas. NPR banned the use of the term "pro-life" because the liberal managers felt it put a happy face on the antiabortion message. They were willing to sacrifice the term "pro-choice," used by supporters of abortion rights, rather than accept "pro-life" (afterward, they would point out that people who support abortion rights aren't antilife). This same crazy dynamic applies to political fights. When I point out that Israel is an occupying force with settlements outside its borders, I am called an anti-Semite; and as you know, when I confess to a fear of Islamic extremism, I am called an anti-Muslim bigot.

By definition, political correctness means—and here I am quoting the *Oxford English Dictionary*—"the avoidance, often considered as taken to extremes, of forms of expression or action that are perceived to exclude, marginalize, or insult groups of people who are socially disadvantaged or discriminated against." Historians have found instances where the words "politically correct" appeared in print as early as the 1700s. The early meaning was much more literal and referred solely to the accuracy of a statement. Offense, real or perceived, did not figure into the definition. For example, "New York has more votes than Rhode Island in the Electoral College" was once known as a "politically correct" statement.

PC began to take on its new, more familiar meaning in the 1960s and 1970s. At first it was a term of self-criticism used by people on the Left, including civil rights activists and leaders of campus groups organizing against the Vietnam War, but especially in the cultural battles being fought over women's rights by leading feminists. The idea back then was that it was ironic for feminists committed to breaking down old social barriers to put up new walls by insisting that women all had to grow hair on their legs, burn their bras, and give up lipstick. That extreme attitude was condemned by women sympathetic to the movement with the dismissive use of the term "politically correct." And the idea was a winner because it brought more people to the movement by allowing women to set their own pace for their liberation from male domination.

What also became apparent during the sixties was the importance of the emerging TV news coverage of left-wing social movements and the strategic importance of controlling the language used by reporters. The general idea, which has some basis in psychology and linguistic theory, is that there is a real connection among language, thought, and action. It was a first glimpse of future culture wars as leaders in liberal movements began insisting on new language in the name of fairness but with the real goal of changing politics and society by establishing a vocabulary of acceptable terms and language for people who cared about equality and justice. Soon it was not acceptable for the television network correspondents covering the civil rights movement to talk about "Negroes" or "Colored people." The proper reference was to "blacks" and later "African Americans." The movement for equal rights for Indians became a "Native Americans" movement. People began to refer to the chairman of a group as the "chairperson" or simply "the chair" in recognition that the chair could be a woman.

Comedians including Lenny Bruce, Richard Pryor, and George Carlin lampooned America's hypocrisy in banning from radio and TV the same vulgar epithets and profanity that were being used every day at home and on the street. Carlin became famous for his routine "The Seven Words You Can Never Say on Television." He skewered the American acceptance of euphemistic language that obscured reality, from sexual practices to racism, that Americans did not want to talk about.

The people jiggering with the engine of popular language used by news correspondents, politicians, and comedians in the sixties succeeded in making everyday people more aware of racism, sexism, and stereotypes of all sorts. This could be described as the post–World War II era of the opening of the American mind. The big idea was increased awareness leading to empathy, a new conception of how America could improve its practice of democratic ideals and finally effect real change in the form of civil rights laws and equal opportunities for women in the workplace. Discomfort in the nation with racial segregation and the government's questionable conduct of the Vietnam War provided a fertile environment for these ideas that challenged the established political order to take root. There was a superficial feel to some of these linguistic changes, but anyone who dismissed them as a passing fad had it wrong. The changes in popular language soon became changes in our textbook accounts of history; literature was scrutinized for its "Eurocentric canon" promoting the "white male power structure."

In a burst, universities agreed to create whole new academic departments, such as Black Studies, Latino Studies, and Women's Studies. "Critical theory" courses also became prominent during that time, essentially teaching that the transformation of Western society can be achieved through unremitting and deconstructive criticism of every institution in Western society. Critical theorists did not view institutions in the traditional sense as just business, government, education, and the like. They viewed these institutions as representations of social inequality when it came to race, class, gender, sexual orientation, and politics. To left-wing intellectuals, this new "critical theory" approach revealed major American institutions as defenders of the status quo—protecting the wealthy, the powerful, and racial majorities. The animating idea behind "critical theory" is that these institutions should be deconstructed in the name of achieving genuine equality.

David Horowitz, a sixties campus leftist turned conservative writer, has written extensively about this period of history. He became a conservative because he was repulsed by the ever-widening constraints of politically correct behavior that made it impossible for him to express a different point of view to his fellow left-wingers without being dismissed as a sellout working for "the man" or an "Uncle Tom."

Horowitz was just one voice in a brewing backlash that extended far beyond the American campus. Conservatives began to point out that the culture of political correctness was a hammer to bludgeon national politics and news reports into conformity with a liberal point of view. The right wing felt the left wing had co-opted the debate by finding a way to shut up people who defended American traditions and conservative principles. As a result, the political right wing began to fight politically correct campus "speech codes" and "hate codes," complaining that American colleges and universities basically indoctrinated top students in leftist thinking. Nobel Prize–winning writer Saul Bellow told *The New Yorker* that political correctness was "free speech without debate." Novelist Doris Lessing, another Nobel Prize winner, called political correctness "the offspring of Marxist dialectics."

After liberal Democratic president Jimmy Carter was rejected in favor of the Republican conservative Ronald Reagan, who had fought political correctness on California's college campuses as governor, the right wing became outspoken in rejecting liberals as an angry minority tearing down American institutions and traditions. With the help of Christian conservative groups like the Moral Majority, the Right convinced people that Christianity, by far the most popular religion in the United States, was under siege by a minority of liberal secularists in the name of political correctness. Even though it had its own rules setting limits on any criticism of Christianity, the right wing positioned itself as anti–political correctness. The conservatives became holy warriors with a mission to protect the faith from the secular PC attack machine. The strategy at work for conservatives was to give political correctness a bad name and, by extension, give liberalism a bad name. To conservatives, political correctness embodied everything that was wrong and evil about liberalism. They hung this idea around their opponents' necks like an albatross and watched with relish as it dragged liberalism into disrepute and damaged left-wing politics.

The intense racial tensions of the era became part of the jousting. The idea of forced racial equality—specifically quotas—became part of the conversation as evidence that political correctness included giving jobs to unqualified people in the name of equal rights. Playing to residual racism in the postintegration South, conservatives convinced a large segment of white voters, the majority in the region, that they were being threatened by liberal Democrats, who represented Northerners, Jews, immigrants, and racial minorities, especially black people. This was the premise of Jesse Helms's famous television advertisement in his North Carolina Senate campaign against Harvey Gantt. A pair of white hands crumples up a job rejection letter as a narrator says, "You needed that job. You were the best qualified, but they had to give it to a minority because of a racial quota." Even black radio talk show host Larry Elder picked up on the angst of whites when he questioned why the phrase "white trash" was acceptable when it was forbidden to talk that way about blacks, Hispanics, or Asians. The argument that whites have never been an enslaved and despised minority in the country failed to halt the slide in political correctness, because the counter-argument undermined the heart of the argument for political correctness—equality for all. In addition, Jews, Irish, Italians, and other white ethnicities had their stories of discrimination and oppression. The serious message being loudly heard across American culture by the 1990s was that political correctness was not just an instance of fun and games among the intellectual class. To conservative white men and some white women, political correctness, affirmative action, and even talk of reparations for slavery were a very threatening reality that made it harder to get a job and get their children into college. It generally made them feel as if they had slipped under the thumb of an intellectual regime alien to their upbringing, their traditions, and their pride in America as the leading force for right in the world.

During Reagan's tenure in the White House, the Republican Party had found it could make huge political gains by playing to the so-called culture wars, in which conservatives became victims of liberal attacks on traditions and institutions central to American life. The most salient examples of the culture wars were incidents of excessive political correctness—such as calls not to have schools teach great books because they were written by "dead white men." But they extended into so-called political wedge issues, such as abortion, gun rights, and gay rights, which gave voters a stark choice of identifying with one side or the other. Conservative politicians found that a lot of white working-class Americans decided to side with them in the comfort of the voting booth because of discomfort with the fast pace of social change required by political correctness.

Members of the Right practiced ideological judo by using the ferocity of left-wing adherence to every politically correct position to mock the Left as self-righteous and given to censorship. They cast liberalism as the opposite of freedom, individual rights, and constitutional protections. University of Chicago professor Allan Bloom wrote a best-selling book, *The Closing of the American Mind*, which argued that political correctness in American schools was undermining academic freedom, intellectual debate, and overall scholarship. Bloom asked how anyone could speak or write in any course of study without fear of offending the high priests of political correctness. Democratic presidential candidate Michael Dukakis was asked by CNN's Bernie Shaw if he would want the death penalty for a man who raped and murdered his wife. Dukakis could not bring himself to say yes. It would have been a repudiation of liberal opposition to the death penalty. Conservatives pounced.

The backlash against politically correct thinking became pronounced in the early 1990s. The *New York Times* published articles about several incidents of PC run wild. "At San Francisco State University, a black professor was reviled by students for teaching in the political science department rather than in

black studies," according to one story. The *Times* also found
instances where a Harvard student was not only rebuked by
other students but punished by the school's administration for
hanging a Confederate flag out the window. At Stanford, students demanded an end to core curriculum in Western civilization and demanded a new approach called "Cultures, Ideas
and Values" that the *Times* said focused on "non-European,
non-white studies."

This coincided with long-standing efforts that had largely
been initiated in the 1970s to eliminate American Indian
names for sports teams. Major schools, including Marquette,
Stanford, the University of Massachusetts, and the University of Wisconsin at La Crosse, all changed their nicknames
over this time period. Marquette, for example, changed from
"the Warriors" to "the Golden Eagles." All of this aggravated
alumni and traditionalists. In this new world it was a crime to
say that a person was blind. To be politically correct you had to
say that person was "visually challenged." A handicapped person was "physically challenged," and a retarded person was
only to be described as "mentally challenged."

It was more than just a right-wing complaint that politically
correct language seemed out of control in the early nineties.
People of all races, men and women, liberals and conservatives, felt that haphazard declarations of "appropriate" language as ruled by the politically correct were ever changing,
making them feel guilty for saying things they didn't know to
be taboo. Writing in the *Washington Post,* journalist Jefferson
Morley wrote that "for many Americans—especially a certain generation of older white males—the fact that their ideals of fair play and tolerance can be violated by implacable,

self-righteous people with power is utterly novel. In a time of declining wages [for blue-collar workers], such an experience is also frightening and radicalizing."

Politically correct thinking became so out of fashion that President George H. W. Bush openly attacked it in a 1991 commencement address at the University of Michigan. He said politically correct thinking amounted to "bullying" and "censorship." While the PC movement, he said, came into being "to sweep away the debris of racism and sexism and hatred, it replaces old prejudices with new ones. It declares certain topics off-limits, certain expressions off-limits, even certain gestures off-limits." The president concluded: "What began as a crusade for civility has soured into a cause of conflict and even censorship."

Robert Bork, who became a conservative icon after he was denied a seat on the Supreme Court—by Democrats on the Left who attacked him as too controversial because he openly expressed a conservative, and definitely not politically correct, judicial philosophy—joined in the attacks on political correctness. In a 1993 debate with Professor Linda S. Greene of the University of Wisconsin Law School, he spoke of the frustration felt by many when he said: "Political correctness, I think, is something that is widespread in this society and it's part of a mood of radical egalitarianism which has taken hold. . . . And we're seeing it in the speech codes, which are judging speech not by what it objectively means, but by how somebody perceives it, over which the speaker has no control."

The sense that PC had gone too far became mainstream. Radio talk show host Rush Limbaugh lampooned hard-line feminists as "femi-Nazis." In 1993 comedian Bill Maher's show *Politically Incorrect* debuted on Comedy Central, and in 1994 James Finn Garner wrote *Politically Correct Bedtime Stories,* which turned classic children's stories into absurd tales of princes who had weak knees and princesses who did not need princes.

Even President Bill Clinton, a Democrat, seemed to sense the change in the political winds when he famously moved to the center after the 1996 election, with more socially conservative policies on criminal sentencing, welfare, and tax cuts for the rich.

Members of the Left, sensing that political correctness was losing steam, tried to fight back. They made the case in books and in debates that instances of political correctness—like those in the *Times* article—had been either greatly exaggerated or completely made up, twisted by conservatives to divide people in order to win elections. Some liberals, like Camille Paglia, a popular feminist professor, went a step further by saying the right wing had distorted political correctness to stop the advance of gender and racial equality in America. Another professor, Doug Smith, asked what was so bad about Stanford students being required to read the book *I, Rigoberta Menchú,* as well as *The Republic* and *The Prince.* He pointed to a double standard in which conservatives showed the same intolerance to a free market of ideas they charged liberals with imposing on the world. "What is so intolerant," he asked, about having students read one book on a Guatemalan peasant woman who comes to support socialism and feminism, as well as the Greek philosophers? "One could easily and glibly describe Plato and Machiavelli as intellectual hirelings whose works are for the most part apologetics for authoritarianism," wrote Smith.

The Left saw arguments over the concept of political correctness rising to the point that the public no longer remembered the problem—inequality, bias, and racism—that politically correct language was intended to cure. In her 1993 debate with Judge Bork, Professor Linda S. Greene put it this way: "If you can force us to discuss censorship instead of discussing . . . sexual harassment, censorship instead of discussing the question how we are going to transform our institutions into more diverse places, then you have set the terms of the debate and prevented a discussion of the real issues. And it seems to be a great cause of glee on the right, among conservatives, that they have been able to change this debate."

By 2001 British essayist Will Hutton, writing in London's *The Observer,* followed the same line of what looked like left-wing surrender to conclude, "Political correctness is one of the brilliant tools that the American Right developed in the mid-1980s as part of its demolition of American liberalism. . . . What the sharpest thinkers on the American Right saw quickly was that by declaring war on the cultural manifestations of liberalism—by levelling the charge of political correctness against its exponents—they could discredit the whole political project."

The whole political correctness phenomenon seemed to have expired by the turn of the century, replaced by political shouting over Clinton's impeachment hearings and then the historic Left-versus-Right fight over hanging chads in Florida and the 2000 presidential election. The terrorist attacks of 9/11 seemed to further bury political correctness when American flags popped up everywhere from the liberal neighborhoods of the East Village in heavily Democratic Manhattan to conservative Republican suburbs in Orange County, California. The threat to the nation made arguments over politically correct speech seem very dated. In addition, the increasing racial diversity of the country took the edge away from heated debates that tied affirmative action to politically correct policies. Attitudes on gay rights also shifted, even among conservatives, to the point that polls showed majorities of Democrats and even Republicans in support of ending the ban on gays openly serving in the military.

Harvey Fierstein, the gay playwright and actor, wrote a piece in the *New York Times* in 2007 that sounded like a farewell to political correctness. He asked Americans to keep their eyes open for "expressions of intolerance" and prejudice in everyday life. "Still, I'm gladdened because our no longer being deaf to them may signal their eventual eradication," he wrote. He ended by cautioning readers that it is wrong to "harbor malice toward others and then cry foul when someone displays intolerance against you."

But I'm not sure PC disappeared so much as it switched sides. Now it is largely the Left that decries limits on free speech such as those imposed by the Patriot Act after 9/11. And it was not just the law giving liberals rightful fits but also the conservative push to shut down debate about the terrorist attacks and halt criticism of the U.S. military response in Afghanistan and Iraq. The most famous instance occurred when Bill Maher on his late-night show, by then on ABC network television but appropriately still called *Politically Incorrect*, said with his usual fearlessness, "We [Americans] have been the cowards, lobbing cruise missiles from two thousand miles away. That's cowardly. Staying in the airplane when it hits the building, say what you want about it, it's not cowardly." Ironically, when he made these statements, Maher was *agreeing* with a conservative guest, Dinesh D'Souza, when he said that the 9/11 hijackers were not cowards because they stayed in the airplanes as they hit the buildings. If Maher had not affirmed D'Souza's comment about the perverse bravery of the terrorists, nothing might have ever come of it. D'Souza, with his conservative street cred, wasn't going to be lambasted as a traitor, was he? ABC was reportedly pressured to fire Maher after advertisers threatened to pull their sponsorship from his program, and Maher's show was canceled the following year, in large part due to ratings and advertising troubles presumed to have resulted from the backlash against his comments. Bush White House press secretary Ari Fleischer criticized Maher and, in a controversial statement of his own, warned people from the lectern in the White House briefing room to be careful about what they say.

That was seen by the Left and much of the rest of the country as a chilling threat to First Amendment rights. The Far Left began hauling out analogies between the Bush White House and Joe McCarthy, the Wisconsin senator who smeared liberals in the 1950s with largely baseless charges of being communist sympathizers. Instead of being called insensitive or offensive for violating a speech code under the rules of politically correct behavior, conservatives attacked antiwar protesters as people who hated America. Even the language being used in newspapers to describe the U.S. war effort became an issue when Vice President Cheney insisted that waterboarding terrorists—flooding a suspect's covered head with water to create the sensation of drowning—was not "torture." Scott

Horton, writing in *Harper's* magazine, said the decision by the top editor of the *New York Times,* Bill Keller, not to label waterboarding as torture amounted to following "politically correct" dictates coming from conservatives. "This is not merely being politically correct; it is being politically subordinate. . . . Bill Keller's political correctness couldn't be more clear cut. . . . This is precisely the sort of political manipulation of language that George Orwell warned against in 'Politics and the English Language.' "

The country music singers the Dixie Chicks were branded as traitors after one of them told a foreign concert audience that they were ashamed to be from the same state as President Bush. Radio stations refused to play their songs and hosted bonfires where they burned their CDs and merchandise. Entertainers like Tim Robbins, Mike Farrell, and Janeane Garofalo, who questioned the wisdom of going into Iraq, were told they should just shut up. They were accused of damaging the morale of the troops and giving aid and comfort to the enemy.

And in a provocative recycling of the term "speech code," reminiscent of the Right's complaints about left-wing insistence on politically correct language twenty-five years earlier, it was now the liberal *New York Times* columnist Frank Rich who used the phrase "speech codes bequeathed by 9-11" to defend, of all people, Rudy Giuliani in his criticism of the rebuilding of Ground Zero.

So while my friends at Fox frequently and courageously expose the use of this tactic of political correctness by the Left, it's important to remember that the Right plays this game too. It shouldn't be given a free pass, because the net negative effect on the discourse is the same, no matter who's doing it.

While the Left mostly uses PC on minority identity issues like race and ethnicity, the Right uses it on issues of piety and patriotism.

Since Reagan, the Right has used wedge issues like abortion, gay rights, and prayer in school to paint its opponents as heretical and hostile to traditional family values. President George W. Bush's victory over John Kerry in 2004 was in part attributed to anti–gay marriage ballot initiatives in electorally crucial states like Ohio. The Family Research Council, the Parents Television Council, the American Catholic League, and other faith-based conservative groups, whose convictions I deeply respect, engaged in their own form of political correctness during the Bush years and before. They too are quick to claim outrage and offense when their interests are challenged. For example, take the Catholic Church's slow response to the scandal over priests abusing children. Church leaders tried to distract the public by casting their opponents as people attacking the church, rather than people attacking sexual abuse of children. They pretend to be the victims to play on loyalty to the Catholic Church and rile up their membership, demonstrate their political clout, and get their leaders on television. Like groups on the Left, they make implicit criticisms of the goodwill and integrity of people who disagree with them. For them, it is about religious sensitivity toward Catholics (and Christians more generally), instead of race or gender. They presume to speak and act for the majority of Christians in much the same way the National Organization for Women presumes to speak and act for all women. Such political correctness should be exposed in whatever form it comes.

The truth about political correctness is that it has never

gone away. It remains a steady feature of American political and cultural discourse and debates. It is a tactic that almost everyone uses when it suits their purposes. Much like negative ads in a political campaign, appeals to politically correct thinking are proven weapons in modern history. Activist groups and news outlets have rows of scalps from public figures guilty of having made politically incorrect "comments" to remind us all of this. My scalp is among them, after being claimed by NPR. Political correctness is indiscriminate. That is perhaps the most insidious thing about it.

As noted, ABC got Bill Maher's scalp a few years back, but he's not done fighting for political incorrectness. He now hosts a lively, uncensored show on HBO and continues to rail against our fear of speaking out. The week after I was fired from NPR, Maher noted on his show that the most popular name for babies born in the United Kingdom last year was "Mohammed" and said he was "alarmed" because he did not want the Western world to be taken over by Islam. "Am I a racist to feel alarmed by that, because I am. And it is not because of the race, it's because of the religion. I don't have to apologize, do I?"

Like George Carlin and Richard Pryor before them, comedians like Maher are uniquely positioned to challenge the PC culture when it's used by the Left and the Right to cut off debates they don't want others to hear. Many examples of PC are ripe to be skewered with ridicule. While some of the send-ups of PC behavior are funny, it's important to recognize that it's really gallows humor. The substance is very serious, and the injury to people's reputations and livelihoods can be very real. As someone who was at the center of one of these

PC media feeding frenzies, I can assure you there was nothing funny about it at the time.

At its core, political correctness relies on tribalism, an "us versus them" mentality. It is about cultivating identity groups and placing people into convenient boxes where they think and act and speak in predictable ways. In recent years, people and groups from all points on the political spectrum have used this fragmentation to their advantage. They use it to attain and expand their political power, whether it's by generating media attention or raising money. They use it to insulate and protect their constituents so that whenever a controversy comes along, they can go to the appropriate box and produce victims who will echo their sense of outrage.

The tremendous growth of media, with cable TV and the Internet offering niche outlets to fit any specific political taste—thereby atomizing the idea of a big-tent, mainstream media where everyone can tell their story and hear the other side—and decades of greater class divisions and political polarization have brought us to this point. There is no clear incentive for anyone involved to change the tone and the nature of the conversation. Politicians who utilize PC tactics regularly win at the ballot box. Lobbyists and special-interest advocacy groups are more influential and better funded than ever before. Their favorite weapon is to charge any opposing camp with being insensitive and even offensive—in other words, politically incorrect. Television ratings and Web traffic numbers are shattering records and soaring with any report about politically insensitive statements, such as the burst of online hits after Ann Coulter labeled the 9/11 widows "witches" and "harpies" or Tucker Carlson pronounced himself a Christian who nonetheless thought football player Michael Vick should have been "executed" for staging dogfights. This problem did not happen overnight, and it will not be fixed overnight.

The goal of these political tactics is changing America to fit one's preferred vision—making sure one's ideas come out on top. The genius of America is that reactionary groups rarely achieve progress. But good arguments, persistence, and appeals to conscience that challenge the majority at critical junctures—see the civil rights movement and particularly Dr. Martin Luther King Jr.—actually *change* the majority and become "mainstream." This dynamic was first expressed by James Madison in Federalist No. 10. The idea is that only the best ideas and movements will survive and have the wide-scale appeal to rise and withstand exposure to vigorous national debate.

Yet as the country has grown more diverse, as women have gained a larger voice in picking winners and losers in the marketplace of ideas, and as Hispanics, Asians, and blacks also have their say in politics and culture, we find ourselves looking across a broken, factionalized landscape. In this new reality, many Americans feel they have lost power, and an increasing number are worried they are in the minority. The best and obvious example is older, blue-collar white males who can easily recall when leadership, decision making, and good taste were largely up to them. The big changes in twentieth-century America—aside from the atomic bomb and technology—have been about social movements for equal rights for women and minorities. They have left much of the nation, including women and minorities, with an identity crisis, a new hunger for some scrap of common identity, and heightened competition for influence over the country's future as we Americans safeguard identities, both for individuals and groups. We are all adopting the vocabulary of the aggrieved, and it comes at the expense of some notion that we all share a common cause. The rising tide has been replaced by zero-sum. The conversation is now a hostile negotiation.

I believe the charged atmosphere of our conversation with one another has taken a wrong turn. And I think it went seriously wrong over the course of the last thirty years—in the midst of the culture war between the Right and the Left.

If the intent of PC was to encourage a culture in which people in power had to be careful of the sensitivities of others, the reality of it was that it inhibited frank conversations. It became nearly impossible to have direct dialogue between any two groups, or even a class discussion about history, without running the risk of offending somebody. As a result, the most important conversations, in which people try to understand one another and solve problems, became more trouble than they were worth. With caution as the wise course of action, many political leaders, professors, and media people on radio and TV began seeking refuge in a polite middle where hard truths are muzzled. Meanwhile, hard-liners on both sides migrated to the political fringes, where honest, potentially fruitful debates are secondary to reaffirming the party line and pushing one another to become more rigid, orthodox, intolerant, and politically correct in their thinking.

It may feel like a flashback to the bad old days of politically correct speech codes and wedge issues. But the truth is this is just a new vintage of the same politically correct wine. In this new age of politically correct thinking, Left and Right continue limiting debate, controlling the media, rousing the base of their most partisan supporters, and hitting hard and fast when lines of group propriety and identity are crossed. The prime targets are anyone who thinks differently and, as was evident in NPR's handling of me, anyone within one's own group who is guilty of straying to talk to the other side and finding points of agreement with what is viewed as the enemy.

Lines have been drawn, trenches dug, bubbles sealed.

If we try to discuss security in the context of Islamic fascism, we are called "racist." If political leaders talk about reining in the unsustainable cost of health entitlements, they are derided for talking about "death panels" and "rationing." If there is a debate about adding troops to a war that is going badly, the people in support of the increased military presence attack critics for not supporting the troops and for being "unpatriotic." If the topic is the rights of gays, supporters are dismissed as lacking religious faith and being "secular." We fall back on labels, labels, labels—speech codes to distract from the true issues at hand that deserve to be discussed and debated.

In a sense, the PC movement hasn't done anything other than make itself more diffuse across pockets of American culture. Hypersensitivity and supercharged responses to the slightest of perceived transgressions are now the norm. What Jefferson Morley wrote in the *Washington Post* in 1995 in assessing the PC movement is an apt description for almost any subclass of Americans who see on the horizon the destruction of their own brand of American-ness by whatever version of heathen they imagine: "Among the less attractive results is the emergence of America's newest victim class: the P.C.

Wounded. Their aggrieved insistence that the injustice done to them is more recent, more unfair, more un-American than that suffered by other groups is just another one of those exercises in comparative victimization that are so common a feature of fruitless political debates."

This remains the case even if it's hard to keep track of who is claiming to be the victim in the latest attempt to stifle free speech. A prime example of how the tables can turn is provided by Mark C. Taylor, a professor at Williams College. In 2006, writing in the *New York Times,* he described how a revival of religious groups on his campus, more than at any time since the 1960s, seemed to signal a reversal of the liberal, politically correct insistence that intellectuals wear suspicion of all religion, especially evangelical Christianity, as a badge of honor. Conservatives have long been critical of hostility toward organized religion at top colleges as part of their defense of values and traditions. But what looked like an end to the politically correct embrace of a campus free of people talking about their faith was a new, dangerous phenomenon that amounted, Taylor wrote, to "the latest version of political correctness." Under the new rules, Taylor said, "the more religious students become, the less willing they are to engage in critical reflection about faith."

Taylor recounted how an administrator at the college insisted he apologize to a student after the student complained that Professor Taylor had "attacked his faith because [he] had urged him to consider whether Nietzsche's analysis of religion undermines belief in absolutes." Taylor refused to apologize. "My experience was not unique," he wrote. "Today, professors invite harassment or worse by including 'unacceptable' books on their syllabuses or by studying religious ideas and practices in ways deemed improper by religiously correct students. Distinguished scholars at several major universities in the United States have been condemned, even subjected to death threats, for proposing psychological, sociological or anthropological interpretations of religious texts in their classes and published writings. In the most egregious cases, defenders of the faith insist that only true believers are qualified to teach their religious tradition."

It is generally accepted that the liberal PC movement and the anti-PC backlash in the eighties and nineties, as well as the conservative wedge issues that emerged in the early 2000s, are all now safely in the rearview mirror as elements of what we remember as the culture wars. But what is clear—from Taylor's case at Williams to my firing at NPR—is that the tactics first used by the Left to impose political correctness and by the Right to emphasize divisive wedge issues are the very same tactics that remain at play in nearly every debate in America. Those tactics are now pushing too many of us to be silent, to play the part of the smiling bartender or risk losing tips. The rules are not nailed to the wall, but everyone seems to know voicing an honest opinion, even expressing a feeling, comes with the danger of being fired, being shunned, having our reputations ruined, and being excommunicated from the church of other true believers—all for simply telling the truth.

CHAPTER 3

PARTISAN POLITICS

A S PRESIDENT BUSH AND I WALKED out of the Oval Office, he suddenly pulled on my arm. He wanted to stop and talk for a moment before entering the Roosevelt Room, which was full of White House staff, producers, and technicians waiting for me to interview him.

"You know I can't say anything about your book," he said, referring to *Enough*, a book I had written about the failure to address the nation's growing culture of out-of-wedlock births, high school dropouts, and acceptance of illegal drug use—especially among poor black Americans. He had sent me a personal letter a few months earlier telling me that he had read it, praising key points. But the president never mentioned the book in public—the kind of coveted, one-of-a-kind endorsement that is sure to draw attention to any book.

Speaking softly, President Bush said he felt if he gave the book his stamp of approval it might cause people who stood to benefit most from the book—the poor, people fighting poverty, churches, philanthropies, and civil rights groups—to dismiss it because they generally disagreed with his Republican politics. His silence wasn't about the book but about the charged nature of the issues. It was a topic he realized he had to approach with extreme caution.

About two years later, at a White House lunch with President Obama and other Washington columnists, I had a similar encounter with the nation's first black president. As the group discussed the recession's impact on working-class men, the president turned to me, the only black journalist in the room. He said I knew what an economic slump can do to a community—fewer men graduating from high school, fewer men marrying, and more men going to jail—because of my writing about the social breakdown in the black community during previous recessions. Like President Bush, President Obama was familiar with *Enough* and, more important, with the ideas it dealt with, but he too never pushed hard for a direct discussion of those ideas, I believe for fear of antagonizing his liberal political base.

How could that be? Let me share a brief story with you.

When Barack Obama, as a presidential candidate, in a rare venture into this territory, spoke to a black church about the high percentage of black men failing to be fathers to their children, he found himself immediately targeted as an Uncle Tom by the former presidential candidate Reverend Jesse Jackson. Acting as the enforcer of politically correct speech for liberal politicians, Jackson damned him for "talking down to black people." Seething under his breath as he prepared to do a TV interview, Jackson was caught on microphone telling another guest that Obama's violation of politically correct speech made him want to castrate the younger man—"cut his nuts off."

With that kind of threat, that kind of retaliating response from one's own party, it is easy to understand why, at every point on the political compass, from the political right wing to the political left wing, from President Bush to President Obama, politicians agree to keep silent on major debates in today's political atmosphere. Both men were aware of the severe price to be paid—scorn, vilification, and being shunned by one's own party, if not converted to a political eunuch—by any leader who plunges into a charged national debate on a particularly sensitive topic.

But I would argue that this period of American history, with its politically correct silences—its widely felt fear of saying the wrong thing—is at strong odds with a tradition of great debate that has historically defined national politics. The history of the United States has been consistently highlighted by a series of essential political debates. From the founding of the country through the Civil War, the Great Depression, two world wars, several cultural revolutions, and the war on terror, robust political discourse in this country has fundamentally shaped and reshaped our lives.

Perhaps the most singular characteristic of the United States' brand of political discourse is its free-flowing, full-throated, even raucous nature. It is far from a polite exchange of ideas. Read through American history and the narrative is defined by debate that is loud, often harsh, straightforward, and frequently personal. The critical debates of the past have been spurred on by politicians who put their arguments, even the effectiveness of their speaking styles, without speechwriters or consultants, up for public judgment. Political careers grew from the power of winning debate. With the leading political lights in the game shining their insights and their words on these debates, other public figures, academics, and business and civic leaders found themselves drawn to the national conversation. Further urgency came from newspapers fanning the flames to increase sales.

Despite the changing nature of the media, the basic recipe for the best of American political debate has not changed all that much since the nation's founding. What has changed is our fear of political correctness. It has replaced the best that we have to offer—robust, honest debate—with hushed tones. Those silences are punctuated by a scatter shot of politically fragmented sound bites, usually from extreme and angry voices. The result is that the media makes more news out of fewer crumbs of competing points of view because the genuine substance of modern political debate is so meager, so hard to find. After the massacres at Columbine, Virginia Tech, Fort Hood, and Tucson, and daily reports on drive-by shootings, how can there not be a major debate over access to automatic weapons? The answer is that it is too risky—it is too politically incorrect—given the power of the NRA and gun lobby and the extreme fear on the Right that the Left's ultimate goal is to ban all guns. The result, in combination with the rise of the twenty-four-hour news cycle, is a media feeding frenzy whenever any major political figure touches on the issue, because the media has so little to chew on. News programs are often reduced to speculation, provocative statements, and opinion masquerading as news because that's all they have to work with. There are exceptions, like Representative Carolyn McCarthy of New York (whose husband was killed and son wounded in the Long Island Rail Road shooting of 1993), who has introduced legislation aimed at reducing the ammunition capacity of gun clips. But it's sad that people like her, who are willing to forcefully advance a position, are the exception and not the rule.

Instead, the modern political dialectic has largely been reduced to winks and whispers. The Federalist Papers and the Lincoln/Douglas debates have been replaced by slogans and talking points and negative ads and, even worse, by warring Facebook posts and YouTube "gotcha" moments. Major politicians, guarded by cautious, highly paid advisers, avoid the risk of honest debate and, even more, the risk of agreeing when an ideological opponent makes a good point.

It is no surprise that this current paradigm for political discourse results in extreme partisanship. There is a lot of money invested in keeping the ideological divide wide and deep.

Direct-mail fund-raising aimed at people with single-issue concerns such as abortion or gun control came of age during the 1980s and 1990s, and it has continued to make a lot of people rich to this day. Newsletters, blogs, radio programs, conventions, and paid speeches shower big money on true believers and on the people holding political power. As Representative Gabrielle Giffords said before she was shot in the head by a crazed gunman, there is a lot of financial and political reward for being extreme and almost none for a politician willing to compromise. All the attention and money goes to elected officials who engage, she said, in "outlandish and mean behavior.... You get no reward for being the normal, reasonable person." With the money going away from people willing to defy political correctness and talk to one another, listen to one another, there are now huge financial obstacles to anyone attempting to bring opposing camps together for rational discussions on key issues.

There may be a silent majority of moderates in America, but they are moving from silent to muzzled in a hurry for lack of money. It is the rare voice that is given a radio program or wins election to office who voices moderate views in America. If the 1990s witnessed the beginning of a schism in the electorate, then the 2000s saw it grow into full maturity. As we look at this game, the question is how anyone's voice can be heard above these well-funded megaphones available to anyone who conforms to the new rules of political engagement and discourse, where partisanship is rewarded while rationality and moderation are penalized and ignored.

In the last decade, I would argue that the national political conversation has been paralyzed by factions of political correctness. There has been little real movement on resolving critical national issues or even defining those issues. The best-known players in this nonconversation are a new class of political figures. Impish, venting archpartisans have created a subculture of celebrity provocateurs who make outlandish statements to grab attention, entertain, and mock but rarely advance the nation's critical debates. As we'll see in subsequent chapters of this book, from national security to entitlements to immigration to social issues, the strategy time and again is to heighten the conflict and widen the divides in this country. Today's most revealing political discussions tend to happen in a vacuum; people talk only to "the base" and preach to an already like-minded audience. That is why it became major news when, as a presidential candidate, Barack Obama talked—behind closed doors—of economically frustrated, small-town

Americans who are holding fast to their guns and God. There are reasons why this is a bold comment and one worthy of discussion. Why didn't we have an honest and thorough debate about it? Well, because it's a fine thing for a Democrat to say in San Francisco behind closed doors, but it's too risky outside of those confines for fear of a talk-radio pummeling or a blue-collar revolt. So rather than be bold, our politicians shrink from challenging themselves or the electorate.

As a result, we have rival camps that resort to spying on each other. That is why groups like Media Matters track and report with alarm what right-wing talk radio hosts are saying to their right-wing audiences. We've forgotten how to say what we think in front of a broader, more diverse audience, to hold an honest dialogue and debate key issues in a frank and solution-focused manner. While previous political debates in U.S. history were hardly models of civil and well-mannered discussion, more often than not they produced real results— they solved problems for better or worse.

Compare that to the last session of the U.S. Senate, historically America's greatest debating society, an arena reserved for leading political minds from every state who, ideally, personify the qualities implicit in the honorary title of "statesman." The 111th Congress saw the most filibusters in American history. Once a rarely used exception to Senate rules, the threat of the filibuster has become the way to stop any debate from taking place. There is little if any value to twenty-first-century debate because parliamentary maneuvering—the filibuster—has become the primary tool for closing debate and blocking legislation. Members of Congress are elected to identify, debate, and resolve problems, aren't they? To serve their constituents within the framework established by the Constitution? The filibuster was created to allow a principled politician to act on conscience and stand tall in opposition to a runaway majority. Today's cavalier use of the congressional filibuster is the exact opposite. It requires a total lack of conscience, a celebration of impeding the Senate's, and thus Congress's, ability to function.

How can government work for the people when "compromise" is now a pejorative? When no politician is willing to have his or her name associated with any hint of compromise with the other side, for fear of being labeled weak or a traitor to his or her party? For another example, look at the ridiculous and counterproductive Senate practice of placing unnecessary holds on political appointees.

Our entire system of government is based on compromise—giving something to get something. In the current political theater, the politicians who adopt the most rigid ideological stances are the ones who garner the most fervent, devoted followings and occasional eye-popping headlines. It's a path to power, whether it's Cornyn, DeMint, or Inhofe on the Right or Sanders, Leahy, or Levin on the Left. The politicians who consistently compromise and work with the other party are punished. They do not get on TV as often and their fund-raising dries up quickly. They are dismissed as traitors to the cause—RINOs and DINOs (Republicans and Democrats in name only)—by partisan commentators. They may be challenged or even defeated in a primary election. The media, financial, and political incentives are stacked in favor of intransigence and against compromise.

The same dysfunction crippling the Senate holds sway in

the House of Representatives. On nearly every major piece of legislation offered in the first two years of the Obama administration, the House voted strictly along party lines, with Republicans in unanimous opposition to the president and the Democratic majority, even when the legislation was originally proposed by Republicans. It was within their rights as the minority party to do this. However, just because you have the right to do something does not mean it is the right thing to do. It leads to paralysis in the government. When I talk with Republican leaders about their strategy of obstructing not only their political opponent but also real debate, they say their primary job is to defeat the rival party and regain power—not to govern or fix the problems of the country. They dismiss the value of debate as a vestige of a past era. They are proud to be the party of no . . . and even "hell no!"

Some rank-and-file Republicans contend that every legislative proposal by President Obama was so misguided that their principles dictated nothing less than complete and total opposition. But if that is the case, why not make your points in a fierce, full-throttle debate? Why not try to win support from honest members of the opposition party through the rigor of arguing your ideas? What happened to winning support from the American people? Unfortunately, part of the problem in the House is that gerrymandering has limited the spectra of constituencies for many individual members. Increasingly, they are rewarded for picking their own choir and preaching to it.

But this dishonest game of political correctness is not played by Republicans alone. Both parties, Democrats and Republicans, use ideological litmus tests. Each has its own politically correct speech within its respective political base. During the Bush years, neoconservatives attempted to expel and marginalize people who questioned the wisdom of the wars in Afghanistan and Iraq, like Congressman Ron Paul. On the Democratic side, politicians rarely speak out against abortion rights, since Governor Bob Casey was prevented from delivering a pro-life speech at the 1992 Democratic National Convention. At both ends of the political spectrum, compromise and moderation have become politically incorrect.

The Constitution that created the Congress was itself the child of debate. Ron Chernow, author of definitive biographies of George Washington and Alexander Hamilton, wrote in a *Wall Street Journal* essay about the Founding Fathers that the "rough-and-tumble tactics" of debate among the nation's first politicians was to be expected and "for sheer verbal savagery, the founding era may have surpassed anything seen today." In Chernow's view, the Founding Fathers led the revolution against Britain by daring to speak out, and after "sharpening their verbal skills hurling polemics against the British Crown, the founding generation then directed those energies against each other during the tumultuous first decade of the federal government." And in their speeches and public writings, the nation's first leaders proved to be more than willing to engage in a war of words, be it on paper or in public.

Those leaders not only spoke up and stood by their positions but demonstrated the capacity to listen, to be persuaded, and to take action for the common good. For example, after harsh criticism of the Constitution emerged, Alexander Hamilton decided to put together a series of essays to make the case for ratifying the nation's founding document. Those eighty-five essays swayed convention delegates in New York to back the new Constitution. Thomas Jefferson described those essays, the Federalist Papers, as the "best commentary of government which ever was written." The Supreme Court has cited the essays in its opinions 317 times across the years—from 1790 to 2005—in citations by both liberal and conservative members of the Court.

Strong, clear lines of debate were critical when the country verged on coming apart over slavery. In Senate campaign debates between Abraham Lincoln and Stephen Douglas in 1858, the men took turns speaking for hours on whether slavery should be allowed to spread into the nation's new territories to the west, which would have lasting consequences for the institution's place and influence in the nation as a whole. Although Lincoln eventually lost the election to Douglas, the press coverage was intense and word of it spread nationally. It engaged the major developments of the day, from the Compromise of 1850 to the Supreme Court's *Dred Scott* ruling in 1857. Lincoln refined his arguments against slavery to write a book that furthered the debate and became the starting point of his presidential candidacy. The historical power of these debates is obvious in hindsight. Yet it is important to remember that Lincoln, despite losing his Senate race to Douglas, did not censor or renounce his arguments against slavery to win more votes. He did seek common ground—he was not calling for abolition of all slavery. But he never backed off his side of the debate for fear of alienating voters in his party. In twenty-first-century terms, he didn't trim his position to conform to national polling data. Here was a major national voice letting everyone see him struggling, grappling with admitting failure, at times, but demonstrating sincerity and love of country as he addressed the hot-button issue of his generation.

The power of debate to shape the nation is clear again during the Reconstruction era that followed the Civil War, as well as later around the foreign-policy debates that led to U.S. involvement in World War I.

In the years between 1890 and the start of the Great Depression in 1929, the Supreme Court put in place laws to foster an aggressive brand of capitalism in the United States. It enforced a strict reading of the "freedom to contract," which included striking down state laws on minimum wages, doing away with limits on how many hours an employee could be required to work, and making it more difficult to unionize workers. The economic collapse of '29 sparked a major debate about the ability of "robber baron" capitalists to regulate and maintain the stable economic markets essential to the nation's future. In 1932 President Roosevelt responded by offering America a vision of a muscular federal government taking a commanding role in the nation's economic affairs. A new Supreme Court set aside legal precedents to open the nation's door to vast new federal regulation of monetary policy, to allow minimum wage laws, to allow child labor laws, and to make it easier for unions to organize workers. The immediate results of FDR's New Deal programs in putting Americans back to work proved popular and helped FDR's Democrats win control of the White House and both houses of Congress (they would keep the White House for seven out of nine terms between 1933 and 1969); they also converted many African Americans from allegiance to the party of Lincoln.

But political triumph did not stop the debate between free

markets and government regulation. "I fear [Roosevelt's Social Security policies] may end the progress of a great country and bring its people to the level of the average European,"
Senator Daniel Hastings, a Delaware Republican, said of the
president and his Social Security plan. "It will . . . add great
strength to the political demagogue. It will assist in driving
worthy and courageous men from public life. It will discourage
and defeat the American trait of thrift. It will go a long way
toward destroying American initiative and courage." Hastings
and other Republicans challenged Roosevelt on diminishing
the rights of individual states to control their own commerce,
as well as unwarranted intrusion through federal regulation of
commerce. Social Security drew particularly harsh critiques
from Republicans as an attempt to "Sovietize America."

The contest of ideas about the federal government's role in
restraining the worst instincts of big business and its role in
providing a social safety net to protect Americans from economic hardship continued for decades. It can be traced from
FDR's time through arguments over President Johnson's Great
Society programs to recent efforts to enact national health-
care legislation. In the 1950s, the future president Ronald
Reagan entered the debate, speaking out in opposition to proposals for what became Medicare, which Reagan called "socialized medicine." Reagan warned that if the government got
in the business of health care, it would cripple the nation and
Americans in the future would "spend our sunset years telling our children, and our children's children, what it once was
like in the United States where men were free." This enduring
debate extended to questions about the use of federal government spending to stir economic activity. As early as 1948 con-

servative scholar Henry Rottschaefer wrote, in commentary that seems like the early-twenty-first-century conservative rebuttals to President Obama's policies, that the country was on a track away "from individualism toward socialism, from acceptance of an economic system operating in response to the profit motive to belief in . . . government planning."

Between those familiar lines of liberal-versus-conservative jousting over social and fiscal policy, a series of shifts took place in how Americans debated. In the years after World War II the right wing revitalized itself as the party of strong, flag-waving opposition to communists. The Republican Party became the home of people who drew their identity as the true guardians of American liberty, with a continued focus on the threat of government growing too big as a result of New Deal policies. The intense, often singular vigilance against communist influences in American life offended Democrats, who did not see the need for the fierce anticommunist attitude. It did not help that some Republicans labeled Democrats "fellow travelers," "soft" on communists, and even "anti-American." By 1958 the John Birch Society had been launched as a conservative group with a limited, hard-line agenda—battling communists and rolling back FDR's big-government programs. The Birch Society sometimes ventured into extremism, such as when members hinted that President Eisenhower, a former general and a Republican, was a communist agent.

But the fervor of the John Birchers proved to be a tonic for Republicans. The Birchers shifted the center of the GOP away from Wall Street to Middle America. Their embrace of patriotism and traditions offered simple, clear themes that stirred grassroots voters and drew media attention to the Republican

Party. Their attacks on liberal elites who did not understand the threat of communism, on people in academia, and on Hollywood also drew attention, although some of it had anti-Semitic undertones. A few conservative intellectuals, notably the writer William F. Buckley, offered a more sophisticated brand of Republican identity. Arizona Republican Barry Goldwater, drawing on Western, libertarian, and conservative ideas of protecting individual rights, made a significant contribution to this contest of ideas about the nation's priorities with his book *The Conscience of a Conservative* in 1960.

The Republican Party also became the home of what was described by politicians in the Vietnam War era as the "silent majority," those frustrated by the rise of racial tensions in big cities and growing protests against sending the U.S. military to fight communists in the tiny, distant country of Vietnam. GOP politicians gained votes by giving voice to calls for law and order in big cities and support for troops abroad. The passage of civil rights laws, particularly the Civil Rights Act of 1964 and the Voting Rights Act of 1965, acted to polarize the Far Left and the Far Right, with each side labeling the other as racist. It was a period that saw a realignment of the political parties, as they began, in the words of law professor Richard Pildes, to "define themselves along different, more ideologically coherent, and polarized lines."

After LBJ's bold civil rights actions, the white South (and thus the South electorally) was all but lost to the Democrats, and as a result their coalition reconfigured and absorbed new support from the black community, urban centers, and new-left factions of youthful progressives, feminists, unions, and the antiwar movement. The Democratic Party became more diverse in the latter half of the twentieth century, even as its ideology became more rigid. Meanwhile, the influx of white Southern voters to the Republican Party also gave a new religious tinge to conservative politics. Thanks to the Supreme Court decision in *Roe v. Wade,* abortion became a polarizing issue as religious conservatives and Christian Right groups, uniting against it, emerged as major voices, driving white, mostly Baptist churchgoers in unprecedented numbers to the Republican Party. Unlike those of earlier eras, many of the debates of the seventies and eighties over critical social issues gained definition and power from third-party groups like the Christian Right. And politicians, to gain favor with these groups, began tailoring their positions on key issues to fit the litmus test. It became increasingly difficult for politicians to express respect for opposing points of view. Discussions among leading political figures and among leading academics were increasingly derided as elitism. Debate, too, fell into disrepute, because nuanced positions and compromise threatened to dull the sharp edges of critical wedge issues— communism, gays, forced integration, the right to have a gun. Real debate presented a threat to people whose fixed political positions gave them strong identities as crusading liberals or law-abiding conservatives.

Economic shifts, too, changed the nature of political discourse in the second half of the twentieth century, as white-collar jobs for college graduates eclipsed blue-collar, industrial employment. More low-wage labor jobs moved overseas, and the number of Americans in labor unions shrank. More educated, affluent Americans—especially whites—moved to the suburbs, removing themselves from racially turbulent cities with higher taxes and higher crime rates. In the midst of so much social and economic upheaval, the desire for simple, clear answers and stability put a premium on fixed political positions. "Whereas Democrats held fast to their New Deal liberal and internationalist vision," St. Louis University history professor Donald Critchlow wrote in describing the political shifts at the end of the century, "Republicans represented the fears of white middle-class and religious voters through a political platform of low taxes, national defense, preservation of family values, regulation of social morality, and opposition to policies that affirmed racial, gender, or sexual preferences in the public sphere."

With personal identity and political identity so closely linked, there was a big jump between the 1970s and the 2000s in Americans expressing strong identification as Republicans or Democrats. Among the nation's political leaders in the House, the percentage of moderates decreased from 30 percent in 1976 to 8 percent by 2002. In the Senate the proportion of members who identified themselves as moderates in the same period fell from 41 percent to 5 percent. Candidates seeking office had to be less willing to speak out and more willing to fit into a liberal or a conservative box.

In the 1992 election, with political polarization on the rise, President George H. W. Bush was viewed by many fellow Republicans as a political moderate and was seen as insufficiently conservative. That led to a primary challenge from conservative commentator and former Nixon aide Pat Buchanan, who spoke of President Bush's inattention to a national "culture war" over family values, gay rights, welfare, and the growth of government and taxation. The "culture war" required

red-blooded conservatives to do battle in the fight over social values. They also had to be resolutely opposed to taxes. The "too moderate" label pressed on President Bush—a war hero, former head of the CIA, and Reagan's vice president—might as well have been translated as a charge that Bush was too willing to listen, debate, reconsider, and respond. "Moderate Republican" became a slur against Bush. Buchanan's primary challenge to the sitting president focused on social issues. Meanwhile, businessman Ross Perot challenged him on tax policy. In the general election Perot harassed Bush for failing, in the face of rising debt, to keep a 1988 campaign pledge on taxes—"Read my lips. No new taxes." Perot got 19 percent of the general-election vote, a record for an independent, with the overwhelming share of that support coming from President Bush's base, paving the way for President Clinton's victory. Bush's defeat made clear that politicians in office can't risk changing position in response to changing realities, unless they want to stir challenges among supporters in their base.

That rigid polarization increased as Republican opposition to President Clinton—epitomized by Newt Gingrich's Contract with America—led to Democrats losing the majority of the House for the first time in nearly half a century. Politicians kept any errant thoughts to themselves to allow their base of supporters to label them as safely and predictably as possible on the liberal or conservative side. Any variance from orthodox policy on the Left or Right became a hot topic on talk radio, particularly conservative talk radio, which grew phenomenally during the early nineties. Bob Grant in New York, Mike Siegel in Seattle, and Rush Limbaugh "coast to coast" became, in the words of the *New York Times,* "precinct captains" who enforced conservative orthodoxy on Republican candidates while stirring anti-Washington, anti-Clinton, antiliberal biases that transformed every conversation about political issues into a confrontation. Conservative talk radio made the 1994 midterm election a referendum on President Clinton, a man they mocked for three hours a day, five days a week as a dangerous liberal pushing the country to the socialist left with his elitist Yale law degree and his feminist wife. After the Republicans won control of the House of Representatives in 1994 in the so-called Republican revolution, the Republican freshman lawmakers made Limbaugh an honorary member of their caucus.

Liberal orthodoxy also came to the fore as President Clinton, in response to the failure of popular left-wing proposals to allow gays to serve in the military and reform the health-care system, tried to regain his political footing with a policy called "triangulation," in which he made himself into the man in the middle, reaching out to the polarized Left and Right. That did not sit well with his liberal base. Clinton was labeled a "New Democrat," code for a Democrat willing to turn away from the legacy of the New Deal that had dominated his party for more than half a century. Even before Republicans gained control of Congress and threatened to make Clinton a one-term president, *New York Times* columnist Bob Herbert wrote: "There is some question now as to whether there is any principle for which Bill Clinton will fight. . . . He has established a long and consistent . . . pattern. . . . The disappointment and disillusionment with President Clinton are widespread."

Herbert's column showed how inflexible the Left was toward politicians who veered off the party message. But it also cut to the heart of an era in which politicians refused to admit to who they were—how they had acted with regard to drug use, sexual behavior, taxes, and family. They kept their thinking on major policy issues hidden as well. Even in formal debates there was little expectation of a real exchange of ideas among political candidates. Typically in primary and general-election debates, candidates refused to agree to formats that allowed for timed debate with point and counterpoint. They kicked out the League of Women Voters, the group that had historically hosted debates, so they did not have to negotiate the rules with anyone who might insist on actual debate. Instead, candidates agreed to joint news conferences in which they answered questions from well-known journalists. The operative rule was for politicians to play it safe by repeating their fixed positions on issues. The media, for its part, previewed debates as if they amounted to horse races, focusing on who was leading and who had to catch up and saving special attention for a put-down or insult of an opponent. It was the era of CNN's *Crossfire*, a show I worked on as a cohost. There was no room for conservatives and liberals to have a reasoned debate of the issues on *Crossfire*. Differences drove the ratings. The producers wanted people shouting, not talking, to one another. I used to joke that the ideal *Crossfire* guests would be Louis Farrakhan on the Left and David Duke on the Right.

This fragmentation of the media has played its part in the polarization of politics too. While the media has always been interested in controversy, scandal, and conflict, it has become consumed by them in recent years. Major news outlets have abandoned any pretense of speaking for the middle by picking ideological sides—for example, the liberal *New York Times* editorial page versus the conservative *Wall Street Journal* editorial page.

President Clinton's impeachment added to the media's embrace of political polarization. There was no time on the top news shows for deliberate discussion of major issues when rumors, political wrangling, and salacious hearings drove ratings. One need only look so far as President Clinton's 1998 missile attacks on Sudan and Afghanistan, targeting a then-little-known (to most Americans) terrorist named Osama bin Laden. Was our focus on this new threat and what needed to be done about it? No, the focus was on whether the president of the United States was launching missiles to distract the public from his sex scandal. I think, at this point, we can all concede that we were the ones missing the real story.

In the 2000 presidential election, the money available to political extremes had become apparent. It was the first campaign in history where the candidates spent less money on TV advertising than the national political parties. The Republican National Committee and the Democratic National Committee combined to spend $79.9 million on so-called soft-money attack ads. Those ads, featuring wedge issues, energized their respective political bases and drew in more money. The candidates participated in this politically correct campaigning by holding closely to scripted, politically correct positions for fear of contradicting any of the ads being run by their most animated supporters. Spending by the political parties fit with third-party attack ads, funded again by "soft money" also removed from direct candidate accountability. For example, in the 2000 campaign the NAACP ran an ad falsely accusing candidate George W. Bush of going easy on two white men who killed a black man by dragging him behind their car until he died. The Gore campaign did not have to respond because it had not run the ad. The truth, however, was that the men had been given the maximum sentence for the crimes they committed. But Bush had strong ties with the black and Hispanic communities in Texas, winning substantial minority votes in his successful campaigns for governor. The NAACP was simply trying to squelch popular support for Bush among blacks nationwide in their attack ad.

In this acid media environment the candidates changed their tactics. The Bush campaign spent its ad money narrowly, avoiding general audiences and open debate in favor of targeting heavily Republican areas, with the goal of getting out as many Republican voters as possible. Even in so-called red states, the GOP did not spend time or money on urban areas with high percentages of young people, minorities, single women, and educated professionals—or, as one GOP strategist described them, Volvo-driving, latte-drinking NPR listeners. They were not in the business of persuading people to vote for them so much as increasing the turnout of known Republican voters. The debate in the media narrowed as the big-city daily papers were attacked as liberal leaning by the openly conservative talk radio and blog universe. Bernard Goldberg's attack on the socially liberal media, *Bias,* became a top *New York Times* best seller in 2001.

The 9/11 attacks provided a rare retreat from rising political polarization as the country rallied around the flag and the president. The pause proved to be temporary. By July 2003 more than half of the public told pollsters that the news media—meaning big newspapers and the broadcast networks—had a liberal bias. That was a sharp rise from the 40 percent who had agreed that the liberal press was out of control in 1985. And in 2003 only 36 percent of Americans said they trusted the media to tell a straight story. Separate realities, with Democrats consuming liberal media and conservatives responding to right-wing media, meant stories that attracted headlines on one side of the political divide got no mention on the other side. Conservatives attacked liberal media for questioning the war effort, while liberals attacked the Bush administration for failing to find weapons of mass destruction in Iraq. The result was the new "law of group polarization," a term coined by Cass Sunstein, at the time a University of Chicago law professor. He made the case that independent-minded voters suddenly found themselves taking sides as they drank in news from echo chambers on the Left or Right that created a clubhouse atmosphere for anyone who shared the host's political views.

During the 2004 presidential campaign the polarization ratcheted up again around the issue of President Bush never having gone to war. His Democratic opponent, Senator John Kerry of Massachusetts, had been on the ground fighting in the Vietnam War. As his party's candidate, Kerry began his speech accepting the nomination with the words "reporting for duty." In response, Republicans began a surprising series of attacks questioning Kerry's military performance on swift boats that traveled up Vietnamese rivers to fight the enemy. They questioned the medals he had been awarded and whether he really threw them away later to protest the war, as he claimed. While the Bush campaign kept its distance, Kerry was attacked as a New England elitist who preferred Swiss cheese to Cheez Whiz and windsurfing to clearing brush. The coded language invited lowly talk as to whether Kerry was less manly than Bush, although it was Kerry who had actually gone to fight the war. Amazingly, the substance of political debate—the nation's wars in Afghanistan and Iraq, the economy, and the solvency of Social Security—became secondary to the character attacks.

Bush won reelection in another close race that reaffirmed the depth of the nation's political divide. But cynicism on both sides of the political divide and a deep distrust of government, the media, and political leaders reached new heights. Going into the 2008 campaign, a backlash, a national desire for candidates who could bridge the two sides, emerged. The candidate who best embodied that impulse, Democrat Barack Obama, gained attention for speaking of one America, rather than of blue states and red states, black and white, liberal and conservative. In his keynote speech to the 2004 Democratic National Convention, he famously challenged the country to move beyond blue states and red states and move forward as the United States. In his second book, *The Audacity of Hope*, he called for a civil, constructive dialogue and an end to the labels of "liberal" and "conservative." After the incendiary sermons of his longtime pastor, Jeremiah Wright, surfaced in the middle of the Democrats' primary races, he delivered one of the most revealing speeches about race relations in recent memory. In that speech in Philadelphia, he spoke of a racial stalemate where black anger and white resentment have largely become distractions that prevent the nation from coming together to solve real problems.

Obama gave the appearance of a candidate willing to engage in debate, a serious man, the anti–sound bite candidate.

His critics responded that he was being treated as a "messiah" by naive followers who failed to see him as a skilled politician. The criticism did not stick, largely because Obama seemed different. He was elected the first African American leader in a country where, as *Newsweek*'s Jonathan Alter has said, the first sixteen presidents could have owned him as property. The historic nature of his candidacy, combined with his God-given talents as an orator and politician, made him a transformational figure. Because of this gravitas, there was a belief that he could succeed where other politicians had failed in changing the political discourse.

In his inaugural speech, Obama spoke to a desire for honest, real political debate to solve the nation's problems. It was a message that played well. "On this day, we gather because we have chosen hope over fear, unity of purpose over conflict and discord. On this day, we come to proclaim an end to the petty grievances and false promises, the recriminations and worn-out dogmas that for far too long have strangled our politics. We remain a young nation. But in the words of Scripture, the time has come to set aside childish things."

Many hoped that President Obama would form a governing coalition that would break down the barriers that prevent us from talking honestly and openly about the myriad problems facing our country. But either Obama never intended to cross the political divide to really debate the Right or he did not have the political skills to do so. Whatever the cause, many of the noble promises of compromising to reach genuine solutions ran up against the cold, hard realities of a political institution—media, politics, and government—polarized and locked into place.

After the election, conservative columnist Ann Coulter sarcastically wrote that Republicans should show President Obama the same amount of respect that Democrats had shown President Bush over the past eight years—meaning not much. Coulter and others in the conservative media often refer to the president as "B. Hussein Obama." The clear intention is to cast him as a foreign influence, as someone different and potentially dangerous.

As a result of this polarizing scare tactic, a segment of our country now believes Barack Obama is not a Christian but a Muslim. According to public opinion polls, the number of Americans who believe he is a Muslim has increased since he has been in office.

Another group, the "birthers," believes that Obama is an illegitimate president because he is not really an American citizen. In their world, led of late by Donald Trump, the president was born not in Hawaii but in either Kenya or Indonesia. The facts are that Obama's birth certificate and archives of birth announcements in Hawaiian newspapers show that he was born in Honolulu, the capital of the fiftieth state. The birthers maintain that these documents are forgeries, part of an elaborate conspiracy to conceal his true identity. How can the American people collectively make a fair, informed evaluation of President Obama and his performance when a growing number of them are wildly misinformed about the basic facts of who he is? What these extreme groups do is use these tactics as a way of dismissing any discussion of President Obama's ideas or agenda. It's far easier to paint them with scandal than seriously debate them on their merits. President Obama himself captured this frustration in April of 2011 when the White House released his long-form birth certificate. In a press conference held at the time, President Obama said, "We do not have time for this kind of silliness."

The speed with which the hope and goodwill inspired by Obama as candidate evaporated during his first two years in office has to be one of the more remarkable tidal turns in modern American political history.

Once again it was driven by the power of polarization. The entrenched, moneyed interests maintain fierce control over what we can and can't say or debate. We are forced to pick column A or column B, one side or the other, limiting the gene pool of our thinking, leaving us with two sides that are equally inbred and unsustainable.

Again, our politicians' partisan views are bolstered by the money they generate—Representative Joe Wilson benefited handsomely from yelling, "You lie!" during Obama's address to Congress regarding health care in 2009. New Deal–era criticisms of federal government initiatives have been resurrected as surefire solicitations in e-mails, newsletters, and direct mail because they bring in the money every time. The mantra "big-government takeover" has been applied to actions ranging from banking regulations to the rescue of GM to health-care reform to Internet regulation (i.e., "network neutrality").

Media, of course, make money from our nondebate too. During the 2010 campaign, Sharron Angle, the Republican Senate candidate in Nevada, claimed that unemployment benefits for people who had been out of work for ninety-nine weeks should not be continued because they would create "a spoilage system," and she refused to do interviews with any media other than Fox News. Rather than debating the accuracy and merits of this claim, the media focused on her taunts to her opponent, Harry Reid, to "man up." Christine O'Donnell endorsed the ideas of partial privatization of Social Security and turning Medicare into a voucher program. Yet the media focused on a comment she had made on Bill Maher's *Politically Incorrect* panel in the 1990s about dabbling in witchcraft with her high-school boyfriend. These were two far-right candidates who deserved serious scrutiny of their ideas. The media could have and should have examined their views (and to be fair, many on the Left did), which I would describe as outside the main-stream of politics, rather than focusing on their personalities, colorful as those personalities may have been.

The sad backdrop against which this all played out is that seemingly overnight, once inside the presidential bubble, President Obama—the man who many hoped could change the national tone—seemed to lose his focus on his promise to work with political opponents, to seriously engage in debate, and to join hands with anyone trying to solve problems. He became fixated on passing laws by winning the votes of fellow Democrats who held the majorities in both the House and Senate. He lost interest in presenting and debating ideas for the American people. The real shift began as Obama had to bail out the banks and provide a stimulus to the economy. The harsh realities of governing, and the admittedly miserable choices before the new president, began to eat away at his coalition. And the repolarization between Democrats and Republicans was supercharged as Obama launched his health-care initiative. Furor erupted on the Right, and the vitriolic criticism, covered in detail by the media, spread the animus to the political center. Many Americans, with unemployment still high, saw the government hemorrhaging money and occupying a larger and larger share of the national economy and their personal lives.

That led to "town hall" confrontations over health-care reform, providing the media a bonanza of visceral conflict. Obama's administration did a poor job of talking to the public about the proposals and focused instead on getting votes in the House and Senate to pass the legislation. The horse-trading, the compromises, the concessions to big business, and the complexity of the legislation drowned out attempts to debate the bill on its merits. But perhaps nothing could have competed for media attention with the ease of airing angry outbursts at "town hall" meetings dominated by seniors who feared reductions in their Medicare benefits and heard scary talk about the plan including "death panels." It was the perfect storm that wiped away the promise of people daring to speak frankly across ideological lines.

Fueling and feeding on the frenzy was the Tea Party, which gained power during the midterm campaigns as a vehicle for expressing anger at health-care reform and tax increases.

The Tea Party is in part inspired by the Tea Party of 1773, where colonists dumped a shipment of British tea in the Boston Harbor to protest the high taxes on it. Speakers at today's Tea Party rallies invoke this spirit and quip that "TEA" is an acronym for "Taxed Enough Already." They claim taxes are too high and Obama has raised them even higher. It is a movement based on a tax protest and purports to be about tax increases. But its advocates ignore the facts in favor of fiery attacks. The reality is that Obama actually lowered taxes for 95 percent of Americans in his first two years. The vast majority of people attending these Tea Party rallies received a tax cut during this time. The much-criticized Obama stimulus package consisted primarily of tax cuts for middle-class Americans. This is a sheer, provable, knowable fact. I don't like to pay taxes. Nobody likes to pay taxes. With an enterprise as large as the U.S. government, there will always be waste, fraud, and abuse. It should be investigated, mitigated, and eliminated where possible. But as Oliver Wendell Holmes Jr. once said, taxes are the price we pay for living in a civilized society. Our visceral disgust at the idea of taxation does not entitle us to misrepresent the truth about Obama's tax policy. If one group of Americans is entering the conversation from a false premise, how can we have a constructive dialogue that results in a fairer tax system that can pay for government services?

The Tea Party movement enjoyed considerable success in 2010. Its candidates mounted strong conservative challenges to establishment candidates in Republican primaries and prevailed in many cases. On the senatorial level, Sharron Angle bested Sue Lowden in Nevada. Ken Buck prevailed over Jane Norton in Colorado. Joe Miller defeated incumbent Republican senator Lisa Murkowski in Alaska. Charlie Crist, a popular Republican governor, fell to Tea Party favorite Marco Rubio in Florida. And last but certainly not least, former governor and longtime Republican congressman Mike Castle lost to Christine O'Donnell in Delaware. All of these vanquished Republicans were seen as insufficiently conservative by the Tea Party. They had said or done something in their career that made them suspect. They were too willing to compromise with the other side. Yet with the exception of Rubio, all of these Tea Party–backed candidates lost in the general election to their Democratic opponents (apart from Miller, who in fact lost to

Murkowski as she triumphed in a write-in campaign). Even John McCain, two years earlier the Republican nominee for the presidency, who had built a career on being a maverick, a voice of moderation and independence in the Senate, was forced to abandon his claim to maverick status and toe the conservative party line after being challenged in his Arizona primary by conservative J. D. Hayworth.

The Tea Party is a fitting representation of our era of no-debate, politically correct politics, where each political side has its own media, and opposing views are almost never given a fair hearing. Conservatives listen only to conservatives, and liberals listen only to liberals. People are spared the inconvenience of facts that don't fit their beliefs and the unpleasantness of seriously considering a point of view other than their own. The ideological media bubbles offer both comfort and protection for the people within them.

With the political and media mainstream holding to their politically correct stands, honest debate loses. The liberal base is safe in its self-righteousness, and the conservative base is safe in its self-righteousness. And the middle has been reduced to the size of a pin.

Some see the current state of political polarization in this country as a threat: "It induces alignment along multiple lines of potential conflict and organizes individuals and groups around exclusive identities, thus crystallizing interests into opposite factions," wrote professors Delia Baldassarri and Andrew Gelman in assessing the state of American politics.

Others see it as a sign of a mature democracy: "The 20th century figures we associate with moderation, compromise, and appeals to the center should perhaps be viewed as manifestations of an earlier, less mature stage of American democratic development," argues law professor Richard Pildes. "Conversely, the hyperpolarization of the last generation should be understood as the steady-state of American democracy, the manifestation of a more mature American democracy, and hence likely to be enduring."

But polarization has changed American politics dramatically by creating a narrow band of political platforms catering to a hyperpolarized electorate. MoveOn.org, DailyKos, and the Huffington Post have carved out liberal niches on the Left, catering to a small but vocal number of ultraliberal voters. On the Right, sites such as Red State and the Drudge Report give attention to fringe movements—like the birthers—which gain legitimacy (and notoriety) in this polarized media landscape that is hungry for extreme stories.

If there is a bright spot in the spectrum of voices, it might be people like Jon Stewart and Stephen Colbert, who—though certainly leftward in orientation—effectively criticize politicians across the spectrum, the partisan machinery, and the media with powerful satire. But as Jon Stewart himself seems to acknowledge regularly, they are not a *replacement* for vigorous and honest debate but a *check* on the impulses that lead us away from clearing our way through the political fog. Stewart once abandoned his satire to tell the hosts of CNN's *Crossfire* that as a serious news program on a channel people turn to for actual news, "You have a responsibility to the public discourse, and you fail miserably. . . . When you have people on for just knee-jerk, reactionary talk . . . oh, it's so painful to watch. . . . You know, because we need what you do. . . . This is such a great opportunity you have here to actually get politicians off of their marketing and strategy." Stewart said the CNN show was "not honest" in advertising itself as a place for serious debate when it actually contented itself with engaging in "partisan hackery."

Political correctness has grown so thick that, like an untended garden, it is now less about the flowers than it is about the weeds. Too much of American politics has become an exercise in institutional madness, hampering the nation's ability to solve urgent problems. More and more, Americans are turning to voices such as Jon Stewart, a court jester of sorts, in the hope of finding any glimmer of light—the truth—through all the mudslinging and haze. If comedy and entertainment are all we expect of our national dialogue, clearly we're abdicating our responsibility as citizens, relying on Jon Stewart to shoulder the burden of breaking routine and snapping us to attention when it's necessary. That's a lot to put on a comedian. But it appears to be just what happened with the Ground Zero rescue workers bill (which ultimately passed, in large part, it would seem, thanks to Stewart's call to action).

In sum, the business of political polarization is booming, at the expense of meaningful discussion and debate on a wide swath of issues of critical importance to the United States. And so far *we* are providing little incentive to the forces of polarization to moderate themselves. I think it starts with demanding real and honest debate on the biggest issues before us. We don't need to suffer talking points and epithets anymore.

CHAPTER 4

9/11 AND OTHER
MAN-CAUSED DISASTERS

I S IT POSSIBLE to talk about Muslims and terrorism without being called a bigot?

The United States is at war with a "far-reaching network of violence and hatred," President Obama said at the start of his 2009 inaugural address. He did not name the people trying to destroy the nation as Muslim terrorists. Later he said America's spirit cannot be broken by unnamed people "who seek to advance their aims by inducing terror and slaughtering innocents." His lone direct message to the Muslim world was limited to "We seek a new way forward" based on mutual respect. The president's delicate approach to Muslim terrorism continued during a visit to India in 2010 when a student asked the president his opinion of jihad. President Obama is renowned for using exact language in service of mature dialogue. But in response to that question he suddenly jumped into a sea of fawning deference, ambiguity, and amorphous thoughts—in other words, political correctness. "Well, the phrase 'jihad' has a lot of meanings within Islam," he said, "and is subject to a lot of different interpretations. But I will say that, first, Islam is one of the world's great religions. And [among the] more than a billion people who practice Islam, the overwhelming majority view their obligations to their religion as ones that reaffirm peace and justice and fairness and tolerance." Later he managed to mention that violence against civilians is wrong.

The president trod carefully to avoid offending Muslims. But no matter how fast he talked, the heavy weight of political correctness dragged his words down, drowning any clear message. But there is a message about Muslim terrorism that every thoughtful, aware person in the world, including Muslims, should be free to boldly speak without fear of offending anyone. That simple, clear message is that it is wrong for Muslims to kill others in the name of their religion. And to people outside the Muslim world the term "jihad" has become familiar as the war cry of Muslim terrorists killing people in the name of their religion. With the world living in fear of Muslim terrorism, the president might have challenged Muslims to speak out against extreme, violent jihadists acting in the name of God. But instead of delivering the bottom line in direct, plain language, the president got bogged down, pulled into depths of politically correct speech that left his audience stuck and with no clear direction. On the path of straight speaking, the president might have said Muslim terrorists are the ones who corrupt the term "jihad" to justify murdering people. They are guilty of creating a link between Islam and murderous violence. Then the president might have explained why it is an act not of bigotry but of rationality to directly ask if Islamic commands for a faithful life can be reconciled with respect for individual rights guaranteed in a nation living under civil law such as the U.S. Constitution. The president's politically correct divergence from the hard truth did not comfort Muslims. It did not reassure Jews or Christians. And it did not spur moderate Muslims to speak out against Muslim extremism. It just left the issue on the table.

The more the president and other leaders twist their words to avoid the hard truth about terrorism and its ties to Muslims, the more fear and suspicion are left to fester. Politically correct attempts to avoid that harsh reality open the door to fear, stereotypes, and outbreaks of pent-up anger that lead to anti-Muslim bigotry. This is precisely the conversation I was having with Bill O'Reilly when I admitted to getting nervous when I see people in Muslim garb on airplanes.

As with much of politically correct speech, Obama's intentions are good; they are noble. The president did not want to paint an entire religion with a broad brush. As the leader of the United States he does not want to shred the Constitution and establish a police state or place Muslims in internment camps. While we don't want that, we cannot delude ourselves into pretending that those impulses—from fear—don't exist. We can decide they are the wrong impulses to act on without being told not to express them. It is censorship to discourage talk about the fact that terrorism in the world today is coming largely from Muslim countries and the people embracing it claim to be serving their Muslim faith by engaging in what they call jihad. It does not make you a bigot to recognize that the major terrorist threat in our time to stable governments and civil societies around the globe is rooted in Islam. It does not make us bigots if we dare to speak the truth: Islamic extremism is a grave threat to U.S. national security. The president must be clear in addressing the challenge of how

Americans can effectively resist this threat without condemning an entire religion.

President Obama's administration came into office bent on
changing the language around the Muslim terror threat. As a
matter of policy the president and his top staff wanted to encourage a new, less belligerent way of talking about Muslims
and terrorism. No more of Vice President Cheney's declaring that he wants Osama bin Laden's "head on a platter." No
more of President Bush boasting of seeking al Qaeda terrorists "dead or alive" and challenging America's enemies in the
Middle East to send more combatants to Iraq with the taunt
"Bring them on." President Obama wanted to clear the air of
right-wing condemnation, a brand of political correctness that
labels any critic as unpatriotic for raising doubts about the need
for U.S. forces in Iraq or the Patriot Act's erosion of civil liberties. It was time to end Bush press secretary Ari Fleischer's
edict that when it came to terrorism and Bush administration
war policies, people had to watch what they talked about.

Again, the intentions are noble. But this approach has resulted in a lack of honest, rational conversation about the
genuine threat of Islamic terrorism. It is an invitation to mock
well-intentioned people for falling victim to the blurry thinking
that comes with political correctness. This is the brilliant and
evil heart of terrorism. It creates blinding fear to the point that
smart, normally articulate people fail to have the honest discussions necessary to craft rational responses to contain terrorists.

In discussing her first testimony to Congress with Germany's
Der Spiegel, Homeland Security secretary Janet Napolitano

said she did not want to use the word "terrorism." Napolitano explained that she preferred to refer to 9/11 and subsequent attacks as "man-caused disasters." The reason, she explained, is that "we want to move away from the politics of fear toward a policy of being prepared for all risks that can occur." The impact was not to lessen fear but to indicate her approval of politically correct restraints on anyone who wanted to talk about Muslim terrorism. Her mandates resulted in derision from administration critics. Fox talk-show host Sean Hannity pointed out that Napolitano's approach undermined confidence in the new administration's determination to keep the United States safe: "Madam Secretary," Hannity said, "if you can't even call it by its name, how exactly do you plan to protect us against it? Shying away from the word 'terrorism' in an effort to be politically correct is cowardly, not courageous." The Homeland Security secretary's sterilized language also had the effect of making it hard for anyone trying to clearly identify and understand a fierce and implacable enemy, a foe with no ties to other countries, a "nonstate" actor, in government parlance, who is willing to crash airplanes into buildings, plant bombs, and carry out assassinations. The one thing clear about this enemy's motivation to terrorize and kill Westerners is that they are acting in the name of Islam.

Similarly, Obama's secretary of state, Hillary Clinton, abandoned the phrase "war on terror." In the spring of 2009, speaking to reporters who asked her why she did not want to use those words, she dodged the issue: "I haven't gotten any directive about using it or not using it. It is just not being used," she said.

Secretary Clinton's announcement was followed by news

of a Pentagon memo asking military officials to avoid using the phrase "global war on terror" in favor of "overseas contingency operations." In April 2010 the president's national-security team decided to edit any mention of "Islamic extremism" out of the National Security Strategy, the basic statement of policy for protecting vital U.S. interests. Under President Bush the document had read: "The struggle against militant Islamic radicalism is the great ideological conflict of the early years of the 21st century." A few months later John Brennan, the president's top counterterrorism adviser, elaborating on a point Napolitano had broached, explained that the new president had concluded that terrorism was not the enemy. Terrorism is a tactic or a state of mind, he said, diving into the sea of political correctness. Taking national pride into the sea with him, he issued the proud but meaningless claim that Americans refuse to live in fear—even as we spend billions on security and go to war to combat Muslim terrorists.

Before completely disappearing beneath the waves of political correctness, he announced: "Nor do we describe our enemy as jihadists or Islamists because jihad is a holy struggle . . . meaning to purify oneself . . . and there is nothing holy or legitimate or Islamic about murdering innocent" people. By that logic the United States is not at war with terrorists, Muslim extremists, or jihadists. Our enemy is to be defined as organizations using violent tactics, such as al Qaeda and its affiliates. There is no longer mention of terrorists or Muslims. And there can be no mention of the gulf that exists between Judeo-Christian religions and Islamists, who would impose perversions of Muslim religious tenets as national laws. Stoning women to death for adultery, cutting off their noses for refusing to become child brides, denying them the right to an education—these things do not happen under civil law accepted by Jews and Christians. That's a fact. And it is a fact that they are accepted under various interpretations of Islam's Sharia law.

The best that can be said about these flights into euphemistic fantasy is that they pleased liberals who were fed up with years of hard-line rhetoric from the Bush administration. The worst that can be said about the administration's policy statements is that they are a blatant departure to the land of muddled thinking born of politically correct speech, a land with eyes blind to the reality of violent Muslim extremists launching worldwide terrorist attacks on people in an office building in New York, people on a train in Spain, people on vacation in Indonesia.

What is frustrating to me as a journalist is that Americans have displayed incredible maturity since 9/11 in dealing with the Muslim terror threat. President Bush visited a mosque in the days after the 9/11 attacks to make a public display of his belief that it was wrong to blame all Muslims for the violence. On September 20, 2001, he told a joint session of Congress: "The terrorists practice a fringe form of Islamic extremism that has been rejected by Muslim scholars and the vast majority of Muslim clerics—a fringe movement that perverts the peaceful teachings of Islam." The Republican president displayed tact and sensitivity at a moment of national crisis. Meanwhile, American faith leaders held joint worship services around the country for Christian, Jewish, and Muslim clerical leaders to come together and offer an example of unity in the face of the potentially divisive fallout from attacks justified as an Islamic mission. This evidence of maturity and restraint gave the nation a basis for an honest conversation on the topic. As an author of several books on black American history, I can give voice to how far the United States has come in dealing with racism and bigotry. The civil rights movement in the United States achieved many of its goals with appeals to conscience, calls to action based on Christian principles, historical reference to the nation's founding ideals of all men being equal, and the power of the nation's commitment to justice under law. These principles withstood riots in the streets, the murder of Nobel Peace Prize winner Dr. Martin Luther King Jr., and bitter, divisive segregationist appeals. Our nation came through the fire, demonstrating the capacity to deal with the racial divide, the deepest cut in our country's history. Even when it came to war, the country has acknowledged its mistakes of the past. During World War II President Roosevelt ordered one hundred thousand Japanese Americans into detention camps, as if they constituted an enemy within. The remorse and shame over that action prevented any similar treatment of Korean Americans during the Korean War or Vietnamese Americans during the Vietnam War. And in 1988 Congress went so far as to vote for an official apology to survivors of the Japanese internment. America has hard-earned status among the nations of the world when it comes to dealing with racial diversity and minority rights.

As for fear that forthright discussion about Muslim terrorism might result in a spike of religious intolerance directed against Muslims, it is a statement of historical fact that if any country in the world has a history of frank, peaceful discussions on religion, it is the United States. The United States is home to remarkable tolerance of varying religious practices, to the point of protecting the rights of nonbelievers; repeated court rulings have come down against the Christian majority labeling the United States a Christian nation. Polling done for a 2010 book on religion in the United States found that an overwhelming majority of Americans said people practicing other faiths can go to heaven. Professors David Campbell and Robert Putnam, the authors of the book *American Grace*, also reported that wide majorities of Christians in the United States, including the most devout evangelicals, stated their belief that Muslims, Jews, Buddhists, and atheists can all go to heaven. Islam ranks among the least popular religions in the United States today, but the authors note that not long ago Judaism and Catholicism, now among the most respected faiths, were among the least respected. Their rise in the esteem of people of other faiths is offered as evidence of the nation's capacity for tolerance and ability to engage in reasoned debate on Islamic terror.

So why would President Obama, NPR, or anyone else on the Left or Right want to stop Americans, and particularly O'Reilly and me, from talking to one another about this threat, as if we are not to be trusted? There is a hunger for better information, a deep desire to engage in these difficult conversations when it comes to Muslims and terrorism. Yet so many supposedly well-meaning people in politics and media don't trust other Americans to take part in these debates. How can Americans avoid these conversations when the FBI and other law-enforcement agencies are tracking Muslim terror suspects and monitoring their conversations in the United States and abroad? When the courts are trying to establish the basis for surveillance and there are legal and ethical questions about profiling Muslims? When government agencies are determining what is within legal limits as they infiltrate places where radical Muslim ideology is being championed, including places of worship, mosques? How can we be told to shut up, be careful what we say, or even be fired for joining a conversation that is under way?

Already the effort to repress conversation on Muslim terrorism is resulting in a deadly form of debate breaking out. In whispered, conspiratorial tones Americans are joining the rest of the world in asking why, if Islam is a peaceful religion, is there a pattern of attacks on Christians in countries with Muslim majorities? Why do Muslims tear down historic Buddhist monuments? Why can you regularly read of Muslims burning schools for girls? Why do imams indoctrinate so many terrorists? Why was Daniel Pearl, an American Jewish journalist, beheaded in the name of Islam? Why is an American political cartoonist, Molly Norris, in hiding because of death threats by Muslims upset at her suggestion of a "Draw Mohammed Day"? Why was the Metropolitan Museum of Art in New York compelled to take down all artwork depicting the Prophet Muhammad from its Islamic exhibition? Why was Theo van Gogh, a Dutch filmmaker, killed by Muslims for making a film about Muslim abuse of women?

Pretending that this pattern of Muslim violence does not exist makes no sense. Moreover, it is dangerous, because it suppresses the necessary public vent of honest conversation, open dialogue, and debate. It exacerbates tension as pent-up fear, worries, and anger emerge. And it is likely to become ugly when acted on by frustrated people tired of being called bigots for seeing what is plain as day but not being able to speak about it. In September 2010, the month before I was fired for talking about my fear of Muslim terrorism, the AP reported that the Justice Department reported that it was investigating several anti-Muslim incidents in four states. In one case a brick was thrown at a window of the Madera Islamic Center in California. Signs left behind read: "NO TEMPLE FOR THE GOD OF TERRORISM" and "WAKE UP AMERICA—THE ENEMY IS HERE!" Justice was also responding to an attack against a Muslim New York City cab driver who had his throat slashed by a man raging against Muslims. The FBI is dealing with growing vandalism at mosques. And famously, there is an uproar with a strong anti-Muslim flavor over a perfectly legal plan to build a mosque several blocks away from Ground Zero, the site of the 9/11 attacks that brought the World Trade Center crashing down. In Oklahoma, a state with a tiny Muslim population, the state legislature passed an anti-Sharia law at the prompting of politicians looking for an issue to drive up their poll numbers. And the pastor of a very small Christian church in Gainesville, Florida, became the center of international attention for announcing plans to burn the Koran on the ninth anniversary of the 9/11 attacks.

These are examples of the growing tensions erupting among Americans as they are told to muffle and muzzle their fears of Muslim terrorism. Political, media, and religious leadership rightly protect the First Amendment rights of Muslims to practice their religion. But they fail to acknowledge and denounce radical Islamist elements preaching world domination through violence that are associated with terrorist groups in the Middle East, such as Hamas and Hezbollah. Such (well-intentioned) censors seem to me to be also opening the door to *more* Muslim terrorism in U.S. schools, in the military, and in jails by deriding those asking questions about radical Islamists as anti-Muslim bigots. If you admit you are suspicious of elements of Islam, you are called a bigot. So lots of people keep their suspicions to themselves. When law enforcement agencies capture Muslims engaged in planning terror plots, as they have in New York, New Jersey, Miami, Dallas, and Washington, DC, in the last year, the politically correct crowd reflexively ratchets up the message that not all Muslims are terrorists and calls for restraint in discussing the blatant links between extreme Muslims, Islamists, and terrorism. I call it censorship. This is a corrupt, self-defeating cycle. It limits the reasoned, rational assessments of genuine terror threats—an essential element of effective response.

The uncensored reality is that there are 1.5 billion Muslims in the world and Islam is the world's fastest-growing religion. The most pressing threat to our nation comes from this religion's determined extremist faction, the Islamists who see jihad as a holy mission to establish a one-world government, a caliphate, under Muslim law. Of course, the overwhelming majority of Muslims are peaceful people who are respectful of others, mean no harm, and are just trying to hold a job, pay the rent, and raise their children. However, if only one-tenth of 1 percent of Muslims are radicalized and intent on harming the United States and its allies in the name of Islam, that makes 1.5 million seeking to bring down democratic governments, ban religious diversity, and overturn Western civilization. That is an astoundingly large number, and by all indications the growth of Islam in the United States and the worldwide reach of the Internet are leading to increasing conflict between those bent on committing acts of terror and the rest of the world. To point this threat out is not bigotry. It is an act of self-preservation.

But the insidious hand of political correctness extends its corrupt fingers to shush people who are trying to introduce some straight talk into discussion of the Muslim terror threat. For example, when President Obama told Bob Woodward, my former *Washington Post* colleague, that the United States could absorb another terrorist attack, conservatives who normally rail against left-wing political correctness played their own game of avoiding hard truths. They hammered President Obama as a weak commander in chief who was effectively inviting another terrorist attack. But the president had done no such thing. He had simply told the truth: that he was doing everything he could to prevent another 9/11 but that even after 9/11 "the biggest attack ever . . . we absorbed it and we are stronger." The president spoke the truth. He was not giving in on the fight against terrorists. He was expressing almost hubristic, pro-American sentiment in noting the strength and resilience of our people and our country. Hard-line conservatives, sensing political vulnerability, turned it into a statement of surrender by a weak-kneed liberal Democrat. To them, the Democrats have long been suspect on national security. But they turned the president's words against him in an unfair way. We do a service when we shed light on a statement that exposes a hidden truth. But deliberately misconstruing comments and turning them into something else is a lie—it's a form of censorship, whether it's done by the Left or the Right.

This is the other side of the political pressures limiting rational assessment of terrorists' power. They undercut honest dialogue about the Muslim terror threat. The not-so-hidden factor at play here is that Republicans are setting the stage to blame President Obama should any terrorist act take place. It has the effect of forcing the president into a defensive posture, hindering decisions about the practical limits of what we can do to prevent terrorism. This is a tit-for-tat game because Republicans are still trying to justify every over-the-top, costly step taken by the Bush administration, including getting into questionable wars. The politically correct thinking suggests that the Bush team was right to keep its deliberations secret to ensure quick response to any terror event. It also reveals how scared the Bush White House was of another terrorist attack. Their thinking was to control the response to any threat and keep Congress and the public out, assuming that they, not Congress, would be blamed if anything happened. As a result, they wanted to make all the decisions. Even after the overwhelming passage of the Patriot Act, which gave the government unprecedented powers to conduct surveillance of any suspected terrorist, President Bush, without consulting Congress, secretly authorized domestic wiretaps, monitoring the e-mail of Americans. Three years later, when the *New York Times* learned what had happened, it wrote that allowing such violations of the privacy rights of Americans "crossed constitutional limits on legal searches." It also created a lack of accountability. It opened American intelligence agencies to charges of fixing their reports to please the White House. It called into question American credibility with other governments. The Department of Defense was similarly tarnished after Congress granted approval in 2002 for a program called the Information Awareness Office. The plan allowed for collecting and analyzing phone calls, e-mails, and personal information. But under the Bush administration the program was discovered to have become a digital "drift net" to grab any and all communications, or what an expert Internet technician later called "vacuum-cleaner surveillance of all the data crossing the Internet." That criticism grew so intense that Congress pulled funds for the program in 2003.

The real question, then and now, which no one is directly addressing, is how far we are willing to go to keep ourselves safe from terrorism. Most Americans, according to polls, are willing to sacrifice some rights in order to allow the government to keep the nation safe. Those polls show more Americans are willing to entrust government with expanded reach into their lives. But Americans don't want to create a big-brother state. Nonetheless, some conservatives, notably former vice president Cheney, want to silence anyone concerned about essential questions regarding constitutional protections—the heart of the American experiment. So, using another brand of political correctness, they demonize those who insist on public debate and demand accountability for American political leaders who go beyond constitutional limits.

The irony in this situation is that it is usually conservatives who are sensitive to any intrusion by big government, whether it comes in the form of a pat-down by airport security or a government health-care plan. The consensus in the intelligence community is that the country is safer today from terrorism than it has ever been. In their language, targets—U.S. airports, buildings, and monuments—have been hardened, and Congress and the Bush and Obama administrations have all greatly increased surveillance under the law. Nonetheless, the unspoken truth that the political alarmists deliberately ignore or sweep under the rug is that America can never be completely safe as long as we live in a free and open society. Nothing is absolute.

That includes the notion of absolute security. Endless redundancies in intelligence and crime-fighting networks dedicated to heading off the slightest terror threats, whatever the cost, are being justified by politicians who fear being blamed by the public and the other party for the next terrorist incident. Yet absolute security from any and every terrorist act is an illusion. And when leaders voice such expectations, they are inviting disappointment. While security is an all-important responsibility of the government, it is not the government's only responsibility. The president and members of Congress swear an oath to preserve, protect, and defend the Constitution of the United States—not the security of the United States. The Constitution declares our rights and liberties and defines us as a nation. Nothing in it offers a guarantee of safety from crazed, jihad-inspired terrorists.

We seem to be caught between the ideas of Benjamin Franklin and those of Abe Lincoln. Franklin once wrote that those who would give up liberty for temporary security deserve neither and will lose both. On the other hand, President Lincoln once said, in justifying his Civil War–era suspension of habeas corpus (the right of any suspect to appear in court and be told the charges against him), that, in essence, extreme times call for extreme measures. The political pressure discouraging mature conversations about the tension between liberty and national security has caused a terrible loss of American unity. Free people have to agree on the *limits* of defense against terrorism if they don't want to sacrifice the very rights that guarantee our freedom and form of government. At every step of the way, from how we define terrorists to how we detain and treat them when captured to how we treat our own citizens during this time of emergency, there is a need for unhindered conversation about these serious topics. We don't need or benefit from censorship. The central question is how to protect the Constitution and the values that underlie America while effectively fighting the enemy. There are no easy answers. But the politically correct mudslinging on both sides makes it nearly impossible to cut through the finger-pointing and get to that all-important debate.

That conversation starts with the question of whether we have the necessary laws to stop the terrorist once we know who he or she is. And that is just the start of the debate. Americans also have to contend with how to treat an enemy who is not covered under the Geneva Conventions, which deal with soldiers representing another country during a time of war. Is it okay to torture a terrorist? Is it okay to hold a suspected terrorist without trial? Does that trial have to take place in U.S. civilian courts? Or does it better serve the nation to try terrorists in military courts?

Unfortunately, open discussion of these questions got treated as out of bounds after the 9/11 attacks. Congress issued a resolution authorizing the president to use whatever force he felt necessary to combat the terrorist groups behind the 9/11 attacks. The president did not have to make his case to Congress or the American people. Public support for the president in the immediate aftermath of the 9/11 attacks was at a record level, more than 90 percent. That level of trust across political, class, racial, and religious lines gave the president the latitude to speak and act for all Americans. The normal appetite for discussion of policy was quieted by a desire for fast action and effective response to prevent further terrorism. Vice President Cheney, speaking on *Meet the Press* after 9/11, said the Bush administration had license to work secretly, outside the normal congressional, judicial, and public oversight and debate. In other words, beyond the constitutional checks on power in America. "We've got to spend time in the shadows of the intelligence world," he said. "A lot of what needs to be done here will have to be done quietly, without any discussion."

The congressional resolution allowed the president to secretly give the CIA authorization to kill al Qaeda operatives, to open secret prisons overseas, and to torture people. In one memo that set off huge controversy when it was later made public, a lawyer for the Bush administration, John Yoo, advised the president that without any public debate or congressional authorization he could start a war anywhere in the world in pursuit of terrorists. In 2002 President Bush issued an executive order denying Geneva Convention protections—specifically safeguards against torture—to terrorist detainees. Attorney General John Ashcroft decided—without public debate—that waterboarding, a technique in which the victim feels as if he can't breathe and is drowning, is not torture and is legal. One Bush administration legal memo concluded that anything can be done to terror suspects as long as it does not lead to organ failure, impair bodily functions, or result in death.

To me, the most distressing aspect of not allowing the American people in on the debate about how to handle terrorism was the president's lack of trust in the Constitution and the law. Decisions on U.S. law that impacted our constitutional rights suddenly fell into the hands of a few obscure political appointees working on secret memos at the Justice Department and the White House. They competed to please the administration by giving the president unprecedented, unquestioned levels of power. American values, democratic principles, and confidence in the maturity of the American people and their representatives in Congress to work through a threat to our nation got left behind in the name of ending the terrorist threat through expansive presidential powers. Anyone asking questions was dismissed as naive, unpatriotic, or sympathetic to terrorists. In my experience, as word of these decisions leaked into the news, rather than comfort Americans, it led to uneasiness over what we believe our nation's values are with regard to using torture, championing human rights, and protecting civil liberties. The president's political rivals began to voice concern that there was no process at work, no legal framework for such vast exercise of power by the president. Talk of naked power grabs and dictator-like mandates had to be quieted by the Bush administration with claims that such extralegal steps resulted in forcing more information from suspects and informants and stopping more terrorist plots. As much as the public wanted to believe in the administration, there was no way to be certain, and earlier events, such as the government's justification for attacking Iraq, had weakened public faith in the administration's words. Americans had been told the United States had to go to war in Iraq because

Iraq had weapons of mass destruction. No such weapons were found. Allegations of a link between Iraq and the terror attacks of 9/11 had also proved unsupportable; the president had openly claimed that Iraq was training al Qaeda terrorists. It was never proven. The crisis of confidence was heightened by dwindling international support for the United States in Iraq and Afghanistan and the handling of terrorists.

The situation became glaringly difficult to reconcile with American ideals. News stories revealed terrorists being stripped naked and dying at a CIA prison in Afghanistan, sensory deprivation of detainees, attacks on the religious beliefs of detainees. Then came stories of prisoners shackled to the floors of airplanes for twenty hours with black goggles covering their eyes and ears. We discovered that in 2003, U.S. interrogators used the waterboarding technique on Khalid Sheikh Mohammed, a top al Qaeda leader, 183 times in one month. The Red Cross issued reports on the deteriorating psychological health of detainees at Guantánamo Bay. And in 2004 Americans saw pictures of male Iraqi prisoners being stripped, paraded in front of American female soldiers, and threatened by dogs at Abu Ghraib—Saddam Hussein's most notorious prison—in Iraq. The news that the United States engaged in such abuse undermined claims that Saddam Hussein's tyranny had been replaced with the promise of American liberty. "I'm gravely concerned that many Americans will have the same impulse as I did when I saw this picture, and that's to turn away from them," said a pained Senator John McCain, a former prisoner of war in Vietnam. "And we risk losing public support for this conflict." McCain called for full disclosure of what procedures had been authorized for handling prisoners in American custody. In 2004 the U.S. Supreme Court ruled that detainees at Guantánamo Bay had the right to challenge their detention.

The enduring controversy over waterboarding of Muslim terrorists inspired several journalists, from Fox News Channel reporters to tough-guy radio talk-show hosts to magazine writers, to undergo the procedure themselves and report on whether they considered it torture. Christopher Hitchens, writing for *Vanity Fair* magazine, had it done to him and not only declared it torture but added that once he understood the full barbarity of the act, he realized that the U.S. government had lied when it said it was not torture. "One used to be told," Hitchens wrote, ". . . that the lethal fanatics of al-Qaeda were schooled to lie, and instructed to claim that they had been tortured. . . . Did we notice what a frontier we had crossed when we admitted and even proclaimed that their stories might in fact be true? I had only a very slight encounter on that frontier, but I still wish that my experience were the only way in which the words 'waterboard' and 'American' could be mentioned in the same (gasping and sobbing) breath."

As the calls from the media and some politicians grew for getting the courts and Congress involved in the discussion about torture and how best to handle terrorists, the Bush administration responded by destroying copies of memos authorizing torture and later by destroying videotapes of interrogations. The intransigence of the administration became the issue. Administration officials' brand of political correctness claimed that anyone who disagreed with them was speaking out of turn and endangering national security. The implication was that even opening the subject up to public debate was an act of treachery.

But eventually even fellow Republicans began to rebel against the administration. Senator McCain got forty-six Republicans to join forty-four Democrats to overwhelmingly approve an amendment to a defense bill mandating an end to the torture of detainees. The administration treated it like a nuisance. When the entire Congress passed the Detainee Treatment Act in 2005—outlawing the use of torture on anyone, anywhere in the world—the White House treated the effort with contempt. Administration officials did not make congressional leaders aware that administration lawyers had privately authorized U.S. military and intelligence agents to use torture. When those memos came to light, Republican senator Lindsey Graham of South Carolina said: "If we change who America is in trying to win this war [then] we will lose."

By 2007 three detainees at Guantánamo Bay had committed suicide. The same year the Supreme Court ruled that the U.S. military must comply with the Geneva Conventions for humane treatment of prisoners. By 2009 a Spanish court had announced that it was considering filing an indictment against Bush administration officials for human-rights violations. The worldwide outpouring of unity with the United States in the days after 9/11 had long evaporated. Fewer countries contributed their troops to the war in Iraq. And U.S. public support for the war dwindled. Polls also showed declining support for U.S. efforts to confront the terror groups directly linked to 9/11, al Qaeda and the Taliban, in Afghanistan. Yet former vice president Cheney continues to critique President Obama as insufficiently committed to the Bush administration's policies for fighting terror. Cheney's criticism comes even as President Obama has sent more troops to fight terrorists in Afghanistan and committed the U.S. military to remain in

Iraq well beyond the previously promised exit date of 2011. President Obama is continuing Bush administration policies on rendition, where prisoners are transferred to other countries for harsh, extrajudicial interrogations, as well as allowing wiretaps without warrants and keeping the Guantánamo Bay prison open while not holding trials for terror detainees. Attorney General Holder may have blamed Congress for not allowing Khalid Sheikh Mohammed's trial to occur in civilian court in the United States, but isn't the buck supposed to stop at the top?

The Obama administration has found it easier to continue those policies than to start the difficult but necessary conversation about the limits of democratic freedoms. How many Americans are willing to sacrifice some liberty, some autonomy, because they believe that it is a necessary price to be paid in a time of terrorist threats? It may be that most Americans are willing to approve a suspension of some rights in the name of fighting terrorism. Most people feel they have nothing to hide. It may be that large numbers of Americans believe the government can already invade computer messages and tap phone lines. But the Obama White House is closing off those questions because it is afraid critics will charge it with being weak, lacking the Clint Eastwood and Jack Bauer gumption to shoot first and deal with the questions later. The president might also be afraid that he will open himself to vicious political attacks if another terrorist attack occurs as he leads the nation through this maze of issues. And there is some truth in that, as Republicans find political advantage in questioning the Democrats' dedication to fighting terrorism. So as a result, the Obama White House is bullied into compliance with policies that candidate Obama campaigned against when he won the White House in 2008. And the nation continues to be denied the much-needed debate on how to reconcile the tension between battling terrorists and protecting our ideals and upholding our nation's founding principles of individual rights.

Starting the American conversation might trigger a parallel discussion in the Muslim community about its lack of debate about terrorism. And that extends to the Muslim community in the United States. Muslims, too, have been victims of murderous terrorism by other Muslims. They also suffer from the taint terrorism brings on their religion. Many Americans do not understand the stranglehold that extremists have on the Muslim world. The most violent minority has succeeded in coercing government leaders into acquiescence. One of the most chilling examples of this dynamic was the 2005 murder of the reformist prime minister of Lebanon, Rafik Hariri, by Muslim terrorists aligned with Hezbollah. The threat of violence is also used as leverage against business and media interests throughout the Muslim world.

The fear of Muslim terrorism within the Islamic community is endemic and a barrier to change. But Americans must call Muslim terrorism by its name, identify it for what it is. In order for change to take place, reformers have to be empowered to take on the extremists who threaten us all.

The lack of democratic reforms in the Muslim world, compounded by economic and educational failures, allows terrorist organizations to play a dual role in Muslim society and thus dodge efforts to call them out as murderers. In some cases, groups such as Hezbollah and Hamas provide humanitarian aid to fellow Muslims. They give jobs to unemployed young men. They are closer to the common citizens than the oil-rich sheikhs, kings, and princes. As a result, Middle Easterners often have a very different perception of Muslim terrorists. To some they are humanitarians and employers. Last year, CNN Middle East editor Octavia Nasr was fired for sending a message on her Twitter account that praised a Hezbollah leader after his death. "Sad to hear of the passing of Sayyed Mohammed Hussein Fadlallah . . . one of Hezbollah's giants I respect a lot." Fadlallah served as spiritual leader for Islamic Jihad, a forerunner to Hezbollah, the group that bombed the U.S. Marine barracks in Lebanon, killing 229 people. The problem is not that one journalist praised this violent Muslim cleric. The larger issue is that she was speaking for millions of people in the Muslim world who have a favorable view of Muslim terrorists and their organizations. Only by confronting the varying perceptions that really do exist can Americans and Western leaders hope to defeat terrorism.

Despite the mistakes made by President Bush in handling Muslim terrorists during his administration, it was he, speaking in 2005 to the National Endowment for Democracy, who pulled away all the pretense, all the politically correct verbiage, in dealing with Muslim terrorism. He offered a basis for identifying the enemy and helping Americans to begin a politically incorrect but direct discussion about what the enemy is trying to accomplish.

"Like the ideology of communism," President Bush said, "our new enemy pursues totalitarian aims. Its leaders pretend to be an aggrieved party, representing the powerless against imperial enemies. In truth they have endless ambitions of imperial domination, and they wish to make everyone powerless except themselves. Under their rule, they have banned books, and desecrated historical monuments, and brutalized women. They seek to end dissent in every form, and to control every aspect of life, and to rule the soul, itself. While promising a future of justice and holiness, the terrorists are preparing for a future of oppression and misery."

John Brennan, President Obama's counterterrorism adviser, advanced the conversation when he said in a 2010 speech that al Qaeda's goal is to "undermine the laws and values that have been a source of our strength and our influence throughout the world." Brennan still would not call the enemy Muslim terrorists, but he said "al Qaeda and its violent affiliates" want to get the United States to end its global leadership and become a confused, scared, suspicious nation that "retreats from the world stage and abandons allies and partners." Their goal, he concluded, is "turning us into something that we are not."

Once we have called the enemy by his name and identified his goal, we have a start on the much-needed, politically incorrect, American discussion of Muslim terrorists. Then we can have an honest debate that breaks through the fog of political correctness and admit to our fears in dealing with a vicious, remorseless, implacable foe hiding behind Islamic ideology and sometimes behind religious clothes. We can begin asking one another how far we are willing to go to defend our nation and whether those means will justify the ends or whether they will undermine the rights and privileges we enjoy and ruin the America we treasure. The doublespeak, the euphemisms, the charges of bigotry, and the delicate dances around the fact of Muslim terrorism serve only to hurt America in the end. They allow the erosion of the philosophical and moral tenets that allow America to stand tall.

I meant what I said when I said that I get nervous boarding a plane with those whose dress identifies them first and foremost as Muslims. Does that offend you? Then let's talk about it.

CHAPTER 5

TAX CUTS, ENTITLEMENTS, AND HEALTH CARE

B Y DECEMBER 2010 the Left-Right debate around extending the Bush tax cuts was frozen. On every side the argument was fixed, locked in, politically correct, and predictable. Republicans repeated their mantra that Democrats are always raising taxes when they should be cutting spending. And Democrats squealed with rage that Republicans were filling the pockets of the rich with tax cuts. President Obama even went so far as to say the GOP employed terrorist tactics, holding Americans "hostage" if they did not get that tax cut for the rich. What no one predicted was a historic presidential outburst.

The forty-fourth president became the first chief executive to publicly say he was fed up with the political correctness, intimidation, and polarization being used against him—by his own party. In the White House pressroom he ripped left-wing Democrats for calling him a traitor and a sellout because he broke the logjam by agreeing with Republicans on a political compromise.

"Now, if that's the standard by which we are measuring success or core principles, then let's face it, we will never get anything done," said the president, who had been charged by fellow Democrats in Congress with capitulating to Republican demands. They said he was running away from his "Gettysburg" moment and "punting on third down." The attacks from his political allies rained on Obama when he agreed to extend upper-income tax cuts in exchange for adding several months of benefits for the unemployed, as well as funding for scholarships, tax exemptions for businesses to buy equipment, and jobs programs. "People will have the satisfaction of having a purist position and no victories for the American people. And we will be able to feel good about ourselves and sanctimonious about how pure our intentions are and how tough we are, and in the meantime the American people are still . . . not being able to pay their bills because their unemployment insurance ran out.

"That can't be the measure of how we think about public service," a fuming, frustrated president added. "That can't be the measure of what it means to be a Democrat. This is a big, diverse country. Not everybody agrees with us. I know that shocks people."

The tax dispute that provoked the president to snap at his own liberal base is much bigger than just one more exchange of politically correct polemics. It is the most stubborn domestic political standoff plaguing America. And it is a threat to the nation's future. Politically entrenched thinking protected by special-interest groups and lobbyists has made it impossible for most of the end of the last century and the first decade of this century to resolve central debates over taxes, deficit spending on entitlements such as Social Security, and the high cost of health care.

The 2010 tax deal, in the end, was a compromise—but there was no substantive debate. Instead, both sides played political brinkmanship until it became clear to everyone that an abrupt hike in all tax rates would have devastating results for both parties. No one took advantage of the golden opportunity to get past their politically hardened positions. Instead, Republicans and Democrats turned away from discussion of how to trim defense, Social Security, Medicare, Medicaid, and other entitlements programs and expenses that threaten to explode the federal budget. And when the gauntlet was again picked up by Representative Paul Ryan's proposed budget plan, and President Obama's own plan in response, both sides quickly retreated into their traditional corners.

The result of a lack of honest talk about this problem—political correctness at its most paralyzing—is a yearly deficit now projected, as I am writing in 2011, to approach $1.1 trillion. And that is down from last year, when the deficit reached a historic high of $1.6 trillion. That is a separate crisis and not to be confused with the sea of unpaid bills deposited in a back drawer over the past decade to create the national debt. That debt is now $14 trillion.

"We're broke," Speaker of the House John Boehner said shortly after Republicans took control of the House in the November 2010 elections. "If we lead with our chin, nothing happens. [And] that's what's happened in Washington for the last 25 years." That straight talk brought Boehner and the Republicans tremendous success in the 2010 midterms. Of course, he blamed all the big spending on Democrats, which is far from the case. That partisan bilge muddied a very important message. But voters had enough clarity about the enormity of the federal deficit, complete with the risk of budget cuts and inflation, to decide for themselves that no matter who had created the problem, it was legitimate to be worried about excessive government spending. The Tea Party movement had emerged with activists, principally seniors over sixty-five, giving Republicans the votes for a historic pickup of sixty-three congressional seats, the largest one-party gain since 1948 and enough to seize control of the House of Representatives.

The Tea Party's righteous 2010 march to the polls to protest ballooning deficits does not, however, indicate that Tea Party seniors opened their minds to ending their reliance on federal entitlement benefits. In fact, many would object to the term "handout" being applied to the checks they get from the federal government for Social Security and Medicare. They argue that they paid into those systems and earned a return. What they don't realize, however, is that both Medicare and Social Security pay out far beyond what most individuals ever put into the system. As a result of that politically inconvenient reality, both programs are in fiscal jeopardy, and the situation is getting worse. Currently, a declining number of workers pay taxes into a system that is increasingly top-heavy with growing numbers of retiring baby boomers.

The seniors' precarious situation is just one part of our growing dependence on federal entitlements. The *Wall Street Journal* reported in 2010 that close to half of all Americans "live in a household in which someone receives government benefits, more than at any time in history."

"As recently as the early 1980s, about 30% of Americans lived in households in which an individual was receiving Social Security, subsidized housing, jobless benefits or other government-provided benefits," the *Journal* found. "By the third quarter of 2008, 44% were, according to the most recent Census Bureau data." This startling reality is never discussed in politically correct circles. Instead, two lines of petitioners dominate conversation. In the first line are people making themselves out to be victims and claiming to deserve the government's support. And in line number two are people complaining that they pay too much in taxes and want those entitlements curtailed. Sometimes the same people are in both lines.

The debate over the budget is likely to become one of the defining issues in the 2012 election. In the spring of 2011, the Republicans and Democrats narrowly averted a government shutdown by cutting a deal with each other in order to fund the government for the rest of the fiscal year. The deal included about $38.5 billion in cuts (though the number can vary depending on how some of the timing of the cuts is measured). Naturally, the Republicans seized on what was generally perceived to be a victory for their side, given the size of the cuts. But equally crucial, President Obama claimed some measure of victory for, once again, appearing to be at the center of a compromise between the two poles of American politics.

But even this game of chicken was seen as only a warm-up for the debate over the 2012 budget, which took off right after the shutdown compromise when Republican representative Paul Ryan introduced the GOP's "Path to Prosperity"—a budget that would aim to cut not mere billions but trillions ($6.2 trillion, in fact) from President Obama's budgets over the next ten years.

The plan was an instant lightning rod. Supporters on the Right claimed someone had finally gotten serious about changing the fiscal path of the country. Detractors on the Left claimed that, as usual, with tax cuts for the wealthy and cuts to services, Republicans were looking to put the burden of sacrifice on the middle class and the poor. Moreover, many Democrats and commentators pointed out that Ryan's assumptions for economic growth (and thus revenues) were far too rosy, therefore helping him to avoid the heretical (at least in Republican circles) suggestion of raising taxes to accomplish any of his goals.

But let's give at least some credit where credit is due—Ryan put out a tough plan that took on the Medicaid and Medicare entitlements (it largely avoided Social Security, except to suggest an environment through which legislators would be encouraged to seek common ground).

President Obama quickly countered with his own budget plan, cutting $4 trillion with a mixture of entitlement cuts and increased taxes. In any event, it is unlikely that Ryan's plan will make it into law. The reason? It is simply too costly, politically, for officeholders to slash Medicaid and Medicare. Even now, despite how fed up the nation supposedly is with entitlements, spending, deficits, and the debt, we somehow supposedly lack the political will to do anything about it.

Tax policy in the United States began to emerge as a core component of campaign rhetoric in the Reagan era. The Reagan revolution was fueled by the promise of large tax cuts.

Unemployment was high for that time, at 7.8 percent, and inflation hit 18 percent just before the 1980 election. The nation was hungry for an economic cure-all, a jolt, and Reagan delivered. His central idea was that simply lowering taxes created economic growth. In the 1960s, President Lyndon Johnson had created programs that widened the social safety net and federal spending. His Great Society plan had been defined by Medicare, federal payments to ensure health care for the elderly, and Medicaid, federal money to provide health care for the poor. Presidents Nixon and Carter had also expanded entitlement spending. All three presidents had allowed tax hikes to pay for the new spending. Running for the presidency in 1980, Ronald Reagan saw no need for increased taxes. He condemned them as a burden on American business and personal freedom and a damper on the spirit of innovation. The California Republican promised that tax cuts would create a "rising tide that lifts all boats." He saw no need to compensate for lost tax revenue even as he proposed increased spending, particularly on defense and also on Social Security. The lost tax dollars, he promised, would be made up by increased economic activity.

Reagan called this tax policy "supply-side economics." Reagan's critics, meanwhile, called this theory nonsense. David Stockman, his director of the Office of Management and Budget, later admitted he knew it would not work. Reagan's vice president, George H. W. Bush, during his 1980 presidential campaign, described it as "voodoo economics." The critics proved to be right. During Reagan's time in office the budget deficit spiked. In the year he was elected the deficit was $74 billion; by 1986 it had nearly tripled to over $220 billion.

For the first time the United States became a borrower nation instead of a nation making loans to other countries.

But this is only part of the story. As former Clinton economic adviser Robert Shapiro wrote for *Forbes*, "Everyone remembers Reagan's 1981 tax cuts. His admirers are less likely to tout the tax hikes he accepted as the 1981 recession and his own tax cuts began to unravel his long-term fiscal picture—a large tax increase on business in 1982, higher payroll taxes enacted in 1983 and higher energy taxes in 1984." Yes, on balance Reagan lowered taxes, and on balance the deficit and debt soared. But what's interesting is that Reagan was not, in fact, allergic to *raising* taxes, and he did it more than a few times. At the very least, Reagan displayed the kind of ideological flexibility that seems so foreign to us now.

President Reagan credited his supply-side theory with victory when the U.S. economy eventually rose out of its late-seventies and early-eighties doldrums, but it was never clear that it was the president's tax policy that had spurred the recovery. What *has* been clear ever since is that any pledge to cut taxes is a political winner for Republicans. It has led Republicans to champion smaller government—requiring fewer tax dollars—and to attack big government as a sponge for tax dollars. Reagan's tax policy also fit with his celebration of less government regulation of Wall Street and big business. He gloried in the vilification of government bureaucrats. Reagan got big laughs when he told audiences the most dangerous words ever spoken are "I'm from the government and I'm here to help." The myth and legend of Ronald Reagan has since been fashioned into a rigid conservative orthodoxy—no matter how at odds with reality it actually is.

The inherent contradiction between Reagan's tax cuts and increased spending and his efforts to disguise tax increases with sleight of hand made it easy for Reagan's opponents to mock his plan. Moreover, it forced his supporters into a defensive crouch as they created ways to refuse to admit the policy's flaws. This brand of political correctness—the unquestioned virtue of cutting taxes—had risen to the fore.

Until Reagan's presidential campaigns, tax policy had not been too polarizing a component of political rhetoric on the Right or Left. The United States did not even have an income tax until the Civil War. Once the War Between the States ended, so did most federal taxation. The government was funded with tariffs and excise taxes. Thirty years later, in 1894, to support a growing national government, Congress tried to enact a flat tax on all income. The Supreme Court overturned it because it did not meet constitutional requirements for apportionment of taxes according to the population of each state. But a national consensus emerged for increasing funding for the federal government as an act of patriotism. In 1913 Republicans and Democrats joined to pass the Sixteenth Amendment, giving Congress the authority to tax each citizen's income. In the years that followed, tax increases stirred no partisan divide because they were directly tied to supporting the military during World War I.

As recently as 1930, 90 percent of all federal revenue was still collected from tariffs and excise taxes. With only minor debate, tax rates went up in the 1930s to compensate for shortfalls caused by the Great Depression and to pay for government programs to put people back to work. Income taxes rose, again following patriotic appeals to pay for increased military defense in the years before World War II. Republican opposition to President Roosevelt's plan emerged over how much to raise tax rates and deciding which income brackets to tax. But at a time of military and economic challenges to the nation, there was enough public support for raising taxes to drown out the Republican opposition.

The first critical change in tax policy came with passage of the Social Security Act of 1935. It included a 2 percent tax on income to pay for a number of new entitlements, the biggest of which included Social Security and unemployment insurance. The federal tax structure for the first time went beyond supporting the military. Now federal taxes also supported social programs. Again, the change was greeted by an economically depressed nation with overwhelming public support. And by comparison with today's arguments over tax policy, there was almost no political rancor. Overall, between 1939 and 1945 there was a tenfold increase in the number of Americans paying federal income tax. In the four years between 1941 and 1945, federal taxes as a share of the gross domestic product climbed from 7.6 percent to 20.4 percent.

After World War II another major shift in tax policy took effect. Taxes became an instrument of federal fiscal policy, calibrated to slow or accelerate business cycles in order to prevent another Great Depression. But by the late 1950s and 1960s, the economy was growing fast and tax policy took a backseat. The country's major political fights had to do with the cold war against communism in Korea, Cuba, and Vietnam; civil rights for blacks; law and order in the cities; and the rise of an antiestablishment youth culture, including rock and roll, drugs, and a sexual revolution. Even with the advent of President Johnson's Great Society programs, there was relatively minor debate over the impact of higher taxes. President Nixon, a Republican, later expanded Social Security benefits. Even then, debate over taxes was minor. It centered on inflation pushing more taxpayers into higher tax brackets, leading to taxes claiming an even bigger percentage of the gross domestic product.

It was when the federal government failed to control inflation in the late seventies that the door first opened wide to political candidates to offer remedies for fixing fiscal policy. The nation's debate over taxes soon became everyday political fodder.

Those developments set the stage for Ronald Reagan to cast Democrats as big spenders who hindered economic growth with high taxes and intrusive regulations. The California Republican attacked Democrats with his "tax and spend" label. Once in office, however, President Reagan, ironically, followed President Nixon's example, implementing another expansion of Social Security. In other words, government spending did not match Republican rhetoric. As a result, it was impossible for top Republicans to have an honest conversation with their own rank and file about federal spending. In fact, avoiding that debate gave the GOP a simple, winning message: cut taxes. (Years later another stalwart Republican, Vice President Dick Cheney, would dismiss concern about deficit spending by saying that President Reagan proved "deficits don't matter.") Reagan's successor, George H. W. Bush, used a Reagan-like pledge—"Read my lips: no new taxes"—to win the White House in 1988. And when he broke that promise by brokering a deal that included some tax hikes, it proved fatal to his run for a second term.

Democratic president Bill Clinton picked up on the Republican antitax message, creating a new centrist image for himself by getting tax cuts for the middle class enacted and balancing the federal budget. George W. Bush, who succeeded Clinton, went much further, making across-the-board tax cuts the center of his presidential campaign, arguing that the government surplus Clinton enjoyed indicated that tax rates still reached too deeply into the voters' pockets. After the 9/11 attacks, President Bush passed a round of tax cuts to rev up a shaken economy. In 2003 he signed into law a new, expensive entitlement benefit for Medicare, a prescription drug benefit, without putting in place any new tax to pay for it. Incredibly, in 2003, with a Republican majority in the House and Senate, he passed a second tax cut. It was during that second round of tax cuts that the modern debate over taxes fell into a mixer of politically correct cement. From that point on, every discussion of taxes featured the Democrats' complaint that Republicans wanted to make the rich even richer, by giving a disproportionate percentage of tax cuts to the wealthy, and the Republicans' reply that Democrats were creating a welfare state with high taxes, taking money away from the small businesses that created jobs.

This frozen, crazy, frustrating dynamic originated with President Reagan's success at increasing costly entitlement programs while refusing to raise taxes sufficiently to pay for those programs and while ignoring the soaring budget deficit in the name of supply-side economics. If taxes are not increased sufficiently to cover new costs, then the only way to reduce the deficit is to cut spending. The fact is that budget cuts have little actual public support when it comes to eliminating specific programs. The problem is that every dollar spent by the federal government has a political constituency. Moreover, most private-sector jobs in the United States are tied to federal spending, a fact that few people generally recognize or acknowledge. Therefore, the government is a huge driver of the overall economy.

Washington is busy every day subsidizing farm commodities; offering tax-code incentives to buy homes, to build homes, to prop up the ailing U.S. auto industry, to promote car buying, and to expand factories and encourage research; and awarding government contracts for technology, for the defense industry, and to airplane and ship builders. Federal money is the foundation for most hospitals, colleges, and universities, highways, transportation systems, and more. On top of those dollars is the pile of federal, state, and local government dollars spent on salaries and benefits for government employees. All of this spending is controlled by politicians. And their re-election campaigns are supported by corporate political action committees and unions representing people with jobs that depend on continued government spending. The incentive for any politician—Republican or Democrat—looking to stay in office is to *increase* government spending to benefit their supporters. There is no reason to cut spending.

Americans react in anger when you puncture their personal myth that they are self-made and nothing like those freeloaders living off the federal government. The highly paid lobbying industry, in Washington as well as in state capitols and city halls, exists to ridicule and defeat any challenge to its clients' claim to a share of the treasury. The lobbyists get wealthy by keeping the money flowing to their clients. Those clients and the lobbyists, powerful people with beautiful homes and fashionable clothes, do not see themselves in the same class as others who get government checks.

This delusion creates its own form of political correctness. Breaking the spell requires an act of imagination. So imagine a curtain of misconceptions falling away to open a rare view on the political self-interest behind the government's massive spending. What is revealed behind the curtain is a wizard— call him Uncle Sam. He is dressed as a politician, constantly switching blue and red ties that identify him as a Democrat or a Republican. No matter which tie he has on at any moment, he is always ready to declare that any budget cut is an attack on poor people, the middle class, and any other group worthy of empathy. The man behind the curtain will even defend rich people from calls to end subsidies for their development deals and corporations. Our political wizard behind the curtain is outraged at any budget cuts that take money away from good Americans such as the deserving, job-producing rich, the all-American farmers who grow our food, risk-taking investors, the hardworking small businessmen, the kind elderly, the children that are the future of our country, the nation's brave soldiers, our courageous first responders who keep the public safe, our precious public schools, America's working men and women, our loyal allies who need foreign aid. . . . The list goes on and on.

The political reality is that both parties use the wizard's tactics to distract American taxpayers while pushing their hands deep into the federal treasury. Republicans may present themselves as the vicars of responsible spending, but history shows that the GOP has been responsible for more federal spending than Democrats over the past fifty years. Jimmy Carter raised the national debt by 42 percent during his four years in the White House, while Bill Clinton in two terms raised the debt only 36 percent. By comparison, President Reagan raised the national debt by 189 percent and joked that he was not worried about the deficit because "it is big enough to take care of itself." Reagan's Republican heirs in the Bush-Cheney administration increased the national debt by 89 percent in eight years and left office with a $1.2 trillion annual deficit. Keep these numbers in mind the next time you hear a Republican lambaste Democrats for reckless spending and preach about the need to cut federal spending. The fact is, both have played central roles.

All the wizards and their distracting tricks of political spin cannot hide the fact that politicians on every side—Republicans, Democrats, independents, Tea Partiers, and socialists—feed at the federal trough. They brag to their constituents about "bringing home the bacon" from Washington. They put earmarks on legislation for personal projects such as the infamous "bridge to nowhere" in Alaska. Then, during campaigns, they shamelessly attack one another over high taxes and endless spending. All the candidates tell the voters their hands are clean, while blaming the other side for the huge yearly budget shortfalls that add to the debt, create financial burdens for future generations, and create the risk of inflation and overall economic instability. It is great political theater, but our tickets to this production are ruinously expensive.

The biggest share of all federal spending, other than

domestic programs, is military defense. Admiral Mike Mullen, chairman of the Joint Chiefs of Staff, said last year, "The most significant threat to our national security is our debt." He explained that a country in financial free fall is not able to support a powerful military. "The strength and the support and the resources that our military uses are directly related to the health of our economy over time," Mullen said. His thinking is based on the fact that the United States spent close to 20 percent of its national budget on defense last year. That $664 billion defense budget was more than the combined budgets of the world's next twenty largest militaries.

Yet anyone who questions excessive defense spending, including the Joint Chiefs and former defense secretary Robert Gates, is condemned as weak on national defense, willing to risk the lives of brave soldiers, and sorely naive about the Chinese threat. The truth? Senators and congressmen will use any argument to protect funding for military bases in their home state. They fiercely guard money to defense contractors doing business in their home state. In several congressional districts a military base or a military contractor is the largest employer. Major defense contractors also fund political campaigns through their political action committees. When it comes to spending money on fighting wars, politicians know they can sign a blank check and pay no political price. In fact, they can claim to be patriots and expect laurels, even as they drive up the debt and put financial burdens on future generations. The most glaring recent example is the Bush administration's decision to censor the cost of the wars in Afghanistan and Iraq. The administration never disclosed it. The wars were paid for with deficit spending, off the books, with no accountability for how the money was spent. The Obama administration has revealed some of the cost but not the full amount. So far it is estimated to be more than five trillion dollars—over one third of our total debt.

With the red, white, and blue razzle-dazzle insulating the defense budget from any serious cuts, any discussion of reducing federal spending turns to America's two largest domestic spending programs, Social Security and Medicare. Again, the politically correct thinking that shoots down any cuts in defense spending also tends to throw up a Teflon defense against suggested cuts to Social Security and Medicare. Anyone mentioning reducing Medicare costs is charged with taking money from ailing seniors. Anyone talking about limiting benefits is denounced for attempts to create "death panels" or "kill Grandma."

Social Security is the government's single biggest domestic spending program. It consists of two entitlements. One is for retired workers and their dependents or survivors. The second is disability insurance for people younger than retirement age who are unable to work and their dependents. In 2009 Social Security cost the government about $670 billion, or 15 percent of all federal spending. Over fifty-nine million Americans currently get Social Security benefits. And with the large number of baby boomers retiring in the next two decades, more than 20 percent of the nation will soon get a Social Security check. The Social Security Trust Fund currently has enough money to pay its bills, but according to congressional budget experts the fund began running a deficit in 2010 that will empty its pockets by about 2037.

The second-largest share of domestic spending goes to Medicare, health-care subsidies for the elderly. It cost the federal government over $500 billion in 2009. According to CBS News, over 10 percent of that amount, about $55 billion, was paid to doctors and hospitals to keep patients alive during the last two months of their lives, "more than the budget for the Department of Homeland Security, or the Department of Education." The report found "20 to 30 percent of these medical expenses may have no meaningful impact [on the patient's health or longevity]. Most of the bills are paid for by the federal government with few or no questions asked."

Together Social Security and Medicare make up 33 percent of the annual federal budget. With Medicaid, federal health care for the poor, entitlements account for about half of the budget. Those programs have to be cut if there is any genuine interest by politicians in reducing the federal debt. But as Congressman Paul Ryan and the Republican Party discovered, with their plan to trim Medicare and drastically cut Medicaid to pull in six trillion dollars in revenue over the next ten years, it is risky for a politician to open the door to charges of trying to kill Grandma by asking politically incorrect questions that challenge spending on people who are elderly, sick, and dying. Seniors vote in large numbers and they control a disproportionate share of the nation's wealth. They contribute to political campaigns, write letters to the editor, and volunteer to work on political campaigns. AARP, the seniors' lobbying group in Washington, is the largest lobbyist in the nation. And then there is the bizarre attack by seniors and their lobbyists on anyone questioning ever-escalating Medicare and Medicaid spending. The same seniors who lament big government and the spread of socialism act as if Medicare has nothing to do with big government and socialism. In fact, seniors object to attempts to reform Medicare as big-government disruption of the privacy of the doctor-patient relationship.

The simple truth is that the federal government has been at the center of the doctor-patient relationship as long as there has been Medicare. Medicare's size and national reach over doctors, hospitals, HMOs, drug companies, and rehabilitation centers puts the government in control of health-care prices and policy. Call it what you will, but Medicare and Medicaid amount to a "government-run" program and by all definitions a socialist program. President Obama has told the story of getting a letter from a Medicare patient who wrote to him to say she did not want government-run health care or socialized medicine and then added: "And don't touch my Medicare." At a town-hall meeting held by Republican Robert Inglis of South Carolina, a senior asked the congressman to "keep your government hands off my Medicare." When the Republican pointed out that Medicare is paid for and run by the federal government, the senior citizen countered that "he wasn't having any of it."

It is a politically inconvenient truth for that man in South Carolina because it does not fit with his anger at big government. But the truth it is. Without limits on Medicare, the program is taking the government on the path to insolvency by driving up the deficit and creating pressure for higher taxes.

The unaddressed issue at the center of every debate about Medicare, Medicaid, and Social Security is to what extent

the federal government should be involved in providing social services to its citizens. Are those services necessary as a
mediating force, a safety net against the excesses of a free-
wheeling capitalistic society where people can fail, go bank-
rupt, get sick, get old, be hurt by the corruption on Wall Street
and abuse of others? Or is fear of failure a sharp spur to hard
work, competition, and retirement planning? And what about
the futures of those who have failed and become street beg-
gars, criminals, and the homeless? What about the blameless
children of the poor, whether their parents are irresponsible
people or simply the victims of layoffs, poor education, or a
medical catastrophe (the biggest cause of families filing for
bankruptcy)? What about orphans and widows?

Republicans have tried to argue that Democrats' efforts to
expand the social safety net are misguided adventures in socialism that encourage dependency. And yet Republican presidents, too, from Nixon to George W. Bush, have presided over
large expansions of entitlement programs. Conservatives' posturing against entitlement spending is not in keeping with the
truth about their actions when they are in power and seeking
votes. They can't seem to have an honest conversation among
themselves, let alone with the nation as a whole.

Democrats often try to close off the debate by dismissing
critics of social programs with self-righteous screeds in which
they portray themselves as defenders of the poor. They remind
us that even the strongest, brightest among us are subject to
the fortunes and misfortunes of life, from professional failure to devastating disease, injury, and, of course, old age and
death. The Democratic base of unions, racial minorities, single
women, and young people without houses and investments has

every reason to try to slap aside any discussion of the limits of government help to those in need.

With neither side willing to compromise on the extent of the government's role in providing a social safety net, for fear that it might lose money or political advantage, political paralysis has taken hold on a topic of critical importance to the nation. For a long time, politicians simply told one another that Social Security was the "third rail of American politics," something to stay well clear of. For the first time, with the national debt becoming front-page news, that is beginning to change, but there's a long way to go.

However, the cone of silence over Social Security spending is enforced by the votes of the senior citizens who get Social Security benefits. According to the Center for the Study of the American Electorate, people over sixty-five vote "at a rate of about 60 percent more than young people and about 10 percentage points higher than the national average." Even ardent Republicans such as Tea Party members who oppose deficit spending and big government find a way to defend Social Security and Medicare spending. And as concern has grown about the fiscal instability of the Social Security and Medicare system, seniors have become more politically active in its defense.

In the 2010 midterm elections, one of the reasons seniors voted in record numbers against what Republicans labeled "Obamacare" was concerns about cuts to Medicare and Social Security. The result? Voters over age sixty-five gave Republicans an unprecedented twenty-one-percentage-point advantage over Democrats in those midterms.

"This is the first time in modern history that older people had their vote influenced by what is going on with old age benefits," said Robert Binstock of Case Western Reserve University in Ohio. In the past, the political priorities and voting preferences of the elderly were much like those of every other voter.

The power of the senior lobby to protect its entitlement benefits was first hinted at during President Bush's effort to reform Social Security in 2005. After winning his second term, President Bush proclaimed that he intended to use his political capital to reform Social Security to ensure its financial stability. Having been elected to a second term, President Bush risked challenging senior voters by starting a conversation about the ailing Social Security system.

His political advisers saw a possible political windfall in the effort. They told me they hoped to win the gratitude of senior voters by ensuring the solvency of their central retirement plan. Their goal was to make the senior vote the cornerstone of what they called a "permanent Republican majority." The Bush White House also hoped to make inroads with blacks, a voting group strongly aligned with the Democrats, by making the case that the current Social Security system cheated blacks. In his memoir, the president later wrote: "Because their life expectancy was shorter, black workers who spent a lifetime paying into Social Security received an average of $21,000 less in benefits than whites of comparable income levels."

The key to the Bush administration's plan was to shift a portion of each worker's Social Security money into a private savings account where it could be invested and benefit from market gains. He unveiled the plan in grand style during his State of the Union speech. Within months the plan was doomed. The AARP, which had helped President Bush win votes in Congress to expand Medicare drug benefits in 2003, quickly distanced itself from the president. Democrats attacked the Bush reform plan as an effort to "privatize" the New Deal entitlement. Labor and civil rights groups opposed it as a plan that helped the rich while exposing retiring workers and minorities to the risky ups and downs of the stock market. Polls showed young people lacked enthusiasm for the reform effort because they did not believe the program had the financial strength to survive long enough to offer them benefits.

Politically correct thinking carried the day, and to the delight of the critics, President Bush's plan was defeated and the conversation quickly died. It provided a clear warning to other politicians that the only acceptable, politically correct posture on Social Security was to leave it alone, despite rising life expectancy, ballooning health-care costs, and huge budget deficits.

The cautionary tale of Social Security reformers is a sign of the danger awaiting both parties if they broach the subject of the runaway cost of Medicare. One of the reasons President Obama and the Democrats suffered a record loss of congressional seats in 2010 for proposing health-care reform was that it included cutbacks on Medicare benefits available to people over sixty-five. That power to punish would-be reformers is growing as the number of seniors increases from the current 13 percent of the population to a projected 20 percent by 2030. Historically, Democrats, as heirs to the Roosevelt and LBJ legacies of creating entitlement programs, have scored better than Republicans when senior voters are polled on which party is more trusted to protect Social Security and

Medicare. But the Democrats lost much of that advantage by advocating health-care reform.

There has been a long history of calls for a national health-care system, of course. And all such attempts have been defeated. Presidents Theodore Roosevelt, Truman, Nixon, and Clinton all tried and failed.

But by the 2008 presidential campaign the issue of health care had come back to life. The high price of health care was a drag on the economy. General Motors complained that the high cost of health insurance for its workers was adding $1,500 to the sticker price of every car it sold. The rising prices also pushed the cost of Medicare and Medicaid higher, burdening the federal budget. Both presidential candidates, John McCain and Barack Obama, produced plans. The key goal was to reduce the cost of health care. By the end of 2009 health-care spending had hit a record high of 17.3 percent of the gross domestic product. The Centers for Medicare & Medicaid Services reported the biggest one-year increase in federal spending on health care since 1960. They also predicted even larger, budget-busting increases to come. Obama proposed requiring every American to have health insurance to bring more young, healthy subscribers into the system. McCain criticized Obama's proposal as another example of big-government overreach because of the mandate for every citizen to have health insurance. McCain countered with a proposal to give people tax credits to encourage them to buy insurance.

After President Obama's victory he made health-care legislation his top priority. In an address to a joint session of Congress in 2009, he offered a vision of increased competition among health insurers, lower prices for prescription drugs, and every American having insurance. He declared now was the time to get it done. Republicans strongly disagreed. When the president refuted criticism that his plan would give health-care coverage to illegal immigrants, one congressman, Representative Joe Wilson, yelled out, "You lie!" The unprecedented insult to the president of the United States was a deep tear in political decorum. It made headlines and hardened feelings. It set the tone for bitter, partisan battles as the House and Senate debated various ideas about a health-care plan. Republican leaders in Congress refused to even join in the discussions. They criticized the Democrats' proposals as a "government takeover of health care." Sharp rhetoric from Republicans about "socialized medicine" and potential tax increases tied to the cost of the reform succeeded in depressing public opinion of the proposals being considered by the Democrats. Representative Michele Bachmann, a Minnesota Republican and a leading voice of the Tea Party, declared that health-care reform was "the crown jewel of socialism." Congresswoman Virginia Foxx, a North Carolina Republican, went to the floor of the House to proclaim, "We have more to fear from the potential of that bill passing than we do from any terrorist right now in any country." The dispute allowed for no independent points of view that might have helped to resolve differences. When the nonpartisan Congressional Budget Office assessed the cost of the final reform bill, it announced that the bill would not add to the deficit. But the bill's opponents said the calculation was wrong because it assumed that Congress would pass future cuts in Medicare spending to pay for part of the new plan.

A Tea Party movement, composed primarily of seniors and Republicans, emerged to condemn the health-care proposal. They labeled it a threat to Medicare and a likely cause for insurance companies to raise the premiums on insurance for all Americans. Sarah Palin, McCain's former running mate, popularized the fallacious idea that the bill allowed federal experts to deny coverage to dying people if the care was expensive, calling them "death panels." Democrats in return attacked the GOP critics. Congressman Alan Grayson, a Florida Democrat, accused the Republicans of not having any new ideas for the government's role in providing affordable care to the sick. "The Republican health care plan is: don't get sick. . . . In case you do get sick . . . the Republican health care plan is: die quickly." The fury on both sides made it impossible to honestly debate the central issue of health care—its costs, its impact on the economy, taxes, and entitlement programs. When Congress went home for summer recess in August 2009, local town-hall meetings with constituents turned into angry confrontations as Tea Party activists, with support from the Chamber of Commerce and lobbyists who opposed the bill, poured vitriol on anyone who supported health-care reform. The president appealed for all sides to come out of their entrenched positions. "What we have also seen in these last months is the same partisan spectacle that only hardens the disdain many Americans have toward their own government. . . . Too many have used this as an opportunity to score short-term political points even if it robs the country of our opportunity to solve a long-term challenge. And out of this blizzard of charges and countercharges, confusion has reigned. Well the time for bickering is over."

It did not halt the acrimony. President Obama had been slow to take control of the debate over health care as the proposal was debated in Congress. He wanted to give Democrats and Republicans the opportunity to put their stamp on the bill before he entered to strike a compromise. But Republicans responded by uniting in total opposition to negotiating. And President Obama's slow entry into selling the need for reform to voters had a negative effect on public opinion. Polls consistently found most Americans opposed to the bill, including people who wanted health-care reform but felt the Democrats' plan was too modest.

On the Republican side a familiar pattern emerged in the attack on President Obama's health-care proposals. Kate Zernike, a *New York Times* reporter, in her book *Boiling Mad: Inside Tea Party America,* wrote, "Conservatives fell into the same positions they had during the Democrats' last major effort, in 1993, invoking fears of health care rationing, long lines for treatment, and, in Sarah Palin's warning, 'Death Panels,' that would coldly calculate whether Grandma got to live or die." In fact, the same charges had been raised against health-care reform going back to the era of Truman, whose health-care plan was seen as a step into socialism.

What was different in the twenty-first-century version of the debate was the indisputable damage the high cost of health care was inflicting on the federal budget because of the rising number of ill and elderly people. Being sick in America is very costly. In 2010 there were forty-seven million Medicare beneficiaries. Even with federal money to help pay their bills, 90 percent of Medicare recipients needed private insurance to pay their medical bills. As Medicare's cost continued to rise, the unfunded liability of the Medicare system reached ninety trillion dollars. The annual report of Medicare's trustees modified this figure to thirty trillion dollars, based on the Affordable Care Act's promises to limit price increases and cut spending. But many observers felt those promises were unlikely to be met.

Health-care costs today account for 17 percent, or one sixth, of the nation's economic activity. Doctor visits, prescription drugs, medical testing using the latest high-tech equipment, and hospital administration add up fast. They make the cost of getting health care in America by far the highest in the world. Yet for all the money we spend, the United States does not rank high on health-care outcomes as compared to other nations. The *CIA World Factbook* for 2010 ranks the United States only fiftieth in life expectancy and 176th in infant mortality. In a comparison of first-world nations—Australia, Britain, Canada, the Netherlands, New Zealand, and the United States—the United States ranked dead last. The nonprofit Commonwealth Fund reported that in 2007 the average health-care spending per person in the United States was $7,290, more than twice any other country surveyed.

While Americans are more likely to be obese than people in other developed countries, other nations had higher rates of smoking and some had older populations. Considering all those factors, the study found Americans are the most likely population in any developed country to go without health care because of the high cost. And Americans had more difficulty gaining access to primary care and after-hours care, according to the study. Every other system covered all citizens; in the United States forty-six million Americans, 15 percent of the population, had no health insurance. These findings are consistent with a 2000 World Health Organization report: "The U.S. health system spends a higher portion of its gross domestic product than any other country but ranks 37 out of 191 countries according to its performance."

The voting power of seniors, the biggest beneficiaries of Social Security and Medicare, combined with ballooning health-care costs, for years have frozen all rational political debate about how to make cuts to save the programs. The media is equally culpable, as they celebrate the latest sound bite from Michele Bachmann on the Right or Alan Grayson and the like on the Left, even though they are minor players in Congress with little influence on the legislative process. The same sclerotic flow of debate has long limited the ability to deal with the out-of-control costs of existing entitlement programs, such as Medicare and Social Security. Eliminating the programs has been so politically out of bounds it has never been discussed. Similarly, budget discussions, until Republican Paul Ryan's plan was announced in April 2011, were limited to mere slices of the federal budget, discretionary spending on small programs, while massive spending on entitlement programs and the defense budget went forward with no scrutiny. Right-wing Republican senator Jim DeMint, a South Carolina Republican Tea Party favorite, has openly declared that all efforts to cut government spending will be done "without cutting any benefits to seniors or veterans," claiming Social Security is off-limits to the budget knife. John Boehner, the Republican Speaker of the House, proposed raising the age at which Americans qualify for Social Security as one way to protect its solvency. But he was quickly chastised and repented. "I made a mistake when I said that," he later explained.

This is the tyranny of political correctness. Comprehensive, genuinely bipartisan reform to better serve the American people—the most important work of the federal government—has been all but stymied. The stilted debate about health-care reform perfectly encapsulates the current dysfunctional political dynamic over tax policy, deficit spending, and entitlement reform.

One earlier politician to look over the cliff of eliminating some of the costly entitlement health spending on seniors was former Colorado governor Richard Lamm, a Democrat. In 1984 he said the terminally ill of all ages should not be burdening society with costly high-tech medical treatments that help them slow the approach of death even if they have no quality of life. "We've got a duty to die and get out of the way with all of our machines and artificial hearts and everything else like that and let the other society, our kids, build a reasonable life," he said. Lamm is still castigated as unfeeling and mean.

Oddly enough, for all the controversy over the Democrats' health-care reform plan and the political fallout that the Democrats suffered in the midterm elections, the bill has slowly begun to gain support from the public. Even as Republicans took advantage of their new majority in the House, won largely as a result of Tea Party–inspired backlash against Democrats, and voted to repeal the law, favorability ratings for the plan increased in the polls. Rather than offering proposals to fix the flaws in the health-care reform that have become evident as the bill begins to take effect, House Republicans instead voted to repeal, calling the reform "Obamacare" and the "Job-Killing Health Care Law Act." In fact, they banned any amendments to the bill. (As a result, they got little support from potential allies among conservative Democrats.)

The Republican repeal effort was pure posturing, since the Democrats' Senate majority would never pass the repeal and President Obama would never sign it if they did.

But as a result, both sides have shut down pragmatic debate when it comes to health care. With Representative Ryan's new proposal, on one side Republicans are going to continue bashing Obamacare as more bloated government, and on the other Democrats are going to criticize Republicans for cutting the health-care services for those who need them most. Both sides are maneuvering for the next election, in 2012. The political posturing is a vivid reminder of how hard it is to have real, honest, and productive discussions about this issue that is of vital importance to so many Americans. In the meantime we are left with the pleasure of mocking the hypocrisy of our politicians.

During the 2010 campaign one Republican candidate, Andy Harris of Maryland, defeated the incumbent Democrat by promising to repeal health-care reform. But reality proved embarrassing and shocking to Harris. When he attended orientation for new members of Congress and was told that his government-subsidized health-care plan would not go into effect until a month after he took office, Harris reacted with outrage. How could he and his family make do without health coverage for a month? Harris asked why he could not buy insurance from the federal government to cover the gap in his insurance, the same public option for health insurance that he had denounced as socialism during the campaign.

The Andy Harrises of the world can't even think honestly about health-care reform. When smart people are so unaware of what they are saying that they make fools of themselves, the power of political correctness to stifle debate becomes obvious.

As *Time*'s Fareed Zakaria noted in an article published just after the Ryan budget was released, despite its many flaws the Ryan budget would be a test for President Obama when it came to the big issues at stake, showing whether or not he could break the stranglehold on the American dialogue. As Zakaria wrote:

> The President has talked passionately and consistently about the need to tackle the country's problems, act like grown-ups, do the hard things and win the future. But he has also skipped every opportunity to say how he'd tackle the gigantic problem of entitlements. Ryan's plan is deeply flawed, but it is courageous. It should prompt the President to say, in effect, "You're right about the problem. You're wrong about the solution. And here's how I would accomplish the same goal by more humane and responsible means." That would be the beginning of a great national conversation. . . .
>
> Obama has an obvious script in front of him. He could turn every item in Ryan's plan into an attack ad, scare the elderly and ride to victory in 2012. But that would probably mean we had pushed off reform of entitlement programs one more time, hoping that someone sometime in the future will lead this country.

I hope that, by the time this book is published, President Obama has risen to the challenge put forward by Zakaria.

His response to Ryan's budget plan shows that he very well may. Many Americans other than Zakaria are counting on this president to lead great national conversations, and indeed many elected him precisely because he seemed the person most likely to do so.

CHAPTER 6

IMMIGRATION, TERROR BABIES, AND VIRTUAL FENCES

WELL AFTER GEORGE W. BUSH LEFT OFFICE, once he'd escaped the punishing grip of right-wing bullies enforcing their brand of politically correct ideas and speech codes on him, here is what the conservative Republican president dared to say about the repeated breakdown of government efforts to resolve the national crisis over immigration.

"I not only differ from my own party but the other party as well," the former president said in a C-SPAN TV interview. "The reason immigration reform died was because of a populism that had emerged." The news here is that the former president was willing to point to his own party's culpability for wasting time with political posturing that stalled much-needed national action on a serious issue.

The former president strained to walk a fine line, pointing a finger at Democrats as well as Republicans for not reaching agreement on immigration. But the "populism" he blamed was almost completely to be found on right-wing talk radio and among the most conservative voices in Congress. When the

former president let it be known that even as the most powerful man in Washington he had been unable to act in America's
best interest because of "a populism that had emerged," anyone paying attention drew an inescapable conclusion. In his
heart Bush blamed bitter, frenzied talk by extremists in his
own party. Extremists impose a cancerous form of political
correctness that demands conformity and kills any possibil-
ity of a reasoned approach to immigration reform and other
issues.

"The failure of immigration reform points out larger concerns about the direction of our politics," President Bush wrote
in his memoir. "The blend of isolationism, protectionism, and
nativism that affected the immigration debate also led Congress to block free trade agreements with Colombia, Panama,
and South Korea. I recognize the genuine anxiety that people
feel about foreign competition. But our economy, our security,
and our culture would all be weakened by an attempt to wall
ourselves off from the world."

"What is interesting about our country, if you study history, is that there are some 'isms' that occasionally pop up,"
President Bush explained in the TV interview on C-SPAN.
"One is isolationism and its evil twin, protectionism, and its
evil triplet, nativism. So if you study the twenties, for example,
there was an America-first policy that said, 'Who cares what
happens in Europe?' . . . My point is that we've been through
this kind of period of isolationism, protectionism, and nativism. I'm a little concerned that we may be going through the
same period. I hope these 'isms' pass."

The former president's remarks set off the right-wing talk-
show hosts. One conservative pundit, Laura Ingraham, said

that "to say that it's all about hostility to foreigners is ludicrous. . . . Maybe President Bush was right. We are suffering from an outbreak of isms. Elitism comes to mind."

It was just the kind of attack Bush had experienced when he tried to grapple with the issue of immigration as president. Those on the extreme Right labeled him a moderate and said he had lost touch and abandoned the Republican Party for attempting to pass immigration reform in 2007.

That year the president supported an immigration reform bill supported by Republican senator John McCain and Democratic senator Ted Kennedy, among others. But the right wing tore into the bill as "amnesty for illegal immigrants." Conservative writer Ann Coulter claimed it would turn America into a "roach motel." And the king of conservative talk radio, Rush Limbaugh, said the bill was the first step on the road to doom for the Republican Party because it invited a flood of likely Democrats into the country. He said it also spelled doom for schools, hospitals, and welfare lines burdened by this mass of newcomers. Any Republican senator who dared to voice support for President Bush and the bill came under fire as a RINO (Republican in name only), a traitor to conservative principles. Senator Lindsey Graham was labeled "Graham-nesty" for his support of the bill. The harsh rhetoric poisoned any chance for reasoned, honest debate, and the bill died. Even as late as 2010 the power of the extremist poison was still being felt. Senator McCain, fighting for his political life in a primary challenge from a strong anti–immigration reform opponent, had to renounce his support for his own bill and take a hard-line position against immigration reform.

The pattern of paralyzing attacks from politicians and the

media that killed the Bush immigration-reform plan fits a pattern that is now standard theater in Washington, courtesy of both sides of the aisle and their supporters.

In the opening act the nation faces a difficult issue. A glimmer of hope appears when a group of Republican and Democratic leaders begin talks and work on a serious, practical resolution. And then the curtain comes down on act 1. In the second act, those statesmen are attacked as elitists for ignoring the will of the people as expressed in popular partisan positions. They are derided as weak-kneed people ignoring supporters on the Left and Right. In the third and final act, the political leaders stop talking to one another across party lines and eventually stop looking for answers as they become preoccupied with countering threats from party members and political supporters to cut off campaign funds. That is immediately followed by announcements that fiery political opponents will challenge those "out-of-touch" members of Congress in upcoming primaries.

That modern political drama in the Capitol also includes a subplot featuring a cast of second-string politicians who make no effort at serious debate in search of answers but gain several minutes of fame for denouncing anyone suggesting new, pragmatic thinking about the issue. They are rewarded with cameo appearances in which they make outlandish statements. In the immigration fight Congresswoman Marsha Blackburn, a Tennessee Republican, got a ton of media attention and praise from talk radio in 2006 when she appealed to fears of an immigrant invasion by declaring, "Every town has become a border town. Every state has become a border state." Congressman Phil Gingrey, a Georgia Republican, won major press coverage in 2010 when he denounced what he described as "anchor babies." He said illegal immigrants regularly plotted to have their children born in the United States to gain citizenship rights granted under the Constitution to anyone born on American soil. That same year, Congressman Louie Gohmert, a Texas Republican, won headlines when he took concern over the American-born children of illegal immigrants in the United States to a new level, warning of "terror babies" who are brought into the country by terrorist mothers and raised to carry out terror attacks in the future. And Colorado Republican Tom Tancredo got more than a cameo when he criticized the pope and the Catholic Church for being less interested in offering a Christian, charitable response to illegal immigrants than in "recruiting new members." The congressman gained further attention when he tied lax immigration enforcement to President Obama. Speaking at a Tea Party convention, Representative Tancredo said, "People who cannot spell the word 'vote' or say it in English put a committed socialist ideologue in the White House—his name is Barack Hussein Obama!"

These congressmen and other politicians have every political and financial incentive to stake out extreme positions. When they make offensive comments about illegal immigrants, for example, they become the subjects of heated debates. Videos of their remarks become YouTube sensations. They get invitations to appear on national television. Speech requests pour in from like-minded groups. They suddenly attract campaign contributions nationally. But while there are plenty of incentives to stake out extreme positions on issues, there is little incentive for them to roll up their sleeves and work out a compromise on issues of critical importance to the future of the nation.

Looking back, the 2007 immigration-reform bill, for example, does not seem so wild and radical an idea as to generate talk of "terror babies" and attacks on the integrity of the pope and worsen an already bitter national controversy. The bill proposed a pathway to citizenship for the twelve million illegal immigrants in the United States. They would have been allowed to enroll in a special "Z visa" program, a point-based merit system that would have taken into account their education, as well as job-related skills, family connections, and proficiency in English. Far from granting "amnesty" to people who entered the country illegally, the law would have required immigrants without proper documents to register their presence in the United States, pay a fine, pay back taxes, and leave the country before applying for legal immigrant status.

The bill also provided more money for border security. Lack of funding for surveillance and armed patrols is a sticking point for many when it comes to immigration reform. Over the last few years Mexico has been ravaged by corruption, kidnapping, human trafficking, and murder associated with the drug trade. There is rational fear, especially among people living in U.S. towns bordering Mexico, of violence and anarchy following the drug trade into the United States. Had the bill backed by President Bush become law, there would be more surveillance technology and more agents patrolling the borders. Anyone who said the bill did not increase border security was misrepresenting the truth. But the lie was repeated again and again until it appeared that the bill's commitment to border security was up for debate, a matter of partisan dispute.

One congressman, Republican Steve King of Iowa, an opponent of the 2007 bill, said the only satisfactory border security is a massive wall across the thousands of miles of the U.S. border. Representative King actually brought a scale model of such a wall to the House floor, and he had a simulated electrified wire on top of his wall. He was outraged when critics said his wall looked like a prison and posed a danger of electric shock to people coming near the wall. The congressman said the electric wire would not kill people but act as a "discouragement" to trespassing. "We do this with livestock all the time."

King's impractical proposal for a wall from the Gulf of Mexico to the Pacific is one more example of how rational debate is derailed by the sensational time and again. This is what President Bush referred to as isolationism run wild. Even if the wall were built, it would not be effective in stopping illegal immigrants from crossing the border. In his 2010 memoir President Bush wrote, "The longest and tallest fence in the world would not stop those determined to provide for their families." Janet Napolitano, former governor of a border state, Arizona, and now secretary of Homeland Security, said it best when she said that fifty-foot-tall walls result in fifty-one-foot ladders. A similarly impractical proposal from opponents of immigration reform is that all illegal immigrants be deported. Senator McCain's response to that suggestion (at least in the past)? To point out that the United States doesn't have twelve million pairs of handcuffs.

But the Democrats are hardly idle in the audience during such Republican political dramas. They actively encourage these displays by issuing expressions of outrage that delight the Far Right and prompt more offensive statements about immigrants. In the case of the 2007 immigration debate, the Democrats claimed that the guest-worker plan created levels of immigrants that amounted to a medieval caste system by stigmatizing low-wage temporary workers. It was a weak argument when compared to the potential passage of a bill that opened a legal door for people to get jobs without worry of being exploited by employers or chased by immigration agents. But the Democrats' posturing allowed them to claim the mantle of being defenders of the immigrant community. Democrats saw political opportunity in the Republican excess. The Hispanic community increasingly identified with Democrats as the pro-immigrant party and voted for them. The rising Hispanic vote is a potential political gold mine for Democrats. The result? Neither Republicans nor Democrats have a strong reason to alter their positions in search of a compromise that might lead the nation to come to terms with a dysfunctional immigration policy, as we shall see.

Many Hispanics, too, have used the national focus on the immigration drama for their own purposes. They dismiss calls that Hispanics deal with legitimate concerns over rising numbers of Mexican and Latin American legal and illegal aliens who make little or no effort to assimilate into life in the United States, even as they clamber to get into the country and enjoy the benefits of living here. The push for assimilation is now often dismissed inside the Latino community as a betrayal of an immigrant's true identity. To this way of thinking, only self-hating immigrants move away from their native roots and the ethnic, nationalistic, and racial parameters of the old country. By that logic it has become politically correct and chic, especially among younger Latino immigrants, to disparage those Latinos making the effort to assimilate. What is hip among some young immigrants is remaining apart from the American mainstream and taking identity from refusal to fit into the American melting pot.

In 2009, the Census Bureau reported that 97 percent of people coming to the United States from Mexico and the Dominican Republic spoke no English at home; 52 percent of the people born in another country report they don't feel confident of their ability to speak English, much less write it. It has never been easier to see identity politics at play than it is today in large Latino communities, dissuading newcomers to America from doing the work necessary for assimilation and consciously breaking with the American tradition of "E Pluribus Unum"—or becoming one people out of many. Today well over half of U.S. immigrants are people of color born in Latin America. In California alone more than a quarter of the population is made up of immigrants. They have to deal with the twin barriers of race and language. And yet inside the Latino community, that very effort is often denigrated. This problem is compounded among illegal immigrants, whose status creates feelings of alienation. Nevertheless, it is critically important for such cultures to assimilate today because there is so much immigration. Self-segregation—remaining isolated and apart from the mainstream in America—is a self-defeating strategy for anyone who wants to be successful in America.

I believe the Hispanic community has to take a firm stand against illegal immigration themselves, in order to break the logjam on overall immigration reform. They need to wave the red, white, and blue. Newly arrived Hispanic immigrants, in the tradition of earlier immigrants, should be trying to be more American than most Americans. The pretenders in this game are people who think they are still back home and celebrate the old languages and customs out of proportion to what they would do if they were back in their native land.

This is a critically needed step to defuse much of the opposition to immigration reform. The congressional failure to act on immigration reform distracts from a legitimate discussion of the threat that immigrants who fail to assimilate pose to American society and democratic principles. But at the moment, the Republicans, the Democrats, recent immigrants, and leaders in America's Latino community are all finding some advantage in not dealing with the immigration problem.

The immigration crisis, as President Bush pointed out, goes beyond anxiety over the high number of immigrants in America today. It impacts language, culture, and unemployment. Yet the distortions caused by outright lies and politically correct assertions on immigration make it difficult for the public to keep track of the critical nexus between economic growth and welcoming talented immigrants into the United States. Somehow the immigration equation is reduced in political debates to low-wage, unskilled laborers who work in factories, kitchens, and fruit orchards. Unattended by this is the nation's critical need to attract the world's best minds, its most ambitious, driven, innovative people, in order to successfully compete in a global economy. It is also necessary to welcome people with money to invest. Yet these critical issues are rarely addressed in the rage in the media that passes for immigration debate.

The heart of the concern raised by our top business leaders

is that there is a shortage of H-1B visas, those documents that allow highly skilled foreigners to reside and work in the United States. Like tickets to a hot concert, they sell out within days of being offered. The limited number falls far short of the demand and the need in a country of three hundred million people striving to compete globally with China and other countries.

After the 9/11 attacks, visas for top foreign students and skilled workers became even more difficult to obtain. The result is a brain drain; the United States is not keeping the top international talent that is often educated at the best American schools. "These policies work against urgent national economic priorities," the Brookings Institution concluded in a 2011 report, "such as boosting economic vitality, achieving greater competitiveness in the global marketplace and renewing our innovation leadership."

The same conclusion was reached by an exasperated New York mayor Michael Bloomberg, who recently said: "Our immigration policy is a form of national suicide. . . . We ship [top students from around the world who come to our nation's top universities] home where they can take what they learned here and use it to create companies and products that compete with ours."

It was the same warning that came from an American-born entrepreneur, Bill Gates, the founder of Microsoft. Gates is a man looking for the best technological talent to boost his American-based company. He recently told a congressional committee on science and technology: "We provide the world's best universities . . . and the students are not allowed to stay and work in the country. . . . The fact is [other countries'] smartest people want to come here and that's a huge advantage to us, and in a sense we are turning them away."

There have been no serious rebuttals to Bloomberg and Gates. The right-wing talk-show hosts carp that the smart foreigners being celebrated by Bloomberg and Gates are taking the jobs of slightly less educated Americans. It is a weak response, because in a global economy the smartest people are always going to be hired or attract the money to start their own business. The only question is where they rev up their economic engines. That populist retort stems, perhaps, from a fear that Americans are increasingly unable to keep up with foreign competitors. If true, that should lead us to insist on structural reform of our elementary, high school, and college education, rather than indulge protectionist impulses that keep smart people out in the name of defending mediocrity.

"Tech giants such as Google and Apple will no doubt move significant development projects out of the U.S. to places where these skilled workers are available," wrote Frank Aquila, a mergers and acquisitions lawyer, in the pages of *Bloomberg Businessweek* magazine. "Smaller high-tech businesses, historically the engine of U.S. growth and job creation, will simply never get off the ground. The consequences are clear: The next generation of innovative companies will not likely be founded here. Instead, due to U.S. policy, these companies will most probably be created in places such as India, China, and Singapore."

Aquila offered a proposal to break up the clogged and closed-minded thinking around immigration that is damaging American economic interests. He wants Congress, which he describes as "stalled" by partisanship over immigration, to allow foreign entrepreneurs who have investment capital to come to the United States to start their businesses and create an invigorating wave of economic activity. "It's a sensible approach, but sadly few in Congress appear to have the political will to move it forward," he wrote. "We may no longer be willing to accept the world's huddled masses, but we must make a place for the world's top scientists, engineers, and entrepreneurs if we want to remain the world's largest and most dynamic economy."

The Brookings Institution estimates that immigrants' productivity (even though immigrants are only 10 percent of the population) increases the nation's gross domestic product by $37 billion per year. According to Brookings, immigrants have founded more than half of Silicon Valley's new high-technology companies. Immigrants founded more than a quarter of all American technology and engineering businesses between 1995 and 2005, the report stated. And in just one year, 2005, American-based companies started by immigrants employed 450,000 workers and produced $52 billion in sales.

"In order to fully reap the benefits of the worldwide talent market, U.S. immigration policy must be reoriented," the Brookings report concluded. "Current policy is significantly and negatively affected by the unintended consequences of the 1965 Immigration and Nationality Act that made family unification its overarching goal. . . . Its main effect was to enable immigrants to bring in family members without regard for the new immigrants' education, skill status or potential contributions to the economy. . . .

"U.S. employers have a large, unmet demand for knowledge workers," the authors of the Brookings report explained. "They are eager to fill jobs with well-trained foreign workers and foreign graduates of U.S. universities—particularly those with degrees in the sciences, technology, engineering and mathematics, the STEM fields that continue to attract too few U.S.-born students. . . . Meanwhile the United States is falling behind in the pace of innovation and international competitiveness. Evidence for the decline in innovation is the decreasing share of international patents."

So how can we better approach this problem from all angles? A big part of finding some solutions begins with better understanding and identifying with the tradition and legacy of immigration in America.

The current political stalemate over immigration threatens the nation's future on so many levels. But at its deepest and most compelling level the debate touches our national identity. America celebrates as a principal tenet of its democratic freedoms the noble claim to be a welcoming host to people of the world, or as the words inscribed on the Statue of Liberty read: "your huddled masses yearning to breathe free." It is fact, and not myth, that America is, overwhelmingly, a "nation of immigrants," beginning with the colonists who settled the nation.

The history of immigration in America includes periods of anger at new arrivals, as well as outright racism. But this country stands apart from any other in terms of its open door to the world. And that attitude began in the colonial period, when immigration to the United States was a rather open and unbureaucratic affair. The major hurdle was the courage to make the ocean voyage to the new land. It was not until 1790 that the newly formed United States adopted a formal immigration and naturalization policy. After two years of residence, any "free white person" of good moral character could become an American. In 1795 the two-year wait was extended to five years as part of the Alien and Sedition Acts. The law gave the president power to deport any foreigner deemed a threat to national security.

During the early 1800s wars, religious bigotry, and political oppression in Europe led a steady wave of people to book passage on ships and flee to America. More than thirty million Europeans migrated to America between 1836 and 1914. *American Heritage* magazine, in a 1981 article, described the historic shift in populace and the country it created:

> By 1830 annual arrivals numbered 23,322 and a visiting Frenchman wrote glowingly of "the great flood of civilization" that was pouring over the American landscape "with a wonderful power and an admirable regularity." In 1840, a total of 84,066 newcomers landed; in 1850 the number had risen to 369,980. Between 1820 and 1860 some 5 million immigrants crossed the seas, their number surpassing in four decades the total 1790 population it had taken nearly two centuries to achieve. With justifiable pride, Oliver Wendell Holmes exulted, "We are the Romans of the modern world—the great assimilating people."

The pace of Europeans coming to America through an open-door policy continued to accelerate. Between 1880 and 1920 about twenty-six million immigrants made the trip to America. The first big shift came in 1924 when President

Coolidge, responding to the post–World War I growth of the isolationist wing of the Republican Party, put a limit on immigration from any one country. Under the new law only 2 percent of the total number of immigrants from any one country already living in the United States gained admission. The Great Depression further slowed the rate of immigration. It was not until well after World War II that pressure from overseas and a booming U.S. economy led to a pro-immigration shift in U.S. law.

The Hart-Celler Act of 1965, strongly influenced by the civil rights movement against racial segregation in the United States, eliminated the immigration quotas of the 1920s. The impact was to open the doors as never before to immigrants from Asia, Latin America, Africa, and other nonwhite, non–Western European nations. Official government estimates mark the increase in immigrants living in the United States rising from 4.7 percent in 1970 to 10.4 percent in 2000. Over the course of the 1970s and 1980s, with Presidents Nixon, Ford, Carter, Reagan, and Bush, the nation's immigration laws became even more liberal, with increases every year in the number of immigrants allowed into the United States.

President Reagan directly addressed *illegal* immigration in the 1986 Immigration Reform and Control Act. His goal was to organize the flow of seasonal laborers, mostly Mexicans, coming into the United States and to offer illegal aliens living permanently in the United States an opportunity to become legal citizens. Cutting a deal with a Democratic majority in the House and Senate, the Republican president agreed to make it easier for immigrants without proper visas to gain legal status. Ed Meese, Reagan's attorney general, later wrote that the path to citizenship carved by President Reagan required immigrants to "pay application fees, learn to speak English, understand American civics, pass a medical exam and register for military selective service."

The Congressional Budget Office estimates that about 2.7 million people became legal citizens under the Reagan-era law. But the congressional debate about the law, and subsequent arguments about its impact, focused a level of political attention on the immigration issue not seen since the 1920s. Conservative leaders began to openly complain about immigrants lacking an understanding of American history and democracy. They complained, as well, about the sharp changes coloring the ethnic and racial makeup of the nation. Many of their complaints gained traction as complaints about continued high rates of illegal immigration.

"President Ronald Reagan signed that [1986] bill into law with great fanfare amid promises that it would grant legal status to illegal immigrants, crack down on employers who hired illegal workers and secure the border once and for all," the *New York Times* later reported. "Instead, fraudulent applications tainted the process, many employers continued their illicit hiring practices and illegal immigration surged."

Public concern about illegal immigration prompted another round of immigration legislation under President George H. W. Bush. The Immigration Act of 1990 was advertised as correcting the problems with the Reagan-era immigration law by offering new avenues for legal immigration. It also raised the number of immigrants allowed into the country to seven hundred thousand annually. And it eased requirements for immigrants to be conversant in English while eliminating bans on homosexuals and people with AIDS. This was also the first immigration law to create "priority" visas for immigrants with "extraordinary abilities," including top professors, researchers, and corporate executives.

But by the 1992 election a public split over immigration emerged on the Right. A primary challenger to President Bush, conservative social critic Patrick Buchanan, made a call for an "America first" policy as a centerpiece of his campaign.

Buchanan's attack on the Republican president, as described in Saint Louis University professor Donald Critchlow's book *The Conservative Ascendancy,* echoed "the prewar isolationist Right that promised to restore American sovereignty through trade protectionism, a nationalist foreign policy, enforcement of national borders against illegal entry, and immigration restriction."

President Bush defeated Buchanan in the primary but lost his bid for a second term to President Bill Clinton. But immigration remained an issue. The persistent conservative complaints about high numbers of illegal immigrants came into play during debate over a regional U.S. trade pact with Mexico and Canada. To win Republican votes for the 1994 North American Free Trade Agreement, NAFTA, President Clinton argued that an improved economic climate in Mexico would reduce the flow of Mexicans coming to the United States illegally to find work. But while U.S. corporate investments in Mexico grew under NAFTA, there was no improvement in Mexican schools, roads, or social services. Combined with an economic slump in the mid-1990s, fear of drug violence, and widespread corruption, Mexico's lack of opportunity and quality of life continued to give its people seeking a better future plenty of good reasons to risk entering the United States illegally.

When Republicans gained control of the House of Representatives for the first time in forty years in the 1994 midterm elections, President Clinton faced pressure to deal with illegal immigrants. His 1996 Illegal Immigration Reform and Immigrant Responsibility Act increased border patrols, reduced government benefits available without proof of citizenship, and started a system for employers to check by phone on any job applicant's immigration status. The plan passed the Republican House and, along with an economic boom in the late nineties, calmed the national anxiety that had heightened over immigration.

Over the next decade, however, Mexican immigration to the United States increased, from four hundred thousand annually to more than five hundred thousand a year, and the government estimated that 80 percent of those people crossed the border illegally. George W. Bush, the former governor of Texas, a border state with a large Hispanic population, campaigned in 2000 to bring "compassionate conservatism" to the immigration debate. That approach by Governor Bush included reforming immigration laws to legally bring together the supply of Mexicans seeking work and the demands of American employers seeking low-wage workers. On September 5, 2001, the president met at the White House with Mexican president Vicente Fox to promote a "guest worker" program, under which Mexicans could enter the country for a set period of time to do specific jobs. The two presidents spoke about the crisis surrounding illegal immigration in terms of exploited workers and the sad loss of life that occurs when people face dangerous currents to swim across deep rivers to get into the United States, or when people walk through the blistering desert risking death to get a job and support their families. They also addressed concerns about the social and financial burden—in terms of crime and added people in hospitals and schools—to states on the southern border.

Six days later, progress in the debate on illegal immigration expired in the fires of September 11, 2001.

After the terror attacks the national focus on preventing future attacks locked on the question of how the 9/11 terrorists got into the country. The answer was not a simple one. The nineteen hijackers had come in legally. Some of their visa applications contained false information and some of their passports had been doctored, but they had been granted legitimate visas by the U.S. government. A Gallup poll the year after the attacks found that the percentage of Americans who felt immigration was a "bad thing" had jumped ten points higher than before 9/11 to 42 percent of the nation. And in Washington the discussion of immigration took on a singular focus—stopping any more terrorists from getting into the country. That meant tightening border security and imposing more requirements on anyone applying for a visa. The George W. Bush administration increased funding for border security by 60 percent. And the Immigration and Naturalization Service was restructured and integrated into the new Department of Homeland Security with a new sense of purpose, namely searching for any potential terrorist hiding in the country.

The immediate result was a reduction in the number of legal immigrants arriving in the United States. About two million fewer immigrants gained admission, dropping from 7.6 million in 2001 to 5.7 million in 2002. There is no reliable measure of the number of illegal immigrants crossing the Mexico-U.S. border, but with increased security it is likely that number also fell.

By 2004 the ongoing fears of illegal immigration, drug activity and violence from Mexico, and terrorism led a former Marine and retired accountant named Jim Gilchrist to found the Minutemen, a group in southeastern Arizona, to defend the "state against an overwhelming siege by drug and human-trafficking cartels." Hundreds of people signed up. Most sat along the border with walkie-talkies, binoculars, and night-vision goggles, looking for any sign of people walking across the border. Some amateur pilots took to the sky to search for il-legal immigrants. President Bush called the group "vigilantes." When Gilchrist was invited to speak at Columbia University in New York, students stormed the stage in protest. Another presentation at Harvard was canceled because of protests. Gil-christ complained that students were violating his right to free speech. Again, conservative groups picked up the cause and talk radio trumpeted the message that left-wing radicals who wanted open borders did not want to hear about the threat it would pose to national security. Fake videos began to circulate of an illegal immigrant being killed by two people identified on the video as members of the Minutemen. The video was tied to two members of the group who said they made it because "we're old men and we're bored." But xenophobes and bigots began flocking to the Minutemen movement. In May 2009 two people in a Washington State Minutemen splinter group participated in the real murder of an immigrant and the man's daughter in a robbery.

Even before those murders, Gilchrist told an interviewer he was "very, very sad, very disappointed" with what had be-come of his movement. "I have to say some of the people who have gotten into this movement have sinister intentions. . . . I very well may have been fighting for people with less character and less integrity than the 'open border fanatics' I have been fighting against. And that is a phenomenal indictment of something I have created."

It is hard to understand the Minutemen as anything but a desperate plea for the federal government to face down hysterical voices and political threats to get ahold of the nation's dysfunctional immigration system. At their best the Minutemen simply wanted to protect the borders against an indisputably large number of illegal immigrants. The group's creation was an outburst by people who feel powerless and ignored, people whose emotions are played on with scare tactics instead of serious debate. It was an expression of frustration with the failed leadership at all levels of American politics. This is what we get when leaders are so easily intimidated and refuse to engage one another constructively in order to find some consensus and solution.

The aggravation over inaction combined with heightened fear of immigrants and concern over the threat to national security also played a role in the 2004 presidential campaign. The overall campaign between President Bush and Democrat John Kerry, a Massachusetts senator, boiled down to competing claims about which party could better protect the country from terrorist invaders. Historically, polls have shown Americans trust Republicans more than Democrats on national security. And President Bush's reelection team, predictably, hammered Senator Kerry as weak on defense. Part of the president's antiterrorism message was a hard line on immigration. But Republicans did not want to alienate naturalized immigrants who had the right to vote. At the GOP convention, California governor Arnold Schwarzenegger denounced Democrats as "girlie men" on the issue of national defense but told his own life story of an immigrant who achieved his dreams by legally coming to America.

After winning reelection, the president held the first-ever prime-time presidential address to the nation on the issue of immigration. He pledged to tighten border security but also to open the nation's doors to immigrants willing to work. The key to this two-step policy would be getting the base of his own Republican Party to agree to a "path to citizenship" for people already in the country illegally.

The "path" required paying fines, paying back taxes, learning English, and going to the back of the line, waiting behind people outside the United States who had applied earlier for immigration papers. To some illegal immigrants the requirements seemed onerous. Well-organized protest rallies by Hispanics calling for immigration reform became regular events. On one memorable day, April 10, 2006, a coalition called the We Are America Alliance mobilized over two million people for marches in major cities. But the legal and illegal immigrants calling for reform to deal with the more than ten million people already in the country—a group of people attending schools, going to work daily, contributing to the American economy—were met by a fierce outcry from conservatives and conservative talk-show hosts. Once again, conflict and not compromise, pitched battle and not progress, were what both sides seemed to crave.

The right-wing media became enraged at the sight of Mexican flags at some of the marches. They cited these as evidence of disloyalty to the United States. Some called for immigration authorities to wade into the marches and demand visas and passports. They latched onto any report of violence, even a car accident involving an illegal immigrant, as evidence that the country was under siege by illegal immigrants. Coverage of drug cartel violence and kidnappings on both sides of the border took on hysterical tones. One talk-show host, incredibly, suggested the illegal immigrants might pose a health risk by bringing leprosy into the country. The fear extended to scenarios in which Middle Eastern terrorists followed the path of Mexicans crossing the southern border illegally.

The frenzied media made honest debate on immigration difficult—some might say impossible. President Bush made several speeches calling for fellow conservatives to support his relatively balanced immigration plan. He went so far as to support construction of a wall along sectors of the border that included a patchwork of physical walls and the use of sensors and cameras to create "virtual fences." The White House got Senator McCain and Democratic senator Barack Obama to sign on as supporters of a billion-dollar appropriation to build and maintain the wall. That bill passed and was signed into law, but there was no follow-up to deal with the need for overall immigration reform.

One proposal to win over conservative critics and allow reform to go forward came in 2010 from Senators Charles Schumer, a New York Democrat, and Lindsey Graham, a South Carolina Republican. The idea was to issue a national identification card. The card, as proposed, is a tamper-proof plastic device that has the citizen's fingerprints as well as biometric scans of eyes and facial characteristics. Some private companies now issue similar cards to frequent travelers who want to speed through airport screenings. But the Schumer-

Graham proposal drew cries of "big brother" from civil-liberty groups, which suggested the government could begin to track people, including critics, and violate constitutional protections of individual rights and privacy. The idea stalled as Graham and Schumer failed to effectively respond to these fears.

President Bush and his top political aides appealed for Republicans to wise up to the potential of the growing Hispanic population as potential future members of the Republican Party. They highlighted all the added money in the bill for security, including funds to put new high-tech surveillance technology on the border. But the conservative talk-show universe gave a bullhorn to every congressman opposing the larger immigration bill. In the end, the Republican majority in the Senate did not pass the bill.

The immigration problem, both legal and illegal, continued apace after President Bush left office. His successor, President Obama, promised during his campaign to deal with the issue during his first year in office but never brought the political attention to what remained of Bush's proposals or any other. In the lame-duck session of 2010, President Obama did try to get Congress to approve the DREAM Act, which had been hanging around in the legislature since 2001 and had been included in Bush's attempted compromise. The Development, Relief and Education for Alien Minors Act allows children brought into the United States illegally to gain citizenship if they serve in the military for two years or finish two years of college. The bill had support from a range of Democrats and Republicans. But even with President Obama's last-minute support, the DREAM Act failed to pass in the final days of a Democratic majority in the House of Representatives.

In response to the failure of the DREAM Act and the broader immigration reform bill, several state governments began to issue their own laws. Most of the laws played to the same angry, extreme voices, the "populism" described by President Bush, which made it politically impossible for national politicians to resolve the issue. In Arizona, for example, Governor Jan Brewer signed into law the Support Our Law Enforcement and Safe Neighborhoods Act. The bill made it a crime for anyone in the state not to have proof of citizenship when asked for it by a police officer. Opponents said the law invited racial profiling because the people most likely to draw suspicion as illegal immigrants are sure to be brown-skinned people with a Spanish accent. Several police chiefs spoke against it because they feared that illegal immigrants would stop cooperating with crime investigations and even become violent when approached by police if they feared deportation. President Obama opposed the bill. President Bush's top political adviser, Karl Rove, also opposed the bill: "I think there is going to be some constitutional problems with the bill. . . . I wished they hadn't passed it."

But the proposal and the law proved a boon to Governor Brewer, who became a champion of the talk-radio, anti-immigration crowd and easily won a reelection fight in which she had previously been an underdog. Her success has prompted other states, including Colorado, Florida, Indiana, Nebraska, South Carolina, and Texas, to consider similar legislation.

Another group of state lawmakers, State Legislators for Legal Immigration, proposed changing the constitutional standard, expressed in the Fourteenth Amendment, that grants citizenship to all children born in the United States. Under the new proposal a child must have at least one parent who is a U.S. citizen or legal permanent resident in order to qualify to become an American citizen. The law fit with concerns previously expressed by extremists and anti-immigrant critics about "anchor babies," and probably "terror babies" too, for that matter.

The radical threat to the Constitution to deny citizenship to children born in the United States is another consequence of the federal government's failure to deal with immigration for the last decade. As I am writing, there is no evidence of anything but continued posturing, political stagnation, and finger-pointing on this critical issue. The Obama administration does not have a record of fighting the good fight to get the debate under way. Its strategy is to work around the edges. It has put money into eliminating the FBI backlog on background checks for people applying for legal immigration and has also put more money into border security to try to defuse concern about terrorism risks posed by lax security. But basically the country remains adrift on immigration, legal and illegal.

"In the end," President Obama has said, "our broken immigration system affects more than a single community; it affects our entire country. And as we continue to strengthen our economy and jump-start job creation, we need to do so with an immigration system that works, not the broken system we have now."

President Obama is echoing President Bush on this issue. Left and Right agree at the highest levels of government that something has to be done. But the years continue to pass without politicians taking the risk of tackling the problem. We are locked into a game of political checkers where no one is going to move for fear of getting jumped.

Midway through the twenty-first century, about 20 percent of the U.S. population will be made up of people born in other countries. Hispanics, the nation's largest minority group, now make up 15 percent of the population. About a quarter of the Hispanic population is made up of illegal immigrants. Polls show Hispanics oppose most of the stringent enforcement plans intended to cut down on illegal immigration. They are almost perfectly aligned in opposition to the anti-immigrant crowd on the Right. Yet within that larger group, native-born Hispanics have the same opinions as the general American population about the need for better border enforcement.

What the polls tell us is that there is a large, unexplored middle ground on immigration. That it is not the divisive issue that political extremists tell us it is. Most Americans, whatever their backgrounds, believe we are a unique nation of immigrants and yet care about our laws of citizenship and national security in an age of terrorist threats. They understand the importance of opening doors for both low-wage workers who do many critical jobs in the United States and highly skilled workers who are key to the continued growth of the U.S. economy.

Why is no one talking to them?

CHAPTER 7

THE ABORTION WARS

AMERICA LONG AGO reached the point where there is no productive way to discuss abortion.

It is the issue that best exemplifies the difficulty of having an honest conversation in America. Ranting and vituperative slander erupt regularly in any public discussion of abortion. Extremists insist there is no middle ground—only their way. That's why even an admission of uncertainty leads to condemnation from those who are either proabortion or antiabortion. Debate degenerates into arguments over abortion that are so personal and hurtful. To escape harsh judgment from those who would ostracize them, many women who have had abortions withhold the truth from parents, husbands, and children. They carry it as a private burden, and an increasing number of doctors do not even learn how to perform abortions, so they can avoid the harassment and arguments that would result from doing the procedure.

Political leaders, both for and against abortion, stick to politically correct scripts for fear of losing ground to another politician who is willing to take an absolutist stance. Even politicians who speak out of sincere belief on abortion knowingly overstate their ability to end abortion or protect women who want an abortion.

It is difficult to discuss any social issue that has strong ties to the volcanic topics of sexual behavior and religious beliefs. But in 1972 abortion went into another dimension, beyond homosexuality and pornography. That year President Nixon captured 60 percent of Catholic voters, previously a reliable Democratic constituency. He won those Catholic voters after announcing his opposition to "unrestricted abortion." However, the next year, in 1973, the Supreme Court ruled in *Roe v. Wade* that abortion was protected by the Constitution. Suddenly, abortion became the number one polarizing issue in the nation. Forty years later it remains the champion wedge issue to divide the American people and the major political parties. Nothing matches its powerful, highly combustible political mixture of sex, death, women's liberation, and religion.

That is why abortion is the epitome of fixed, intractable, polarized American politics.

Every presidential candidate is compelled to support abortion rights if they are Democratic, or stand against abortion rights if they are a Republican.

Every Supreme Court nominee is scrutinized for any indication of how they will vote on abortion.

Catholic leaders threaten to deny politicians the right to communion if they disagree with the church hierarchy, without acknowledging that there is a major divide on the issue of abortion among the most faithful Catholics.

People who call themselves liberals can be intolerant

when it comes to abortion. Teddy Kennedy famously said of Supreme Court nominee Robert Bork that "Robert Bork's America is a land in which women would be forced into back-alley abortions." Faye Wattleton, the former head of Planned Parenthood, a group that provides abortions, once charged abortion opponents with modern-day "McCarthyism." Abortion supporters have made a hideous trademark of a twisted coat hanger as a reminder of the back-alley alternative to legal, supervised medical abortions.

The ugly talk, of course, has also come from people trying to stop legal abortion. During the health-care reform debate in 2010, Congressman Randy Neugebauer, a Texas Republican, felt free to slander a Michigan Democrat, Bart Stupak, as a "baby killer." Incredibly, Stupak is an opponent of abortion. Nellie Gray, who organized the first mass protest in Washington against abortion, warned that like Nazis who killed Jews during the Holocaust, any member of Congress supporting abortion rights "will be held accountable, just as the Nuremberg trials found individuals personally responsible for crimes committed against humanity." Representative Trent Franks, an Arizona Republican, has called abortion worse than slavery. Abortion opponents carry signs with pictures of bloody aborted fetuses. They badger and traumatize women entering abortion clinics.

There is little room in this charred landscape for hope or compromise. This harsh language, the personal insults, the reliance on religious dogma and threats of violence make it easy for most Americans to shut up when it comes to abortion. The fact that both political parties see benefit in keeping up the attacks has made it impossible to have an honest debate or to compromise and achieve national consensus on abortion. People become angry, hurt, and bitter from being assaulted with charges that range from oppressing women to child-killing. The response to such slander is predictable. People on each side harden their positions and join in trading dogma. Tragically, the ill will is so thick it derails the need to resolve the myriad social and economic problems that surround abortion. Abortion takes up so much attention, emotion, money, and energy that by comparison political leaders appear indifferent to or bored with the tragic daily circumstances confronting too many American women and children—poverty, hunger, homelessness, joblessness, and abuse.

The obsessive focus on abortion results in the nation agreeing to a separate and artificial reality.

The alternate universe of bitter words never admits the reality that polls have painted a fairly consistent picture of what the American people think about abortion. It is a world described by President Clinton in which abortion is "safe, legal and rare." A strong majority of Americans seem comfortable with that rational approach, according to the polls. For most of the last forty years, most Americans have told pollsters they approve of a woman being allowed to have an abortion. And studies show that one of every three American women, across all religions, races, income levels, and age groups, will have an abortion before the age of forty-five. The most recent data on abortions in the United States, from the Guttmacher Institute, reports that despite the blanket opposition of the Catholic Church and evangelicals, 28 percent of the women having abortions identify their religion as Catholic and 37 percent say they are Protestant.

The study showed that about half of the women who have abortions, 45 percent, have never been married and are not living with a man. More than 60 percent of the women who have abortions already have one or more children. And many women who have abortions are poor: 42 percent of them have incomes below the poverty line ($10,830 for a single woman with no children), and another 27 percent are limited to incomes less than twice the federal poverty level.

That sad picture offers no evidence to suggest that brutish husbands, pimps, or psychopaths are forcing these women to have abortions. There is no indication that wanton, loose women casually use abortion in place of contraception. The survey indicates that the average woman having an abortion is an adult—57 percent are between the ages of twenty and twenty-nine—who is making a difficult, personal decision, often while struggling to feed herself and her children, to terminate a pregnancy.

Given that reality, even if the *Roe v. Wade* decision giving women constitutional protection for abortion was overturned, abortion would not stop. If a conservative Supreme Court majority overturned *Roe*, it would open the door to each of the fifty states setting its own rules for abortion. Under those circumstances, states such as California and New York would likely allow abortions, while states like Alabama and Oklahoma would likely ban them. In the post-*Roe* world with no constitutional protection for abortion, the world so passionately desired by abortion opponents, women living in a state that did not allow abortions would be able to travel to states that allow abortion. Poor women and young women without the means or support to make the trip might be forced to find doctors or midwives who would do abortions illegally. Or those women would keep children they didn't want and might not be able to adequately take care of. Ideally, in that scenario, they would put those unwanted children up for adoption. But the overwhelming majority of abortions would continue unabated.

The fact is that abortions occur every day in America, and that has been true regardless of what the high court, Congress, the president, or any religious community says about them. This is not an expression of opinion. It is a recognition of reality. Abortion is a painful subject, but no meaningful debate can take place while opponents pretend it can simply be abolished.

The language around the abortion debate is so charged it has become a seductive, paralyzing toxin when applied to other topics. To avoid getting stung in the abortion debate, journalists are now instructed by the *Associated Press Stylebook* to refrain from using the terms "pro-life" and "pro-choice." The problem with these terms is that they can be taken to imply that people who hold the opposite view are not just wrong but morally deficient in their character. If you identify as pro-life, then you are communicating to all those who disagree with you that they are bad people who are "anti-life" and "prodeath." On the other hand, if you put a "pro-choice" sticker on your car, some people will take that to mean that you are impugning the other side as intolerant, small-minded people who are "anti-freedom" and "anti–individual privacy." So the *Associated Press Stylebook* instructs journalists to use the more neutral terms "anti-abortion" and "abortion rights" in telling stories about abortion.

I am going to stick with that language because this book is

not about who is right or wrong on abortion. I don't want to give anyone a convenient reason to ignore the damage being done by the abortion debate to all civil dialogue.

And both sides try to drag everyone into their miserable argument. In addition to the coded words and disturbing symbols, hyperbole is a ubiquitous tactic used by both sides. Supporters of abortion point to pregnancies that result from rape or incest to argue their case. In one of the 2004 presidential debates, Senator John Kerry, the Democratic nominee, posited this scenario to justify his opposition to parental notification laws. What Senator Kerry and the "pro-choice" crowd neglects to mention is that only about 1 percent of all abortions terminate a pregnancy that resulted from rape or incest. Opponents of abortion use similar tactics. They focus on "partial-birth abortion" of late-term fetuses and detail images of limbs being pulled off bodies to make a graphic, emotionally upsetting case for their point of view. And like their opponents, they fail to mention the dire circumstances that require the use of such a procedure or that it is rarer than the 1 percent of abortions tied to rape and incest. On every side politicians and interest groups have a penchant for manipulating the facts about abortion to shift the debate in their favor. Restraint and respect for the other side of the argument are viewed as evidence of lack of conviction. They are seen as weakness.

This dangerous minefield surrounding discussion of abortion is now creeping into discussions of all social issues. As the new standard it has reduced debate to the use of smear tactics, slogans, and questioning the integrity of anyone who holds a different point of view. On gay marriage, school prayer, allowing monuments with religious symbols on public land, and even the celebration of Christmas by public institutions, the debate is always shaped to mimic the failed, frustrating, and purely political pattern of discourse on abortion. The reason the abortion debate has the power to set the beat for every other discussion of social issues is the tremendous success the issue has had in building political movements.

Since the 1980s, Christian conservative groups such as the Family Research Council, Focus on the Family, and National Right to Life have become major players in Republican Party politics because of the power derived from flying the flag of opposition to abortion. On the other side, Emily's List, the National Organization for Women, and NARAL Pro-Choice America have become major players in Democratic Party politics by trumpeting their defense of the right to abortion. On both sides there are big money, major lobbying organizations, and powerful political allies available for any candidate willing to advocate one view loudly, drowning out all nuances, and to vilify all opposing voices. Abortion has become the one and only litmus test applied by these groups to judge all political leaders. These groups have succeeded in forcing the nation to go along with their one-note, narrow standard for electing leaders, writing laws, and setting budgets. And this goes beyond candidates for elected office. Anyone seeking to be an activist in the base of either the Republican Party or the Democratic Party basically takes a pledge for or against abortion with no explanations allowed. Again, it is the ultimate litmus test.

The abortion issue has become a critical factor in even the most routine business of the U.S. Congress. Every year since 1976 Congress has passed the Hyde Amendment to ban federal funding for abortion. Medicaid—federal supplements to help the poor get proper health care—is not allowed to pay for abortions. The Hyde Amendment effectively denies a legal medical procedure to poor women. This is a significant issue of fairness and social justice worth discussing. But that discussion is not allowed. Neither side wants to risk upsetting the status quo, which is benefiting them both. The politics of abortion have made it a zero-sum game with extremists on both sides setting the rules and everyone else remaining muzzled.

One critical aspect of the fear of discussing abortion is acceptance of the idea that there is a major religious component to this debate. It is a fact that the Catholic Church and millions of Americans interpret biblical scripture as condemning abortion. The Constitution gives those citizens the right to religious freedom and the right to practice their understanding of God's word. However, the First Amendment to the Constitution also says that Congress shall make no law respecting establishment of religion. The United States is a secular nation governed by the rule of law. Religious beliefs are not a legitimate basis for making law. The separation of church and state is an established principle of our government. Even though colonists of the revolutionary era were very religious people, they joined in near unanimity in opposing the establishment of an official religion for their new country. The animating idea that led them to that decision was a very conscious desire to not replicate the European models that many had fled in search of religious tolerance. Yet when it comes to contemporary arguments about abortion, the use of religious doctrine threatens to erase the line between religion and government. And when similar tactics are mimicked in arguments about other hot-button issues, from gay rights to prayer in school, it makes it impossible to achieve progress. It clogs the arteries that have carried the blood of American democracy.

It may sound radical—because it is rarely said for fear of giving offense—but religion is not the law in this country. Inspirational references to the ideals of religious teachings are not the basis for our laws. The Founding Fathers, the abolitionists, and leaders of the civil rights movement all called for America to aspire to become a loving community, with justice and charity. But attempts to dictate political, military, or social policy on the basis of religious doctrine amount to imposing constraints on dialogue that are not accepted by all Americans. Using religion to foment division between Americans may be the vilest form of coded speech because it is so contradictory to the reasons this country was founded. The word "God" does not appear in the Constitution. The only reference to a deity is an expression of the date—"The Year of Our Lord"—which is about as bland a reference as one can imagine. The document has been described as the "godless Constitution." So how, in a country governed by that Constitution, can the Bible or any other religious text be the final word on what rights a woman has regarding abortion? The sad thing is that advocates and opponents, as well as politicians, know this but still find it politically advantageous to pretend they don't. And it is ironic that many of those who favor the strictest interpretation of the Constitution are the most liberal when it comes to violating its very first principle.

The power of religion has been a constant force in American life from the start. The Founding Fathers repeatedly referred to the God-given right to freedom as the basis for their Declaration of Independence from the tyrannical rule of King George. But that religious framework did not extend to the principles articulated in the Constitution. In designing the Constitution the Founding Fathers "believed themselves at work in the service of both God and man, not just one or the other," wrote Jon Meacham in his book *American Gospel.* "Driven by a sense of providence and an acute appreciation of the fallibility of humankind, they created a nation in which religion should not be singled out for special help or particular harm. The balance between the promise of the Declaration of Independence, with its evocation of divine origins and destiny, and the practicalities of the Constitution, with its checks on extremism, remains perhaps the most brilliant American success."

Even so, religion was a point of controversy in national politics from the start. Thomas Jefferson's ties to atheists during his time in Paris were used by his political opponents to portray him as a godless man, a heathen lacking any moral compass who was not fit to govern the new nation. He was widely quoted as having defined his stand on religion with a pithy line: "It does me no injury for my neighbor to say there are twenty gods or no god. It neither picks my pocket nor breaks my leg."

Religion became a major force in American life in the early 1800s, with churches and revival meetings becoming the center of social life in small towns and cities. The evangelical tone, with its optimism and promise of personal salvation, fit with the promise of emerging democratic institutions. Alexis de Tocqueville wrote in *Democracy in America* that the new nation was far more taken with religion than any country in Europe. "I do not know if all Americans have faith in their religion," he wrote, " . . . but I am sure that they believe it necessary to the maintenance of republican institutions. This opinion does not belong only to one class of citizens or to one party but to the entire nation; one finds it in all ranks."

The power of religion to create a common bond and to organize Americans was evident in the spread of organized religion in the United States during what historians call the "Second Great Awakening." Churches became a regular stop for politicians seeking office, and the era marked "the beginning of the 'Republicanizing' or nationalizing of American religion," according to Gordon Wood's book *Empire of Liberty*. President Lincoln used references to biblical scripture regularly in his speeches. He capitalized on the religious undertones of the Declaration of Independence to rally his fight to keep North and South as one nation, as well as to compel Americans to deal with the immorality of slavery. Lincoln's speeches, correspondence, and diaries are full of references to God and the moral importance for a God-fearing country of freeing the slaves. "The Battle Hymn of the Republic" stirred antislavery passion with its lyrical appeal to the power of a fierce God who is marching forward to crush the bitter fruit of slavery, the grapes of wrath.

In the twentieth century, religious themes again became central to national identity in the fight against communism. After World War II American politicians framed the ideological struggle between the military superpowers of the day, the Soviet Union and the United States, as a conflict between godless communists and God-fearing Americans. In 1954 the Pledge of Allegiance was altered to include the phrase "one nation under God." And in 1956 the country's motto, featured on its currency, became "In God We Trust." Also during this time, press baron William Randolph Hearst openly promoted a young evangelical and conservative preacher with a fiery, anticommunist message—Billy Graham. "The principles of Christ," Graham said at his many crusades, "form the only ideology hard enough to stop communism. When communism conquers a nation it makes every man a slave. When Christianity conquers a nation it makes every man a king." Graham became a permanent fixture at mass rallies for tens of thousands promoting "born-again" American Protestantism that was tied to fighting the devilish communist menace. Democrats and Republicans in the White House welcomed Billy Graham as a spiritual adviser, but his hard line against communists led conservatives, especially President Nixon, to embrace his willingness to mix Christianity and patriotism. Religion also made news during this period thanks to the Supreme Court's rulings limiting prayer in public schools. And the 1960 campaign saw John F. Kennedy's Catholicism become an issue. No Catholic had ever been president, and he felt compelled to speak against suggestions that he might take directions from the pope and not the Constitution.

Beginning in 1965, arguments about the role of religion in American life erupted again. This time the women's liberation movement and the debate over a woman's sexual freedoms ignited political passions and arguments over whether the nation was losing its moral grounding. Those social debates became a fire-and-brimstone political fury when the Supreme Court issued rulings on the "right to privacy." The Court, in a series of decisions, said women had a right to contraceptives under its reading of the Constitution, as a matter of privacy. And then the 1973 *Roe v. Wade* decision inflamed social conservatives by giving constitutional protection to abortion. The high court's ruling, along with Nixon's political success in winning the Catholic vote as a result of his opposition to abortion, gave rise to a new political force—a vocal, organized antiabortion right wing that spoke in defiance of any "right to privacy," invoking scripture and the importance of a fetus's competing "right to life."

The Republican Party had to reverse its abortion position to accommodate the new political reality. "Before the early 1970s, Republicans had promoted global and national population control through family planning, including contraception, sterilization and abortion," wrote Donald Critchlow in his book *The Conservative Ascendancy.* And in the United States abortion had been a moral issue but never a political issue. The social consensus on abortion created informal rules that stood apart from the strict laws regulating abortion. Americans accepted termination of pregnancy as a private medical decision until the so-called quickening of a fetus, the moment when a woman is able to feel the baby moving inside of her. The law, however, was more rigid, with explicit bans on abortion in most states. Before *Roe* was decided in 1973, only four states—Alaska, Hawaii, New York, and Washington—legally allowed abortion on request during the first six months of pregnancy. Another sixteen states allowed abortion when the health of the mother was in danger or after rape or incest. And thirty states barred abortion completely. The feminist movement of the 1960s organized in much of the country around campaigns to pressure state officials to relax laws banning abortion. And the vast majority of women at the center of the movement were white college graduates and suburbanites, and many of them were Catholics. It was the effort of these women that promoted the *Roe* case in an attempt to force state governments to acknowledge that women nationwide had a right to have abortions. The Supreme Court's decision legalized abortion in line with the understanding of quickening, or in the words of the Court, the "viability" of the fetus. However, the Court left it up to the states to set their own standards for when a fetus was viable and to impose restrictions on any abortions scheduled after viability.

The uproar that followed the *Roe v. Wade* ruling was immediate and energized both sides of the debate. The decision was a boon to the women's rights movement, and it was a boon to conservative religious leaders, who started groups including the Moral Majority to preach against the country becoming a modern-day Sodom and Gomorrah. In the Republican Party, Nixon's winning strategy of opposition to abortion rights became the new standard for top officials. Critchlow describes the organized ferocity of the antiabortion coalition that emerged in the 1970s as intentionally designed to be a political weapon, "a wedge to lure traditional Roman Catholics and evangelical Protestants away from their Democratic loyalties."

Gerald Ford, Nixon's vice president, was criticized in GOP circles as weak on abortion because he never gave strong antiabortion speeches and cited the Court ruling in response to questions intended to get him to personally condemn abortion. Ronald Reagan, who challenged Ford in the 1976 Republican primary, rose to near victory by highlighting his opposition to abortion.

In the 1980 presidential campaign Reagan turned his opposition to abortion into a pledge to appoint federal judges, including members of the Supreme Court, who honored the "sanctity of innocent unborn life." The Republican Party was now the party of opposition to abortion.

By 1981 the political furor around abortion made it, in the words of *Time* magazine's Walter Isaacson, "without question the most emotional issue of politics and morality that faces the nation today." Writing in a *Time* cover story, Isaacson predicted that the conflict had the potential to "test the foundations of [the Constitution's] pluralistic system designed to accommodate deep rooted moral differences." He quoted Dr. C. Everett Koop, later the surgeon general, as saying, "Nothing like it has separated our society since the days of slavery." And national data on the doubling of the number of abortions since the *Roe* decision, from 744,600 to 1.5 million, gave further power to the debate. In his first years in the White House, President Reagan tried to get Congress to pass a "Human Life Statute" to codify when a fetus was to be considered viable and therefore protected from abortion. Congressman Henry Hyde, an Illinois Republican, was the bill's biggest supporter and made incredibly grandiose statements to try to get it enacted: "Defining when life begins," he said, "is the sort of question Congress is designed to answer, competent to answer, must answer." The law was never enacted, but during the early 1980s the Supreme Court ruled on efforts by several state legislatures, inspired by the increasingly powerful antiabortion movement, to restrict abortion through the use of parental notification requirements and even requirements that abortions take place only in hospitals. Those limitations were struck down as unreasonable barriers to a woman's right to have an abortion. That did not stop the effort to find a way to undercut the *Roe* ruling. In 1986 the Court had to deal with a form issued by the state of Pennsylvania to all women seeking abortions. The wording counseled against terminating any pregnancy. Associate Justice Harry Blackmun, in his majority opinion, wrote that "the States are not free, under the guise of protecting maternal health or potential life, to intimidate women into continuing pregnancies."

Between 1973 and the late 1980s the Supreme Court's persistent defense of the underlying premise of the *Roe* ruling—that a woman's right to make a private decision on having an abortion was protected by the Constitution—led abortion opponents to shift tactics. Instead of focusing on efforts to force the Court to look at a variety of state restrictions, the anti-abortion movement concentrated on changing the makeup of the Court. The goal was to seat judges opposed to abortion while opposing any judge who supported protections for abortion. President Reagan had long promised to nominate judges who opposed abortion, and he had successfully nominated three associate justices of the court, Sandra Day O'Connor, the first woman to sit on the high court; Anthony Kennedy; and Antonin Scalia. Foes of abortion rights expected these justices to be ready to support them in future cases limiting or upending the *Roe* decision. But there was uncertainty when another Republican president, George H. W. Bush, who had been vice president under President Reagan, successfully nominated David Souter to the Court. President Bush had given all necessary reassurances to abortion opponents when he ran for office. But throughout his career he had never been a leading voice of opposition to abortion. President Bush's White House, like President Reagan's, claimed to have no abortion litmus test for its nominees. But among the leaders of the movement to stop abortion the assumption was that the Republican presidents had been privately assured that their nominees planned to shift the balance of the Court majority and weaken if not reverse *Roe*. The moment for change in the Court's handling of abortion seemed to be in place, because Souter took the seat of a leading liberal and abortion supporter, William Brennan.

Associate Justice Souter was seated in time for the next abortion case, *Planned Parenthood v. Casey*. In a surprise to most of the country, he joined with O'Connor and Kennedy in a plurality decision that upheld *Roe* but also clarified the right of states to regulate a variety of abortion procedures so long as the rules did not place an "undue burden" on a woman's right to choose. Opponents of abortion were livid.

The Republican orthodoxy requiring opposition to abortion was matched by the Democrats' orthodoxy requiring support for abortion rights. During the 1992 Democratic National Convention, the governor of Pennsylvania, Bob Casey, was denied the chance to address the delegates because he planned to speak in opposition to abortion. The *New York Times* later reported that the governor of one of the nation's largest states was "not permitted on camera for fear that his sour note on abortion would disturb the symphony of [convention] unity." The governor was incensed and took personal offense at buttons sold at the convention that depicted him, a Catholic, as the pope. "To me, it was simply a case of anti-Catholic bigotry," he later wrote. "What was going on here? What had become of the Democratic Party I once knew?"

President Clinton helped to quiet the debate over abortion during the midnineties with his position that abortion should be "safe, legal and rare." Even when Republicans won control of the House of Representatives in 1994, they did not focus on ending abortion as part of the "contract with America." But in the 2000 campaign for the Republican nomination the issue returned with political punch. Two staunch opponents of abortion, Gary Bauer and Steve Forbes, ran for the nomination. Texas governor George W. Bush announced his support for a constitutional amendment banning abortion except in cases of rape or incest or when the mother's life was in danger. He used his standing as a "born-again" Christian and his opposition to abortion to distinguish himself from his biggest challenger, Arizona senator John McCain. Bush enlisted antiabortion groups such as the National Right to Life Committee to run advertisements portraying McCain as wavering on abortion.

Abortion stayed in the news that year when another case, a challenge to a Nebraska ban on partial-birth abortion, was struck down by the Supreme Court, in *Stenberg v. Carhart,* as an attempt to criminalize abortion in violation of both the *Roe* and *Casey* decisions. After Bush narrowly won the presidency, he spoke of promoting a "culture of life," and in 2003 he acted on his pledged opposition to abortion by signing a ban on partial-birth abortions, a law that would eventually be upheld in 2007 by a newly conservative majority on the Supreme Court. Meanwhile, abortion opponents pressured the president to name people to the high court who could be counted on to limit if not overturn *Roe*. Pat Robertson, who had made banning abortion a central message of his nationally televised evangelical programs, blasted the justices for allowing abortion. Robertson launched "Operation Supreme Court Freedom" in 2005 as a prayer project for all Christians to ask God to replace the current justices of the Supreme Court with "righteous judges." Robertson embraced a new tactic in which judges who disagreed with him on abortion rights found themselves charged with ignoring the Constitution and "legislating from the bench." In one televised prayer he asked God for more vacancies on the Supreme Court, "that we might see people who respect the Constitution and who respect the fundamental law of the land. . . . Lord, give us righteous judges who will not try to legislate and dominate this society. Take control, Lord!"

Reverend Robertson got his wish when President Bush got two strong conservatives, both Catholics, on the Supreme Court, including the new chief justice, John Roberts. By the end of President Bush's second term, the conservative majority made up of Roberts, Sam Alito, Antonin Scalia, Anthony Kennedy, and Clarence Thomas all were practicing Catholics. This is the Supreme Court that upheld President Bush's ban on partial-birth abortion.

In the 2008 election Senator McCain, the Republican nominee, tried to attack Democrat Barack Obama as a man with "poor judgment" on social issues, beginning with his association with 1960s radicals and his left-wing Chicago minister, Reverend Jeremiah Wright. When the Supreme Court's ban on partial-birth abortion was decided in 2007, then-senator and presidential candidate Obama tried to stay out of the bitter fight while quietly expressing his views: "I think that most Americans recognize that this is a profoundly difficult issue for the women and [the] families who make these decisions. They don't make them casually. And I trust women to make these decisions in conjunction with their doctors and their families and their clergy. And I think that is where most Americans are."

With Senator Obama's clear statement of support for abortion rights, McCain did not have to worry about losing antiabortion voters to the Democrat. But McCain's campaign wanted to use Obama's support for abortion to weaken his standing with moderate voters. They wanted to introduce doubt and raise questions about whether he was too left-wing to be trusted to handle a range of social issues, from stem-cell research to gay rights. The *New York Times* reported that McCain's talk about Obama's "poor judgment" was also "code" to suggest the Democrat was likely to appoint "liberal, activist judges." The Democrat's response was to avoid speaking directly about abortion. As for the kind of judges he was likely to put on the federal courts and the Supreme Court, Obama cast himself as concerned with delivering justice to all. "What I do want is a judge who is sympathetic enough to those who are on the outside, those who are vulnerable, those who are powerless, those who can't have access to political power and as a consequence can't protect themselves from being—from being dealt with sometimes unfairly, that the courts become a refuge for justice."

Candidate Obama's goal, as a senator with a very liberal voting record and the first African American to win his party's presidential nomination, was to avoid any statements that allowed opponents to paint him as radical and out of the mainstream. He definitely did not want to get involved with blunt, provocative stands on abortion when it was to his advantage to focus on Republican responsibility for the economic crisis and two controversial wars. Even when he ran for the Democratic nomination and had to reassure the party's base of his support for abortion, he similarly avoided making direct statements, preferring thoughtful expressions about the issue that he hoped would appeal to moderates. "When you describe a specific procedure that accounts for less than 1 percent of the abortions that take place, then naturally, people get concerned," he said regarding partial-birth abortion, "and I think legitimately so. But the broader issue here is: Do women have the right to make these profoundly difficult decisions? And I trust them to do it."

Shortly after President Obama took office, the abortion debate flared up again. A doctor who performed late-term abortions in Kansas, George Tiller, was shot through his eye and killed at his church in Wichita. Tiller became the eighth abortion doctor killed by antiabortion advocates in the last twenty years. In addition, several abortion clinics had been bombed. The president condemned the violence, especially the shooting, but deferred on offering any new arguments in support of legal abortion. The détente that the Tiller killing brought about between abortion and antiabortion activists was quickly scrapped as the health-care reform debate heated up. The concern was whether health-care reform might allow for coverage of abortions. Some old allies in the campaign to end legal abortion found themselves at odds.

"One of the most prominent voices in the anti-abortion movement," *U.S. News & World Report* wrote, ". . . has carved out a much different position in the healthcare debate. The U.S. Conference of Catholic Bishops, while fiercely opposed to abortion rights, has lobbied for decades for universal healthcare coverage as a fundamental right. 'We think the right to have basic healthcare is corollary to the right to life,' says Richard Doerflinger, associate director of the Secretariat for Pro-Life Activities at the bishops' conference, which represents the Roman

Catholic Church's roughly 270 American bishops. 'And that society has some obligation to help provide it.' "

The Catholic Church's position—opposing abortion while supporting health care—put Democrats in the position of wanting to separate the issue to benefit from the power of church backing for the president's top legislative priority. Congressman Bart Stupak, a conservative Democrat from Michigan who opposed government funding of abortion, refused to commit to support the health-care bill unless it included a ban on paying for abortions through health insurance exchanges set up by the government to provide insurance coverage. President Obama eventually signed an executive order banning abortion payments under the health-care reform plan. But that compromise did not satisfy a vituperative, antiabortion Republican, Representative Randy Neugebauer, who, as mentioned earlier, damned Representative Stupak as a "baby killer." That blasphemy stands as the epitome of the kind of horrid, lowball personal attack that makes rational discussion about abortion nearly impossible. Presidents ranging from Obama to George W. Bush largely stay out of the debate beyond perfunctory nods to the appropriate side given their party affiliation. But leaving the debate to the crazies means the crazies lead on the issue, and on abortion their destination, time and again, is more accusations and arguments. There are no winners here.

Even after the health-care reform bill passed, the bitterness continued to boil. In the 2010 midterm elections Republicans won back control of the House of Representatives and gained control of several state legislatures, largely due to voter concern over high unemployment and government spending. But with Republicans back in power in Congress and twenty-nine governors, almost all Republicans, opposing abortion (instead of the twenty-one who had before the election), there was an immediate shift from economic discussions to the reliably divisive abortion issue. In Congress the Republicans tried to make the Hyde Amendment permanent. And in statehouses some 350 bills were introduced to restrict abortion. "The lawmakers are drafting . . . bills that would ban most abortions at 20 weeks after conception, push women considering abortion to view a live ultrasound of the fetus, or curb insurance coverage, among other proposals," reported the *New York Times*. In addition, the Catholic Church called attention to new data indicating that the nation's biggest city, New York, had twice the national average of abortions. New York archbishop Timothy Dolan called the finding that 40 percent of all pregnancies in the city ended in abortion "chilling" and urged city leaders to pass more laws limiting the right to abortion.

But the key to further debate is not the religious beliefs of opponents and proponents. As much as the religious Right may try to make it a religious issue, the debate can never be settled by trying to impose constraints on the dialogue through religious doctrine. Any one set of beliefs tied to one church is never going to be accepted by every American because America, while heavily Christian, has always been a nation of varied denominations with a range of beliefs. A faith-based debate is not in the spirit of the separation of church and state, which remains at the core of the American belief in secular governance. Even more to the point, there is never going to be a consensus based on an effort to abolish abortion rights. No matter anyone's opinion, abortion is far too common, and has been for decades, to reasonably expect it to be effectively removed from American life.

To the casual observer the American people appear incapable of moving past the abortion divide. But the reality is that many political parties, lobbying organizations, and zealots don't want to give up the issue. Their strategy is all about a desire to keep the conversation locked in failure.

Abortion is a premium "wedge" issue for producing money and votes. The base of the discussion is presented as a matter of differing religious values. And clashes come fast and with sharp edges when religion is introduced into America's public sphere. There should be a big fight because, again, one of the country's founding principles is the separation of church and state. And don't be fooled by people who claim the words in the Constitution say that it is "freedom of religion," not "freedom from religion." The attempt to make such a distinction is a common refrain from religious advocates who complain about the country losing its basic religious values and becoming too secular. That thinking leads to a hard-line split between "heathens" and "fundamentalists," as each side is harshly depicted by its opponents. It is no surprise that this antagonism takes center stage come major national elections. Political strategists use these debates to excite their base voters, pro or con, but also as a form of negative advertising to attack the character of opposing candidates. American presidential campaigns have increasingly become contests in which voters pick a candidate based on which one most closely shares their values. And like clockwork the political debates come down to competing religious perspectives. And as a result, a great deal of debate on any issue with a values or religious angle immediately is reduced to fearmongering and demonization. That is the regrettable situation with high-profile debates on the leading wedge issues of our time—abortion, gay rights, gay marriage, and teaching evolution in school, as well as government-funded celebrations of Christmas. They all fit into the same fixed pattern of debate with the same prescribed divisions being held in place by the gravity of big money and the power to excite voters. And they all orbit around the same attempts to force religious beliefs into public-policy debates.

The gay rights debate has taken center stage for much of the first decade of the twenty-first century, from state and federal policy on gay marriage, civil unions, and gays serving in the military to a major Supreme Court ruling on antigay speech. The issue emerged as a wedge in the presidential politics of 2000, 2004, and 2008. In the 2000 election George W. Bush opposed gay marriages and so did his Democrat opponent, Vice President Al Gore. Unlike Bush and the Republicans, the Democrats and Gore did favor gay civil unions.

The political dynamic continued to change in favor of increased gay rights, and by 2004, the year of his reelection campaign, President Bush proposed a constitutional amendment to prevent same-sex marriage. In the president's words, after centuries of social standards, "a few judges and local authorities are presuming to change the most fundamental institution [marriage] of civilization." Senator John Kerry, the Democrats' presidential candidate in 2004, feared a backlash if he went beyond a middling acceptance of gay unions, shutting down debate on the national level and crushing any chance of compromise.

That pushed the debate to the state level, with politicians

ranging from California governor Schwarzenegger to San Francisco mayor Gavin Newsom taking the lead. (The governor twice vetoed bills to legalize same-sex marriage, before becoming a supporter of gay marriage, while the mayor was aggressive in granting gay marriage licenses in San Francisco.)

By the 2008 campaign, even with six states having passed laws to allow gays to marry, the Republicans continued to oppose gay marriage—but so did the Democrats. The courts and the opinion polls might have moved, but the politics of the issue, especially on the liberal side, had become paralyzed with fright.

The repeated references to the Bible in the divisive gay rights debate led *Newsweek*'s religion editor, Lisa Miller, to write: "First, while the Bible and Jesus say many important things about love and family . . . neither explicitly defines marriage as between one man and one woman. And second, no sensible modern person wants marriage—his or her own or anyone else's—to look in its particulars anything like what the Bible describes."

Fox News Channel's news analyst Kirsten Powers also addressed the Bible's role as the final word being cited by opponents of same-sex marriage: "Many complained that they weren't anti-gay, that they just opposed same-sex marriage because the Bible, they said, defines marriage as between a man and a woman. Yet, we don't live in a theocracy. The Bible is not the governing legal document of the United States. The Constitution is. But if people really want to use the Bible as our governing legal document, then we need many constitutional amendments, including one that bans divorce except in the very narrow circumstances the Bible permits it. This would be a tough one for Evangelicals since their divorce rate is almost identical to that of atheists and agnostics. This might explain why we don't see evangelical leaders pumping hundreds of thousands of dollars into campaigns to keep the government from providing divorce."

In the military, gay rights made more progress over the decades. In 1950 President Truman signed the Uniform Code of Military Justice, which outlawed homosexuals from any branch of the military. President Reagan, in 1982, said explicitly that "homosexuality is incompatible with military service." President Clinton campaigned in the gay community by promising to lift the ban, but once in office he ran into a political uproar over the issue. He tried to find some middle ground by agreeing not to ask service members if they were gay. Over the next fifteen years, however, his "don't ask, don't tell" policy resulted in twelve thousand people being dismissed from the military. In 2010 a U.S. district judge ruled "don't ask, don't tell" unconstitutional. And after the 2010 midterm elections a lame-duck Congress, with bipartisan support, repealed "don't ask, don't tell." The rapid end to the controversy leads to the question of whether there was ever a real issue here, or if politicians spent several years simply playing for political advantage by appealing to traditional bias against gays. And if the opposition was a matter of religious teaching and tradition, how did bedrock values change so radically and so quickly? The answer seems to be that religion and tradition had long ago taken a backseat to the business of money and political power. Money and power pushed "don't ask, don't tell" as a successful wedge issue and found it useful to point to religion and tradition as the reason for keeping that wedge issue alive in national politics.

The same dynamic is at the heart of political fights over

prayer in public schools and at graduation ceremonies. The Supreme Court has banned prayer in public schools since the early sixties, and President Kennedy supported the Court. His response to the controversy was to say that children and adults who wanted to pray in school had a clear, constitutional alternative: to pray in churches and at home. And the same dynamic is at the heart of arguments over another school controversy, the teaching of evolution. Some fundamentalist families have complained that it is wrong to teach their children anything other than the biblical assertion that God created man. This wedge issue goes back in U.S. history to 1925, when Tennessee legislators made it the law that state-funded public schools teach nothing that contradicts the creation of man by divinity. The famous lawyer Clarence Darrow argued that the origin of man as told in the Bible does not belong in any school's government-approved curriculum. Nevertheless, the fight has persisted. But as in the wedge-issue debates over abortion and gay rights, the overarching question is why any science class or academic text should be written to conform to religious teachings. Science is not religion and religion is not science. And why would any divinely inspired religion need to debase itself by wading into the muddy depths of human efforts to postulate scientific theories, devise test regimens, and then gauge and measure them in the name of scientific findings? It is the nature of religion to delight in faith as opposed to concrete evidence. Faith is a matter of belief in supreme powers beyond human understanding. And there are several different versions of the creation as told by various religions. Unless a child is going to a parochial school affiliated with one denomination, any complete textbook would have to list all the competing versions of the creation. At that point the schools would be teaching comparative religion, not science.

But these fights over religion and public policy stir passion, garner donations, and provoke voter turnout. They pit the faithful against nonbelievers and even against faithful people with other beliefs. The political power here is significant. The question is who gets to decide on everything from abortion to gay marriage to school prayer to the teaching of evolution. The contest for power in American life is eternal and essential to the work of democracy. When those power plays slip into orthodoxy, they cross constitutional lines and the law. Religion is not the law in America. The Constitution is the law. And we Americans live in a nation founded on freedom from any one religion's imposed rules. That seems to include abortion, gay rights, and school prayer.

CHAPTER 8

THE PROVOCATEURS

I N THE MOVIE *The American President*, actor Michael Douglas plays a president who walks into the White House briefing room and delivers a powerful response to a political opponent's personal attacks on his character. "We have serious problems to solve, and we need serious people to solve them," he begins. "And whatever your particular problem is, I promise you Bob [his opponent] is not the least bit interested in solving it. He is interested in two things and two things only: making you afraid of it, and telling you who's to blame for it . . . [so he can] win elections." In the final line of the speech, he calls out Bob: "This is a time for serious people, Bob, and your fifteen minutes are up. My name is Andrew Shepherd and I am the president!"

Like all good works of fiction, that scene is so memorable because it touches on something so real.

Today's provocateurs in politics and the media seed conflict everywhere. But nowhere do they show a genuine interest in bringing Americans together to achieve positive results. If they did, they might be out of a job, after all. We are no longer living in the 24-7 news cycle. This new era is being called the "1,440-7" news cycle, where media are competing for the audience's attention every minute of every day. And one surefire way to get attention in the 1,440-7 news world is to say something outrageous. As a result, we have an entire graduate class of professional provocateurs. We all know them. They are my friends, my colleagues, and occasionally my adversaries in the media. Rush Limbaugh. Rachel Maddow. Sean Hannity. Lawrence O'Donnell. Glenn Beck. Even my colleague and antispin meister Bill O'Reilly has been accused of the role, although I find his show balanced in a way few talk shows on the Left or Right can match.

As is true of the medium, talk-show hosts are entertainers as much as they are commentators, and being bland as toast wins neither reviews nor ratings. Whether on the Left or the Right, whether on MSNBC or Fox News, each is aware of their target audience. Each offers provocative commentary that grabs our attention and fires up debate. The problem is that talk-show hosts aren't on the air to compromise or bring opposing sides together; they have a strong point of view, which they fiercely express. By their very nature they are designed to spark debate, not search for answers; focus our concerns, not reach a bipartisan compromise. But in sparking debate that plays off of our fears and concerns, they also act to drive out rational discussion and reasoned debate. Their very function as hosts and provocateurs can serve to drive us apart.

The influence of talk-show hosts on today's political culture is pervasive and worth exploring in more detail. Some have called such pundits and provocateurs perpetual conflict machines. Others have called their shows echo chambers, where the hosts simply preach to the choir. Whatever you call this phenomenon, the point is that the current state of media and public affairs is stifling the genuine give-and-take of honest debate. Every day a stream of snarky, loud, and sometimes angry voices from the Left and Right are giving reinforcement, reassurance, and endless coverage to one or the other political extreme. This is what lies behind our common perception that "the crazies are the ones doing all the talking." To a large extent, they are.

But when these provocateurs—in politics and the media— are challenged on their crass appeals to fear, anger, and hate, they counter by charging their critics with "political correctness" and claim objectors are attempting to censor them. It is a strategy that has stymied many critics. Casual observers see the deterioration of important debates on the issues into a carnival sideshow, with the clowns running an entertaining, distracting, emotionally charged, but not very informative spectacle. I believe most Americans would passionately embrace reasoned, honest debate on the issues, but they don't know how to stop the drivel and personal attacks. And critics in government certainly don't want to risk speaking out too loudly for fear of being targeted for attack by provocateurs on the other side. It has made it harder for the American people to see when politically correct thinking is really being used not to open a debate but to shut one down, such as the NPR response to my debate with Bill O'Reilly about Muslims and terrorism.

The reality of much of American media today makes a movie fantasy such as *The American President* ever more appealing—

someone in authority finally stands up to politics and media run amok. The nation would love for a political Superman to take to task the growing horde that has no interest in solving the serious problems facing America.

Let's face it, these professional rude boys (and girls) thrive on arousing people's passions. They make money by making our problems even worse. The more bitter the divide over an issue, the more intractable the problem, the brighter they shine. So they make us afraid of problems; they belittle and demonize those with a different point of view as enemies—even political allies who are not willing to be as extreme or radical in their views. We are given superb political theater but little in the way of education. It is like watching a docudrama at times. Yes, it is based on the facts, but they have been embellished, made more entertaining, with none of the painful searching and uncertainty of real life.

The provocateurs delight in coming up with demeaning, cutting sound bites that quickly go viral on the Internet and cable news. My colleague Glenn Beck has been guilty of this repeatedly. Such attacks and personal put-downs attract attention, as well as condemnation from critics. Nonetheless, the spotlight, good or bad, brings the provocateurs to the attention of even more people, putting more people in the seats for their carnival act. And that puts more money in their pockets. It is entertaining among their constituents, to be sure. But their vitriolic displays scare good people away from getting involved in politics, and they have led smart, well-informed people in the political middle to stay away from important debates. The perpetual conflict machine these agitators have created favors entrenched constituencies that are looking not so much for real debate with new ideas and hope for compromise as much as for confirmation of the beliefs they already hold. Their audiences are captivated by the explosive anger they see on the air, arousing their own anger and frustration.

This phenomenon has reached the point where our provocateur culture inhibits the functions of government. Our public servants increasingly respond first to the loudest voices behind the biggest microphones, who can make them or break them in the opinion polls and at the ballot box. The result is a chronic hardening of political views that is destroying the flexibility needed for effective democracy. But today's politicians feel they have little choice but to play along. After all, the prophets of doom and destruction get people to attend rallies, to give money to politicians, and to get out and vote. Candidates running for office, and even those politicians in elected office now, find it to their advantage to mimic the screaming, hectoring, and finger-pointing instead of looking for compromise and solutions. Anyone who varies from their party's hard line is condemned and ultimately muzzled.

The First Amendment to the Constitution gives everyone the right to speak without fear of government censorship or reprisal. It allows me to earn a living doing what I love to do—talking and writing about politics. Of course, it does not guarantee there will be an audience when I exercise that right. Sometimes bells and whistles, fireworks and sparkles are needed to attract an audience. Sometimes we need political theater to get us into our seats. But this need also creates programs with attitude and opinion. Most of the programming day at Fox News Channel is taken up with news presented by working journalists collecting the facts and presenting compelling stories. The channel strives to maintain and grow an audience by providing a mixture of honest, original, and engaging analysis and news. But it also offers a variety of potent talk shows on the issues of the day with hosts and guests who have big personalities. Fox CEO Roger Ailes recognizes that the media is a demanding, competitive business and the audience cannot be taken for granted. Attractive, engaging, provocative people and compelling arguments are always in demand.

Whenever I appear on Fox News or write a column for The Hill, I try to meet the economic demands of those outlets by advancing the conversation, avoiding the predictable, and making a constructive contribution to the discussion. I make a conscious effort to avoid ad hominem attacks or name-calling. I attack ideas and point out their consequences, rather than attack the people who hold them. I don't say things just for the sake of being provocative. I criticize both liberals and conservatives when I think they are wrong and agree with them when I think they are right, trying to keep my arguments grounded in honesty, civility, and rational thought. As a result, the larger-than-life media personalities—who never entertain any doubt of their fixed position—occasionally shout me down and upstage me. But I give them full credit for having me on in the first place to present what is sometimes a contradicting point of view. I want both left-wing and right-wing audiences to pay attention to what I have to say because they know me as someone who is straight with them, who doesn't come at the issues from a fixed ideological position. I put a premium on telling them what I really think, and they seem to value that. My bet is that the audience wants to hear what I will say, too, even if they can't count on me as reliably conservative or liberal.

Of course, caustic political commentary and satire has a cherished, well-established tradition in American history. Mark Twain, H. L. Mencken, Will Rogers, Dorothy Parker, and scores of other satirists could have been described as political provocateurs in their day. We celebrate their work and can recall their most memorable quotes. When they wrote, the media environment was smaller, slower, less complicated, and less significant in American politics. But as media has evolved over the last several decades, political commentators have become an entirely different species. Today political partisanship has become institutionalized as media technology has increased outlets for niche points of view on the extremes of the political spectrum, and the money and celebrity flow to those voices at the extremes through radio shows, book deals, and Web traffic.

Much of the history of provocateurs in America is part of the glorious history of free people speaking freely—democracy in action. These voices emerged to challenge the status quo or in some cases to defend the status quo against the forces of political correctness, both good and bad. Some of our nation's most heated debates took place during the postrevolutionary era as Thomas Jefferson, James Madison, and Alexander Hamilton argued passionately over the details of our nation's democratic blueprints, the Declaration of Independence and the Constitution.

Thomas Paine is among the most renowned of the founding-era provocateurs. He is the original American agitator, an immigrant to the United States who wrote the inflammatory

Common Sense. His treatise, which railed against British colonial domination, was intended to inflame and goad Americans to rebellion. He wrote in bold language: "Everything that is right or reasonable pleads for separation. The blood of the slain, the weeping voice of nature cries, 'TIS TIME TO PART." His words made the American Revolution much more than an uprising. He transformed it into a holy crusade for all humanity. "The cause of America is in a great measure the cause of all mankind," Paine wrote.

By the late 1800s, Paine's pugnacious phrases seemed polite and poetic compared to the daily vitriol printed by the two great newspaper magnates of the time, William Randolph Hearst and Joseph Pulitzer. Their coverage of the news, from crime to political scandals to war, was a study in sensationalized accounts, including outright distortion and lies, in a battle to sell more papers in New York City. The high-decibel contest between Hearst's *New York Journal* and Pulitzer's *New York World* gave rise to the term "yellow journalism." It describes alarmist, sensationalist journalism that is driven by a desire for attention and is willing to incite and provoke readers with little regard for the facts. Hearst and Pulitzer became infamous for starting a real war. They whipped up so much anger at Spain through inflammatory stories about Spain's handling of American vessels that they incited the United States to go to war with Spain in the Spanish-American War.

Radio had emerged in the early twentieth century as a form of mass media. The best-known voice of early thunder on radio was Catholic priest Charles Coughlin. Father Coughlin spewed an inflammatory mix of political outrage, social controversy, and division. President Roosevelt used radio to reach out to a country struggling to recover from economic depression; his use of radio was a first for a president, and his occasional fireside radio chats from the White House became a signature of his presidency. Father Coughlin first gained prominence as a supporter of President Roosevelt's New Deal programs. But he turned against them with equal fury. He blamed Jews for the Great Depression, sympathized with Hitler, and became an ardent opponent of U.S. involvement in World War II. He once broadcast a question that combined isolationism and anti-Semitism: "Must the entire world go to war for 600,000 Jews in Germany who are neither American, nor French, nor English citizens, but citizens of Germany?" His popularity fell, however, when he was linked to a group trying to overthrow the government.

The cold war, with its strong anticommunist sentiments, produced several early versions of today's provocative media personalities. Fear of communist infiltration into the United States stirred the audiences of that era. Radio shows, pamphlets, and speeches were sponsored by the paranoid, far-right John Birch Society.

The civil rights movement of the 1950s and 1960s, too, produced a class of racial provocateurs. Several states added some version of the Confederate flag to their state flags. Alabama's Governor George Wallace propelled himself to national prominence and a third-party candidacy for the presidency using a "states' rights" argument, as well as championing the "good" of racial segregation. In June 1963 Governor Wallace drew world attention when he physically stood in a schoolhouse door to block black students from entering the University of Alabama. With TV cameras rolling, and in defiance of the

U.S. Justice Department officials standing next to him, he announced that the federal action to integrate the school was "in violation of rights reserved for the state by the Constitution of the United States and the Constitution of Alabama." Later, he stirred warlike passion by proclaiming, "In the name of the greatest people that ever trod this earth, I draw the line in the dust and toss the gauntlet before the feet of tyranny and I say, 'Segregation now, segregation tomorrow, segregation forever!' "

Wallace's success as a political provocateur was aided by his prominence as governor of the state. But it was also bolstered by the growth of mass media—radio and TV—that trumpeted his words to every corner of the nation.

In the era of domestic social upheaval during the 1960s and 1970s, the leaders of the feminist movement, the student protests against the Vietnam War, and the civil rights movement all capitalized on the growth of TV news and commentary to build support for their causes. Every cause now had to make strategic decisions on the use of visuals, signs, and symbols intended to display disdain for the establishment, as well as when to stage marches for maximum television coverage, how to increase time on TV by employing Hollywood celebrities to speak for a cause, and how to enlist musicians and messages in movies to agitate for change.

Ronald Reagan's presidency saw political polarization reach another level. President Reagan's professional acting and speech-making skills, combined with the birth of TV cable news and the talk/news radio format, turned politics into televised contests of rhetoric and staging. Working with a public relations expert, Michael Deaver, as his communications director, the president led the nation with bold language and powerful settings for his speeches. He stood at the Berlin Wall to challenge Soviet leader Mikhail Gorbachev with the line, "Mr. Gorbachev, tear down this wall." He did not hesitate to label the Soviet Union "the evil empire." He antagonized his liberal critics by talking about poor women as welfare queens in "pink Cadillacs," taking the bold economic position that if the rich got richer the poor would also be helped because "a rising tide lifts all boats." Consideration of one Reagan nominee for the Supreme Court, Robert Bork, transformed televised Senate confirmation hearings into a stage for political fights over abortion, race, gun control, and every other hot-button issue. As noted earlier, during the Bork hearings, Senator Ted Kennedy unleashed his own inflammatory attack on the nominee. "Robert Bork's America," the senator said, "is a land in which women would be forced into back-alley abortions, blacks would sit at segregated lunch counters, rogue police could break down citizens' doors in midnight raids, schoolchildren could not be taught about evolution, writers and artists could be censored at the whim of the government, and the doors of the Federal courts would be shut on the fingers of millions of citizens."

Talk shows began to combine the techniques of news programs with entertainment shows. Phil Donahue's TV show, which was syndicated nationally for a record twenty-six years, set the standard for putting serious conversations on the air in the afternoon, but his show also became known for tackling taboo subjects and bringing lightning-rod personalities on to discuss them. Up-and-coming TV producers followed in his footsteps and often took the format to greater extremes. Geraldo Rivera had his nose broken on an episode of his talk show dealing with "teen hatemongers," which featured a member of the White Aryan Resistance Youth and a black guest. Maury Povich became known for revealing the results of paternity tests to couples on live TV, with all the predictable emotional outbursts and tears. Jerry Springer's show actually rang a bell as guests regularly jumped from their seats in rage to fight one another. Oprah Winfrey's show became the genre's most popular in the nation as a more respectable talk show for suburban female viewers, yet it has never strayed far from family feuds, Hollywood's latest celebrity crisis, and talk about sex and health. But Oprah realized ratings gold in clashes over the day's explosive social issues.

As talk shows became TV sensations, radio programming turned up the volume too, with insults, sex talk, sensational political stories, and caricatures of what hosts saw as politically incorrect politicians. Don Imus and Howard Stern soared in the ratings with a combination of humorous put-downs and a willingness to make controversial, even insulting, statements to incite their audiences. Imus's focus was political, with senators, congressmen, and business leaders often joining him to trade gossip, jokes, and put-downs. Stern rode the persona of an overgrown schoolboy skipping class with his friends to have a smoke in the boys' bathroom and trade titillating locker-room talk about sex. The wild success of both shows inspired countless imitators in local radio markets. And the success of these shows led to the explosive growth of reality television, pitting people against one another to reveal that which is most base, primitive, jealous, and violent in us, as reality TV devolved from shows like *Survivor* to *The Real Housewives* and *Jersey Shore*.

As far back as the late 1970s, Patrick Caddell, a political

adviser to President Carter, recognized this critical shift in the media, and its power contributed to a change in the nature of governing. He warned the president that it had the power to drive trends and opinions of such force that they could swamp even the most sincere and able leader. Caddell told Carter, "It is my thesis that governing with public approval requires a continuing political campaign." That meant that even victorious candidates, once in office, had to keep campaigning; they needed to see governing as a separate, sometimes secondary, task if they wanted to hold on to the power that comes from strong public approval. In that sense, a permanent campaign became the equal of a Hearst-Pulitzer circulation battle, a ratings war, and a competition between brands—a quest to seize eyeballs, to capture hearts, and to stir passions. Politicians need to absorb the lessons of the media about tapping into the biggest possible audience and holding that audience. The key lesson is that there is nothing less dramatic than a few people talking rationally, ignoring extremists and know-nothings, while making steady, incremental improvements in public policy. Even an uninformed, uneducated rube can beat a brilliant statesman in opinion polls if the rube has passion, presents himself as a victim of Washington's arrogance, and is willing to take a stand and put on a show of populist outrage.

In politics, the heated media culture of the 1980s and 1990s saw the rise of three major political personalities who fit the mold of provocateur—Jesse Jackson on the Left, Pat Buchanan on the Right, and Ross Perot as a political independent.

Jackson had first used the power of television in the immediate aftermath of Dr. King's assassination, when he appeared on air the next day wearing a shirt that he said was stained with Dr. King's blood. Throughout the next several decades, his public statements and appearances on TV and radio spoke of his ambition to become the next Dr. King. By the 1988 presidential campaign, Jackson was widely acknowledged as the "president of Black America," a meaningless title except in its power to command the attention of the media and win Jackson his own cable TV show.

Pat Buchanan, a former aide to President Nixon, positioned himself as a social conservative and a man of principle willing to lead the charge in what he called "the culture wars." It was Buchanan who had coined the term "silent majority."

Buchanan became a regular on political TV and radio shows and eventually landed his own. He was one of the original cohosts of the cable TV shouting match *Crossfire*, which created the spit-flying, barbed-put-down, Left-versus-Right template for political panels and programs that have come since. He ran a lucrative newsletter aimed at conservatives seeking hard-line right-wing views.

Like Jesse Jackson, Buchanan made a run for president. In 1992 he used his hard-right stands on social issues to attack President Bush as a political moderate who made "backroom" deals with Democrats and did not deserve a second term.

Ross Perot, like Jackson and Buchanan, also ran for president. In an amazing turn, the wealthy corporate executive ran as a populist, a man trained by his success in business to get things done. The hero and protagonist of a best-selling book and TV series, *On the Wings of Eagles*, about how he organized the rescue of employees being held hostage overseas, Perot presented himself in the news media as a serious leader. He spoke as a no-nonsense pragmatist with a particular distaste for President Bush. In nonstop media interviews, including regular appearances on cable TV's *Larry King Live*, he labeled President Bush a weak leader with no economic know-how and lacking in strong principles.

"This city [Washington] has become a town filled with sound bites, shell games, handlers, media stuntmen who posture, create images, talk, shoot off Roman candles, but don't ever accomplish anything. We need deeds, not words, in this city," Perot said. One of his most telling campaign pledges fit the ever-escalating media culture of the time. He said that as president he would govern by participating in "electronic town halls," where people could speak out and also register their preferences for policy and legislation.

But Perot's erratic behavior, dropping out and then reentering the presidential race in a media frenzy, and his charge that government agents had tried to ruin his daughter's wedding, as well as his choice of the unknown and out-of-his-depth Admiral James Stockdale as his vice-presidential running mate, undermined Perot's candidacy. Nonetheless, he won 19 percent of the vote, a record for an independent candidate.

But most of all, Perot, Buchanan, and Jackson left an industry of extreme political pundits in their wake, politicians and talk-show hosts who gained a level of wealth and political power never known to earlier political commentators such as Will Rogers and H. L. Mencken. They prided themselves on being outside observers of the process.

The current crop of provocateurs, too—from Glenn Beck to Arianna Huffington—have become players in that process. They are rewarded for being the ones who shout the loudest and make the most outrageous attacks, who garner the highest television ratings, the largest radio audiences, and the most Web site traffic. They net lucrative book contracts and receive rapturous standing ovations at political conferences. And they have discovered they can make or break like-minded political candidates with their commentary and endorsements. Voices of moderation and calm persuasion have a hard time being heard over the loud, grating voices of today's political provocateurs. And the Internet and the communications platforms it has created—from Facebook to blogs—have supported the emergence of even more provocateurs: people paid for screaming out any controversial idea, any conspiracy theory. Most of these agitators act without fear of being held to account for distortions or outright lies. When challenged on the facts, they run behind the First Amendment and charge that their freedom of speech is being taken away. The acolytes in their audience could care less about spin and distortion—unless it is committed by their political foes. They just want to hear a rousing speech by a talk-show host who agrees with them.

This psychological phenomenon is one surprising result of technology's ability to deliver more cable channels, more radio stations, infinite Web sites, and Twitter feeds. With the greater variety of platforms to get news and opinion, most readers, viewers, and listeners are drawn to platforms and personalities of their choice, in the same way hometown audiences become fans of a baseball team. They believe their team can do no wrong. They revel in the company of like-minded thinkers. They really don't want to hear news that makes them question their political prejudices. They don't want opinions that challenge the logic of their political thinking by giving a contradictory point of view. They want consistency. They are glad to dismiss critics, the loathsome "mainstream" or "right-wing" media, and opposing political parties. They bond with others as outsiders and get a kick out of personalities who use mocking tones to debase the insiders or elite who disagree with them.

It is this new political culture that produced Al Franken and Rush Limbaugh, stand-up comic and disc jockey with brash political views, two funny guys who have risen to unbelievable prominence in the nation's highest councils of serious political debate.

Limbaugh is the loudest of all the voices in the conservative media echo chamber. A college dropout and failed disc jockey, he created a one-man political show made possible by the repeal of the Fairness Doctrine in 1987. Radio stations no longer had to air opposing views, and Limbaugh is credited with being the first and certainly the best to take advantage of the new law. He beats one ideological drum for three hours a day— the drum of social conservatism. He has made himself into the voice of opposition to everything liberal, from abortion to war protests to concern over torture of captured terrorists and civil rights activists. He lambasted women's rights activists as "femi-Nazis," declaring, "Feminism was established so as to allow unattractive women easier access to the mainstream of society." He mocked AIDS activists by introducing any discussion of the disease with Dionne Warwick's hit song "I'll Never Love This Way Again." On Limbaugh's show, members of the military who did not agree with President Bush's decision to invade Iraq were "phony" soldiers. He showed no fear of making the kind of racial politics put-downs of black people that have sunk other talk-show hosts. Limbaugh once told a black caller to "take the bone out of your nose and call me back." His take on the majority of black Americans identifying with the Democratic Party? "They're only 12 percent of the population. Who the hell cares?" One time he remarked that all composite pictures of criminals look like Jesse Jackson. A big football fan, he nonetheless disparaged the large number of professional players who are black by saying: "The NFL all too often looks like a game between the Bloods and the Crips without any weapons." This episode was cited as one of the reasons NFL power brokers blocked Limbaugh's attempt to buy an ownership stake in the St. Louis Rams football team in 2009. After the plan fell through, liberal comedian and talk-show host Bill Maher joked that this had dashed Limbaugh's lifelong dream of one day owning black people.

Limbaugh's comedic talent, his mimicry, his use of music, and his buffoonlike boast that he is taking on the Left with "half my brain tied behind my back" led the *New York Times* to describe him as a "vaudevillian." When Michael Steele, chairman of the Republican Party, described the radio talk-show host as merely "an entertainer" who stirred up his audience with "incendiary" and "ugly" comments, he found himself deluged with rebukes from the Rush "ditto heads" and threatened with a loss of financial support for the party. So despite Steele's political standing within the party, he bowed his head, offered a personal apology to "El Rushbo," and appeared chastened, even abject, when he beseeched the entertainer to go easy on him. As President Obama entered the White House at a time of war, terror threats, and economic crisis, Limbaugh baldly said, "I hope he fails." He later tried to explain that he was talking only about the president's liberal policies, but the unapologetic comment, indifferent to the needs of the nation but crafted to grab attention, fit Limbaugh perfectly.

Limbaugh's sharp tongue has made him the most successful radio broadcaster of all time. His eponymous radio show, which began in 1988, now has an estimated weekly audience of fifteen million listeners. According to a *Newsweek* report last year, he is by far the highest-earning political personality, earning $59 million annually. For reference, Glenn Beck came in second at $33 million. In third was Sean Hannity at $22 million. Limbaugh's stature is all the more impressive when you consider that his show saved the AM radio frequency from irrelevance. Conservative talk-radio hosts ever since have copied the Limbaugh model.

The success of right-wing talk radio in shaping national political opinions and policy eventually prompted the question, Why don't liberals have their own talk shows? The answer was that liberals did not feel alienated from what conservatives called the "mainstream media." The older, white majority of conservatives had long complained that they were ignored or marginalized as religious extremists, sexual prudes, and bigots by the major newspapers and broadcast networks. And the liberal tilt in Hollywood produced popular liberal-leaning TV sitcoms going back as far as *All in the Family,* in which a conservative blue-collar worker was presented as uneducated, full of blustering resistance to treating women and blacks as equals. The movies promoted liberal themes, including racial integration, premarital sex, and disdain for the American military, from *M*A*S*H* to *Platoon*. On the radio dial, NPR got its start in the early seventies as a network of college stations. Its first big news story was the Watergate scandal and the congressional hearings that followed, with President Nixon as the villain. NPR was immediately adopted by the campus protest crowd and liberal intellectuals.

Conservatives had complained for decades that liberals tended to win tenured faculty positions at the nation's top universities. NPR became an extension of liberal campus counterculture. To conservatives, the arrival of right-wing talk radio on the AM dial created a singular outpost for their views in a liberal media landscape. But to liberals and Democrats the success of conservatives like Limbaugh and their power to push national politics to the right was maddening. Liberal counterprogramming finally hit the airwaves in 2004 with a new radio outfit called Air America Radio. And its star, the Left's answer to Rush Limbaugh, was the comedian and satirist Al Franken.

Unlike Limbaugh, Franken was a top-notch student who graduated from Harvard with a degree in political science. And he had been a star on a hip, liberal-leaning TV show, *Saturday Night Live*, for fifteen years. In 1996 Franken wrote a *New York Times* best-selling book with the insulting, scathing title *Rush Limbaugh Is a Big Fat Idiot and Other Observations*. In 2004 Franken was selected to host Air America's main show. He was seen as the man to take on Limbaugh as well as the successful Fox News Channel and its lead personality, Bill O'Reilly. Franken initially called his show *The O'Franken Factor*. But the show's preoccupation with mocking conservative radio and cable personalities did not lead to ratings success. Franken left it within three years as the network struggled to pay its bills and then collapsed.

But Franken found another outlet in real-life politics. He

had written a second book, titled *Why Not Me?*, a satirical account of a fictional Franken campaign for president. And in one of those bizarre moments when life imitates absurdist art, Franken actually ran in 2008 for a real U.S. Senate seat in his home state of Minnesota and won in a very close race over a Republican incumbent. In the Senate, he made news when he rolled his eyes and made faces of disgust while Republican Senate minority leader Mitch McConnell spoke in opposition to a Democratic nominee to the Supreme Court. That prompted McConnell to rebuke him with the comment "This isn't *Saturday Night Live*, Al." (Franken later wrote a handwritten letter of apology to McConnell for using his comic training on the floor of the Senate when real issues were being debated.) But what was astounding was the elevation of Franken, a man best known for clowning and political satire, a man with no prior political experience, to a seat in the U.S. Senate. Franken may now be maturing in the job, but his background is as a heckler and provocateur.

There is a vast constellation of stars like Limbaugh and Franken now blanketing the media and politics. On the Left there is Michael Moore, the most successful documentary filmmaker of all time. He is a folk hero of the American Left who is praised on college campuses, on the liberal cable channels, and in the progressive netroots community. Arianna Huffington, the Republican pundit turned liberal firebrand, created an incredibly successful Web site, the Huffington Post, which provides liberals with news and opinion. The Huffington Post has been so successful that she was able to sell it to AOL for $315 million earlier this year. Lawrence O'Donnell, one of MSNBC's most popular liberal commentators, now hosts the network's 8:00 p.m. show, which competes with Bill O'Reilly.

On the Right, Rush Limbaugh's legacy has spawned a plethora of conservative talk-radio hosts who have followed in his path: Sean Hannity, Michael Savage, Laura Ingraham, Mark Levin, Neal Boortz, and Mike Gallagher. Each one has achieved success by parlaying his or her radio show into television appearances and book deals. Perhaps the most fascinating example is Glenn Beck, who attracts the third-biggest audience in conservative talk radio, behind Limbaugh and Hannity. Like Limbaugh, Beck never graduated from college and had a checkered career as a disc jockey playing pranks and hit records. Beck began his political talk show in 2000 on a Tampa, Florida, AM station, mixing conservatism and conspiracy theories. In dark, whispered voices he claimed liberals were plotting to destroy America, while also confessing to his life as a recovering alcoholic and conveying occasional religious messages.

In addition to his radio show, with a weekly audience of about ten million listeners, Beck had a 5:00 p.m. show on Fox News that garnered higher ratings than the combined ratings for prime-time programs on CNN and MSNBC. His books instantly catapult to number one on the *New York Times* bestseller lists. Though not as partisan as Limbaugh, Beck's message is clearly conservative and highly critical of the Democrats and President Obama. He famously remarked that the president was a "racist" who had a "deep-seated hatred of white people." In fairness, he apologized and retracted that remark later. But he routinely calls the president a socialist, a communist, and a Marxist and has likened him to Adolf Hitler. He often compares the agenda of Obama and the Democrats to Nazi Germany, Maoist China, and Russia under the Soviets.

The philippics and outlandish tirades against the Obama administration form the engine for Beck's success. Without them, no one would pay attention to his warmer, fuzzier, and sometimes legitimate claims about history, morals, and values. But rather than spark a genuine debate, Beck seeks to ignite our ire and go on the attack. There is no progressive conspiracy to destroy the United States of America from within, and it is absurd to suggest that there is. Although to Beck and those who follow him, it may well seem as if I am dismissing the idea because I am a part of the conspiracy. For that matter, you must be too, if you agree with my ideas. I can see the chalkboard diagram now.

These provocateurs cross the political spectrum and are paid salaries normally associated with Las Vegas entertainers. Personality is key here. Anyone can say provocative things and voice controversial opinions. The people whom I have mentioned are effective because they are always skating on the edge of outrageous controversy, always pushing the limits of supportable facts, logic, and respect for people who hold opposing political views. Their audiences want to see how far they can go without crashing. Perhaps they share the sense that the rest of the world is crazy and they are not going to take it anymore—they are going to set the record straight and tell it like it is. And our hosts deliver daily jeremiads that confirm we are not the only ones who believe these politicians and world leaders and corporate moguls and pampered movie stars and athletes are a bunch of thieves, liars, and idiots. The iron fist hammering the table with the microphone belongs to a man or woman—conservative or liberal—who is not interested in talking *with* people. He or she is in the business of talking *at* people. The closest these dominating radio and TV personalities come to an exchange of ideas is attacking their rivals on another network. The insults fly, and then their respective audiences are roused to defend their heroes, and the ratings climb even higher as more and more people tune in for the spectacle.

Now, there is nothing wrong with talk radio being dominated by conservative personalities or Hollywood being dominated by liberal writers and actors. Competition among political ideas is essential to American democracy. It might be hard to find a liberal radio show as influential as Rush Limbaugh's program, but there is no absence of liberal ideas and personalities elsewhere in the political universe and the media. At the height of their powers, the conservatives on talk radio could only watch as perhaps the most liberal member of the Senate, Barack Obama, was elected president. That is why I will stand side by side with Rush and Sean in opposing attempts to manipulate that marketplace with the return of the Fairness Doctrine. President Obama has also said he opposes the return of a government-imposed mandate that each individual station provide equal time to all sides of a political issue. At this point that kind of legislative response to the provocateurs will not serve to disseminate more ideas and opinions. It amounts to a liberal strategy designed to take down Limbaugh and the other conservatives who dominate one format—talk radio. I am for the government offering tax breaks to support more programs with local talk and news. Having been muzzled myself, I don't think muzzling other voices or having the government dictate programming decisions is in keeping with the First Amendment promise that Congress will make no law restricting freedom of the press.

The real danger here is beyond the scope of government's power. The excess of provocateurs corrupting public dialogue in America sets up a fight on every issue for every American. This rebellion against the provocateurs will have to be done in the tradition of colonial patriots, who came out of their homes and formed private armies to fight British tyranny. Individual Americans are going to have to turn away from the entertainment associated with extremist, at times buffoonish, demagogues on the air and their imitators who are now running for public office. They will have to personally raise the bar for conversations about important social and political issues. In other words, we have to take matters into our own hands. Ordinary Americans need to join the fight against the scourge that is undermining our essential American belief in letting people speak their minds. The dominance of the paid agitators has led to a loss of critical-thinking skills by American citizens—we need to think for ourselves. The screamers, the self-righteous, and the arrogant on radio, on TV, in print, and on the Internet create an environment in which a lot of people in the middle don't bother speaking up because it's hard to shout above the bombast and noise. A lot of us, I suspect, feel an urge to take cover until all the shouting and name-calling stop. We are waiting for someone else to tell the provocateurs that their fifteen minutes are up.

I fear that a backlash against the provocateur culture is creating cynicism about the entire political process. Revulsion for politics and debate is now common among Americans, especially young people. And that path leads to political apathy. Two thirds of the American people tell pollsters the country is headed in the wrong direction. Yet increasingly, politicians themselves begin to act like the provocateurs in the media, resorting to the same crass schoolyard bullying and name-calling. In one of the most offensive campaign ads of the 2010 political campaign, a Florida Democrat, Representative Alan Grayson, referred to his Republican opponent, Daniel Webster, as "Taliban Dan." Labeling someone, even in hyperbole, a member of a brutal regime that slaughters its own people, and Americans for that matter, is bad enough. But on top of that, the vitriol behind the statements was based on a lie. Grayson used a video clip that showed Webster telling women to "submit" to their husbands in keeping with the tenets of an extremist interpretation of the Bible. But Grayson had edited the clip to distort what Webster had actually said. In reality, Webster had cautioned religious men not to use literal translations of some Bible texts to oppress women. '

The independent political watchdog group FactCheck.org was appalled by Grayson's blatant attack on his opponent and the truth. "We thought Democratic Rep. Alan Grayson of Florida reached a low point when he falsely accused his opponent of being a draft dodger during the Vietnam War and of not loving his country," reported FactCheck.org. "But now Grayson has lowered the bar even further. He's using edited video to make his rival appear to be saying the opposite of what he really said."

The 2010 election also saw Sharron Angle, the Republican candidate for a Nevada U.S. Senate seat, tell a group of voters that she would employ gun violence—"Second Amendment remedies"—to deal with members of Congress who did not go along with her ideas. She made headlines with the sensation-alist but totally false charge that her Democratic opponent, Senate majority leader Harry Reid, wanted to give Viagra to sex offenders. Angle also ran ads suggesting Reid was giving tax breaks to illegal immigrants. Those TV ads depicted the people crossing the border to come into the United States as thuggish, threatening, and dark skinned, in a crass attempt to stir up voters' fears and win votes.

This low level of political discourse is chasing away tal-ented people who would otherwise put themselves forward as candidates for office. Who wants to be subjected to shrill and malicious attacks? Who wants to be called names and verbally kicked around by opponents who are not held to account?

In every democracy, no matter what the era, the language of politics is often personal, often harsh, and at times down in the gutter. This was true of political opponents of Presidents Thomas Jefferson and Abe Lincoln. But the proliferation of media through high technology in the last twenty years has led to 24-7 stabs from sharp voices, and I fear the body pol-itic is bleeding to death. There is no off-season for political attacks, especially around election time. We now live with a permanent campaign; it is a year-round sport. From terrorism to budgetary crises to immigration to the war in wherever, the talk-show static is so loud that voices of elected officials try-ing their best to resolve thorny political issues can barely be heard. The result is that a genuine dialogue about important issues gets put off far too long. The urgent need for solutions, combined with our anxiety over a faltering economy, multiple wars, and demographic shifts that have raised the number of racial minorities and immigrants, has created a political pressure cooker. The only sound to be heard is the angry steam venting from overheated people.

That is what happened during the debate over health-care reform in 2010. America's great tradition of town halls where citizens can express concerns to elected officials devolved into circus-tent spectacles, in which every shriek mimicked the harsh rhetoric, angry tone, and personal insults that typify the media provocateurs Americans listen to and watch daily. And the hostile tenor of the meetings was set by those provocative personalities. During a debate on health care, freshman Senate Democrat Al Franken, sitting as presiding officer of the Senate, cut off Senator Joe Lieberman, the senior senator from Connecticut. "Wielding Gavel, Franken Shuts Lieberman Up!" is how the incident was delightedly described in the liberal-leaning Huffington Post. Given that a request to finish a brief ten-minute speech is commonly granted in the Senate, the decision had the flavor of disrespect. And the fact that Senator Franken, a former entertainer, was the lead actor prompted Senator John McCain to lament the demise of civility even among senators. "I've been around here for more than twenty years," McCain said, "and yesterday on the floor of the Senate, the senator from Connecticut was finishing his remarks . . . and was objected to by the newest member of the U.S. Senate—and in the most brusque way." Later he added: "That's how the comity in this body has deteriorated. We got to stop—we got to stop this kind of behavior."

Senator McCain's complaint came barely two months after Representative Joe Wilson of South Carolina broke traditional decorum at a presidential address to a joint session of Congress to yell, "You lie!" That disrespect was unprecedented, and the congressman was wrong on the facts, as well. At a Massachusetts town-hall meeting during the same period, Representative Barney Frank went toe-to-toe with a woman who held up a sign featuring President Obama portrayed as Adolf Hitler. She asked her congressman why he was "supporting this Nazi policy." Frank responded: "On what planet do you spend most of your time?" The honest answer is that she is living on a planet full of provocateurs on her radio, TV, and Internet.

Former Alaska governor and vice presidential candidate Sarah Palin used the Internet to contribute to the poisonous atmosphere in town-hall meetings in 2010. Just before the congressional summer recess and the beginning of the town-hall meetings, she wrote on her Facebook page: "The America I know and love is not one in which my parents or my baby with Downs Syndrome will have to stand in front of Obama's 'death panel' so his bureaucrats can decide . . . [a citizen's] level of productivity in society [and] whether they are worthy of healthcare." This misleading description of the provisions of national health-care reform was surprising, and disappointing, given that Palin regularly confronted the media for making things up about her.

Some people might regard the passionate outbursts during the town halls as over-the-top but within the limits of democracy in action. But something different was going on here. The fact that there were so many threats of violence and vicious, personal insults exchanged and posted on YouTube leads to questions about the direction of American political culture and the impact of the provocateurs. Where are they taking us? Is this where we want to go as a country? Surely there were serious people who came to these town halls wanting to get answers to questions about the health-care bill and to hear informative debate on the issue. Polls had consistently shown for decades that Americans, both individuals and businesses, have been burdened by the high cost of health care and wanted reforms. But the town-hall meetings were not about weighing the comparative impact of reform proposals. The goal seemed to be an exercise in mockery, cynicism, and even contempt for the political system. There is no way the town halls were good for debating legislation. Spectacles like these undermine the functioning of governments of any political stripe and are a threat to a vital, healthy democracy.

Robert Reich, who was secretary of labor in the Clinton administration, wrote about touring the country to see some of the town halls. He realized that the provocateur media culture had been hijacked by the lobbyists and businessmen opposed to health-care reform to create a circus that fed the right-wing radio talk shows and TV cable programs in an attempt to shoot reform down. It then inspired more threats and further hysteria at future town hall meetings.

"On our drive across America," Reich wrote at Salon .com, "my son and I have spotted spiffy white vans emblazoned with phrases like 'ObamaCare Will Raise Your Taxes,' and 'ObamaCare Will Put Bureaucrats in Charge of Your Health.' Just outside Omaha we drove close enough to take a peek at the driver, who looked as dutifully professional as the spanking new van he was driving. This isn't grassroots. It's Astroturf. The vans carry the logo 'Americans for Prosperity,' one of the Washington front groups orchestrating the fight against universal health [coverage]." Reich went on to write that these front groups used the ethos of the provocateurs to "stage ersatz local anti–universal health rallies, and fill hometown media with carefully crafted, market-tested messages demonizing healthcare reform."

Reich is obviously a partisan with a point of view. And not everyone opposed to health-care reform is an agent for the lobbyists or a member of the Republican Party. But his observation that professional political and industry groups were deliberately creating media spectacles to advance their financial and political interests is exactly right. It must be noted that liberals also use the tactic. When Wisconsin governor Scott Walker proposed budget cuts and new restrictions on collective bargaining for public-sector unions, opponents did not make their case in debates. They staged spectacular protest rallies that played to the cameras and microphones and starred celebrities like Michael Moore. Those protests clearly had a lot of Reich's "Astroturf" in them. In this case unions and the state's Democratic Party supplied the artifice. In fact, fourteen Democratic state senators actually fled the state, preventing the majority Republicans from being able to move the bill through the legislature. The spectacle of the Democrats in hiding included one state senator being interviewed on *Good Morning America* from an "undisclosed location."

On the one hand, stripping public unions of their right to collective bargaining is drastic, especially without full discussion. Moreover, the unions had accepted many of the governor's proposals—they had agreed to contribute more to their pensions and health-care plans. It was the governor's attempt to unilaterally strip the unions of bargaining rights that set off the ruckus. Now we are left with boiling-mad, entrenched parties who are incapable of civil, reasoned debate in service to the public good. One side, the Democrats, left the legislature in an act of theater and political gamesmanship instead of agreeing to talk. But Governor Scott did not seem open to debate and persuasion, at least from the Democrats' perspective. Nonetheless, he is the elected governor of the state of Wisconsin. As President Obama famously said: "Elections have consequences and at the end of the day I won." This is equally true for the Republicans in the Wisconsin state house. To have Democratic legislators run away to deny the governor the quorum necessary for a vote when he had enough votes to win amounted to hijacking our republican form of government.

To me, what happened in Wisconsin confirmed that we have entered an era of stunt governing. This goes beyond the pointless screaming discussions among extremists and provocateurs on the talk shows. Now governing, too, has become one big sideshow in which serious issues and the needs of the people can't be honestly debated and settled; government officials reduce themselves to Beltway versions of the provocateurs. They introduce meaningless legislation to ban Sharia law in Oklahoma or call for President Obama to make public his birth certificate. There is no substance to these acts except to produce headlines and more peppery grist to be chewed over on the partisan talk shows. An outrageous waste of taxpayer time and money by elected officials is tolerated and accepted. And rational voices attempting to do the hard work of seeking compromise on big issues know that highly partisan primaries will ambush and punish them for even talking to the other side of the aisle. The provocateurs have led the way to an age in which stunt governing and ineffectual leadership now are the rule. The megaphone of the provocateur culture has over-whelmed deliberation and genuine attempts at legislation. The voice of honest debate in America has been muzzled. And as those voices of honest debate have grown silent, the quality of our political institutions has been diminished. Those town-hall meetings, school-board meetings, and joint sessions of Congress determine the viability of the American experiment and all the dreams it embodies. We can't afford to lose them.

CHAPTER 9

THE LIMITS OF FREE SPEECH

THE JOURNALIST AND HISTORIAN IN ME sees Washington, DC, as a poetic, living tribute to America's passion for free speech in all its glory: radical, liberating, informative, artistic, rebellious, and defiant.

You can see the original text of the First Amendment enshrined on parchment paper at the National Archives. In fact, it is written all over the permanent face of the capital. Forty-five words of the First Amendment are inscribed on a four-story-high stone tablet facing Pennsylvania Avenue. The words appear on the front of the Newseum, a museum dedicated to words and images created by journalists. The pledge "Equal Justice Under Law" stands above the entrance to the Supreme Court and applies to all who come to the court to use their freedom of speech to argue a case, to present briefs for the Court to consider, or to read the decisions of the justices based on their interpretations of the laws.

The Founding Fathers employed free speech to "solemnly publish and declare" the right to break away from colonial rule and form their own government. On the marble steps of the Lincoln Memorial is a marker showing where Martin Luther King Jr. stood to deliver his passionate "I Have a Dream" speech, an oral petition for Congress to pass the Civil Rights Act of 1964. The federal city, home to the Library of Congress and the Smithsonian museum, is filled with the history and artistic representation of our debate and dissent. It is a right protected by the Constitution.

Allowing people to speak their minds, express their feelings, and let the chips fall where they may in the marketplace of ideas is the essence of America. To many, freedom of speech is nearly synonymous with democracy in the United States and has been ever since free speech was enshrined in the Bill of Rights.

George Washington, the nation's first president and leader of the Continental Army, translated the idea of freedom of speech and freedom of the press into the central purpose of the Revolutionary War. He told soldiers in 1783 that as they fought for freedom they fought for the right of free expression, "for if men are to be precluded from offering their sentiments on a matter, which may involve the most serious and alarming consequences . . . reason is of no use to us; the freedom of speech may be taken away and dumb and silent we may be led, like sheep, to the slaughter."

Washington's pledge lives on.

"Ours is the most outspoken society on earth," wrote journalist and historian Anthony Lewis in his 2007 book *Freedom for the Thought That We Hate: A Biography of the First Amendment.* "Americans are freer to think what we will and say what we think than any other people, and freer today than in the past. We can bare the secrets of government and the secrets of the bedroom. We can denounce our rulers, and each other, with little fear of the consequences. There is almost no chance that a court will stop us from publishing what we wish: in print, on the air, or on the Web. Hateful and shocking expression, political or artistic, is almost all free to enter the marketplace of ideas."

But even in America, the freedom to write, to publish, and to speak does have limits. There are legal limits on obscenity, as well as laws against hateful speech, threats, and intimidation. As the Supreme Court decided decades ago, you cannot falsely yell "fire" in a crowded theater, thus potentially causing people injury, without consequences. You cannot yell "bomb" on a plane or in an airport. There are sensible limits to free speech where words would cause danger or mass panic.

There are also times when public officials and presidents, during political turmoil and war, have curbed our right to free speech. The first and best-known such law in American history was the Sedition Act of 1798. Under that law it was a crime—punishable by fine or imprisonment—to speak out against the government. During the John Adams administration, a number of prominent newspaper publishers affiliated with the rival Republican Party paid fines and some went to jail for violations of the Sedition Act. The Espionage Act of 1917, a World War I–era law, punished speech the government considered "disloyal." More than two hundred people were convicted under the act. The law was later the basis for criminal charges against newspapers that published the 1970 Pentagon Papers, revealing government officials lying about the Vietnam War.

During the cold war the House Committee on Un-American Activities had the power to put citizens in jail if they refused to testify about any connections they might have had to communist groups. In most cases, the Supreme Court upheld the committee's right to do so, despite charges by witnesses that their free speech rights—including the right to not speak— had been violated. Numerous writers, directors, and actors, particularly in Hollywood, found themselves blacklisted due to alleged communist links. The hearings put a chill on all speech; everyone feared being mistaken for a communist.

Such examples of the government infringing our freedom of speech stand out, in part because they occur so infrequently. On the whole, the story of America is the story of our ever-increasing commitment to freedom of speech. As the nation has become more racially diverse and socially liberal, there has been more accommodation of controversial public speech and art, even as we have agreed as a society over the years to limit epithets and pejorative slang in public to allow for wider acceptance of women, the disabled, religious and racial minorities, and gays. (Many Americans of a generation ago would find today's rigorous standards for socially acceptable speech to be inhibiting.)

Sexually explicit speech, books, and movies have often posed the biggest challenge in our history to free speech. Since the late nineteenth century, there have been numerous state and federal legislative efforts to control titillating material. Beginning in the 1860s, almost every state passed laws to ban books, such as D. H. Lawrence's *Lady Chatterley's Lover* (published in 1928), that contain sexual themes. This was followed by twentieth-century efforts to control sexually explicit movies through Hollywood's Hays Code. But the Supreme Court, in *Roth v. United States* (1957), began to dismantle limits on sexual themes in art. The justices adopted a "prurient interest" standard for judging obscenity: "The proper test is whether, to the average person, applying contemporary community standards, the dominant theme of the material taken as a whole, appeals to prurient interest." The ruling's impact was to loosen restraints on art while allowing for subjective assessment of "community standards."

By 1973 the high court had swept obscenity further onto the sidelines with *Miller v. California,* which built on *Roth* and said that any sexually arousing material that violated a state law could be outlawed only if it lacked "serious literary, artistic, political or scientific value." Once again, the limits of free speech were loosened.

In *FCC v. Pacifica,* in 1978, the Court decided that the Federal Communications Commission could impose limits on "patently offensive" speech being broadcast over the airwaves—but that such words were not restricted in books or stage acts.

Freedom of speech has even been extended to hateful speech, symbols, and actions, as long as they don't incite violence. In 1978 the Supreme Court upheld the right of a group of Nazi sympathizers to march in Skokie, Illinois, a town with a large Jewish population. Along the same lines, the Court struck down a Texas ban on flag burning. And in 1992 the justices ruled against a Minnesota ban on burning a cross on the lawn of a black family because the state law did not allow for First Amendment protections for expressing an unpopular point of view. (Later the Court found that if a cross burning could be shown to be an act of intimidation, then it was beyond free-speech protection.)

In his book *Nigger*, Randall Kennedy, a black Harvard Law School professor, thanked the court for extending the First Amendment to hateful speech, such as the dehumanizing title of his book. In Kennedy's thinking, by denying First Amendment protection to hateful speech, the justices would have opened the door to a greater danger to American blacks and all minorities. With subjective standards for judging hateful speech, he saw the potential for a boomerang effect, with the government and the most powerful groups in America labeling the radical speech of minorities fighting for their rights as hate speech. He summed up the high court's handling of racially provocative language by writing: "The cumulative effect of [the Court's] speech-protective doctrines is a conspicuous toleration of speech that many people—in some instances the vast majority of people—find deeply, perhaps even viscerally, obnoxious, including flag burning, pornography, Nazis' taunting of Holocaust survivors, a jacket emblazoned with the phrase 'Fuck the Draft,' *The Satanic Verses, The Birth of a Nation, The Last Temptation of Christ. . . .* Resistance against censorship [has] always been an important and positive feature of the great struggles against racist tyranny in the United States, from the fight against slavery to the fight against Jim Crow."

Kennedy's position fit with *New York Times* writer Anthony Lewis's conclusion—that First Amendment protections have steadily grown in the United States because they are so central to America's core beliefs and definition of itself as the "land of the free." As Lewis wrote, "In Germany it is a crime, a serious one, to display the swastika or any other Nazi symbol. In eleven European countries it is a crime to say that the Holocaust did not happen, that Germans in the Nazi years did not slaughter Jews. So it is in Canada, and the Canadian Supreme Court has decided that Holocaust deniers can be prosecuted and punished despite the country's Constitutional guarantee of free expression. In the United States, the First Amendment protects the right to deny the fact of the Holocaust."

But there is one area in which the modern Supreme Court has allowed limits on free speech: national security. Currently, free speech is being tested by a massive leak of 250,000 State Department messages about U.S. foreign policy, including negotiations over war with the heads of foreign states. The Justice Department wants to prosecute Julian Assange, the man who published some documents on his site, WikiLeaks, under the Espionage Act that was used during World War I. That law has not been reviewed by the Court in light of more liberal, expansive readings of First Amendment rights in the last fifty years. A 2005 case prosecuted under the Espionage Act fell apart when a federal judge ruled that prosecutors had the burden of proving that the people involved did not just want to make money but also intended to harm the United States.

That the United States has a lenient, if not extreme, view of the right to spout almost any variety of language was reaffirmed in early 2011, when the Court ruled in *Snyder v. Phelps* that it is within First Amendment rights to conduct a protest at a funeral. The funeral was being held for a Marine killed in the Iraq War. The protest was against the U.S. policy allowing homosexuals in the military, although the dead serviceman was not gay. Members of the Kansas-based Westboro Baptist Church of Topeka carried signs with messages that said, "America is Doomed" and "God Hates Fags."

The 8–1 Supreme Court ruling fit with a prior ruling that

allowed movies showing cruel, violent acts against animals. Chief Justice John Roberts wrote in the Westboro case: "Debate on public issues should be robust, uninhibited and wide-open." He said such speech regarding debate of "public issues occupies the highest rung of the hierarchy of First Amendment values." Roberts wrote anecdotally that "speech is powerful. . . . It can stir people to action, move them to tears of both joy and sorrow and—as it did here [in the Westboro case]—inflict great pain."

Most Americans would not consider disruption of a dead serviceman's sacred last rites to be socially acceptable behavior. But they embrace the wide boundary lines of acceptable speech.

The key here is that we do not censor others' speech. The best instinct of American society is that we encourage people to express their points of view, even if they in turn unleash opposing points of view. Nonetheless, we do judge it.

While the government does not legislate politically correct speech, in many cases the people who are the subject of the speech play a key role in deciding whether they consider a word or phrase offensive or "politically incorrect." Native Americans are asked if they are offended by sports teams with names like the "Fighting Sioux" and the "Redskins." After the 2011 assassination attempt on the life of Congresswoman Gabrielle Giffords in Tucson, Arizona, a shocked nation condemned metaphors about putting politicians in the "crosshairs" and "targeting" them for defeat. Yes, speech codes that arise from topical events tend to evaporate over time. But the point is that this self-policing mechanism is triggered in us in the first place and embraced by large swaths of America. It highlights a paradox of free speech in our country. It is a right so fundamental and so sacred to our national character that we as a society tend to censor *ourselves* in order to maintain a commitment to its principles.

What goes unsaid in this compact is that preserving the liberty to say what is on your mind is never more important than in political debate. Americans assume they can disagree with the highest elected officials in the crowd without some Gestapo-like police force appearing at the door to silence them. The First Amendment guarantees that Congress will make no law that allows such a travesty.

Where we do place limits on free speech is with speech that threatens physical assault or intimidation. At that point both social censure and legal prohibition agree that the offending individual or group has crossed a bright line into what is impermissible. But as we've seen, there is a large buffer zone before the bright line, policed and patrolled by special-interest groups, political groups, religious groups, and slanted niche media. They constantly push social and political debates up to (and sometimes across) the bright line of impermissible speech when they don't like what they are hearing. Such people pretend to honor open dialogue. But what they really honor is their own particular brand of dialogue. Their purpose is to stifle honest intellectual and emotional interaction and preclude full debate. This is particularly offensive in the media, where news analysis, commentary, and opinion play a large role in helping busy people make sense of the gushing hydrant of news. Every minute of every day there are events, both real and staged, to be made sense of, not to mention speeches, announcements, and personalities competing for our attention.

The deluge can confound anyone watching the news. What does it all mean? Is it just noise to fill a twenty-four-hour programming vacuum?

Viewers have a hunger for background, context, and historical reference to make sense of the cascading reports on our fast-paced world. And if there was ever in fact objective journalism in reporting it, it is a vanishing idea. My friend and political jousting partner Brit Hume, who worked at ABC for twenty years before joining Fox, has said the media can never be objective—but reporters can at least be sure to be fair. Hume makes the point that Fox News can appeal to conservative viewers simply by featuring stories that challenge (liberal) media preconceptions and fall outside the framework of other news organizations. He calls it as easy as "picking up change off the street." By recognizing and admitting our own biases, reporters can allow the audience to consider the source as they consume news and information. When news organizations pretend to be without bias, they fall victim to arrogance and elitist tendencies in the way they select stories, tell stories, and choose the people they feature as authoritative voices. They superimpose a single framework of what they consider to be acceptable and right thinking about news. In a sense, these news organizations act as surrogate parents, claiming to know what is best for us. They take away our desire to think for ourselves. They unconsciously subvert free speech by eliminating opinions, ideas, and stories they disagree with. They deny the truth about the cultural and political frame of their news presentation and commentary. But if you pay close attention, you realize that any idea or opinion at variance with their viewpoint is, subtly or overtly, portrayed as politically incorrect.

Today one major unsettled area of dispute over the First Amendment has to do with political fund-raising and political advertising. Do political action committees of corporations, unions, and nonprofit groups have the same First Amendment rights as individuals? In America's reverence for free speech, these questions currently polarize the Supreme Court justices and pit Democrats against Republicans.

In January 2010 the Supreme Court ruled in *Citizens United v. Federal Elections Commission* that Congress had no right to ban political advertising on TV and radio within sixty days of a general election and thirty days of a primary. Justice Anthony Kennedy wrote in the majority opinion that "speech is an essential mechanism of democracy, for it is the means to hold officials accountable to the people." He reasoned that the First Amendment's truest meaning is found in the "right of citizens to inquire, to hear, to speak and to use information to reach consensus" as a "precondition to enlightened self-government." Along the lines of previous rulings that gave the greatest protection to speech employed in the course of public-policy debates, the majority of justices in the *Citizens United* case viewed campaign contributions as the equivalent of speech. The decision said the First Amendment has "its fullest and most urgent application to speech uttered during a campaign for public office." Justice Kennedy later added that the government may not discriminate against any person or class of speakers by setting limits on their free-speech rights.

Justice John Paul Stevens offered a strong dissent. He expressed the fear of his liberal colleagues that corporate money unleashed by the ruling would flood the political system. Stevens wrote that "the Court's opinion is thus a rejection of the common sense of the American people, who have recognized a need to prevent corporations from undermining self-government since the founding and who have fought against the distinctive corrupting potential of corporate electioneering since the days of Theodore Roosevelt." Later in his dissent Justice Stevens explained that the majority's ruling ignored the context of free-speech applications. Corporations, he argued, cannot run for office and cannot vote, and because "they may be managed and controlled by non-residents [foreigners], their interests may conflict in fundamental respects with the interests of eligible voters." Justice Antonin Scalia presented the contrary view of corporations in his concurrence with the majority ruling. He wrote that the First Amendment is "written in terms of 'speech,' not speakers." He said any fair reading of the First Amendment would allow the groups of people who make up political organizations, such as the Republican and the Democratic parties, to issue statements without fear of censorship although they are not individuals. "The association of individuals in a business corporation," he contended, "is no different—or at least it cannot be denied the right to speak on the simplistic ground that it is not 'an individual American.'"

The ruling set off a huge, immediate political row. The Obama White House issued a statement the day of the ruling calling it a win for "big oil, Wall Street banks, health insurance companies and the other powerful interests that marshal their power every day in Washington to drown out the voices of everyday [individual] Americans." The *New York Times* reported that Democrats feared that the ruling favored Republicans because Republicans "are the traditional allies of big corporations [and] have more money to spend than unions."

The reaction to the ruling was so strong that it renewed questions about whether the conservative majority of the Court was essentially an arm of the Republican Party. Similar charges had been leveled against the Court in 2000, after it issued a ruling on counting ballots in Florida that put Republican George W. Bush in the White House. A few days after the *Citizens United* ruling, the anger over the case was on public display at President Obama's State of the Union speech.

"With all due deference to separation of powers," the president said to Congress and his national television audience, "last week the Supreme Court reversed a century of law that I believe will open the floodgates of special interests—including foreign corporations—to spend without limits in our elections. I don't think American elections should be bankrolled by America's most powerful interests or, worse, by foreign entities." Television cameras focused on the justices of the conservative majority that had passed the decision; Associate Justice Samuel Alito was seen shaking his head at President Obama's speech, mouthing the words "not true" in response.

According to polling data, the American public was of mixed mind about the ruling. Most felt that campaign donations are a protected form of free speech under the First Amendment and agreed that donations from corporations and unions deserved to be treated just as donations from individuals. But several polls found the public disagreed with the Supreme Court's ruling. A report from the Gallup polling organization said that one of its polls had found that "the majority [of Americans polled agree] it is more important to limit campaign donations than to protect this free-speech right."

That was an incredible finding, one of the few where Americans are not in lockstep with the principle of free speech. When confronted with hate speech, obscenity, and even cross burnings, the public understands that First Amendment protections are paramount in a democracy. But they are concerned over the imbalance that results when money amplifies the speech of certain people or organizations. The people with money are the rich. And for most of American history there was no effective regulation of campaign contributions. Congress created the Federal Election Commission to track the flow of money into politics only after the Watergate scandal. In the 1970s the Supreme Court struck down limits on how much a candidate can spend on a campaign as a violation of the candidate's free-speech rights. Several congressional efforts at tightening the amount of money going to campaigns and regulating how candidates spend money also faced defeat in subsequent decades. But by 2002 a new set of rules for political contributions had been enacted—the McCain-Feingold bill, which limited money raised by politicians to $2,000 per individual donor and halted all political advertising by outside groups within sixty days of a general election.

The *Citizens United* ruling threw out the limits imposed by McCain-Feingold. The impact was immediate. The nonpartisan Sunlight Foundation's review of spending in the 2010 midterm election found $126 million in "undisclosed money," more than a quarter of all money that groups outside the candidates' campaigns had spent to influence the outcome of political races. An additional $60 million was raised by "outside" groups that did disclose which corporations and individuals gave them the money. And the Sunlight Foundation found that the new flood of money did in fact favor Republicans. "By a nearly six to one margin," Sunlight reported, "Republicans outspent the Democrats among groups that failed to disclose the source of their money [$59 million to $10 million]."

With the *Citizens United* ruling as the governing law, political insiders are now predicting that the major-party candidates for president in 2012 will be the first politicians ever to spend more than a billion dollars to run for office. That is a gargantuan leap from the $33 million that President Carter raised in his winning race for the White House in 1976. And it is a far cry from President Clinton's reelection fund of $108 million. Or President Bush's $356 million in 2004. Running for president, the U.S. Senate, or even the city council is now becoming a function of fund-raising prowess, and that is a potential barrier to people without access to big donations.

That is why despite faithful adherence to the principle of free speech, Americans worry about the power of money to distort the political process. But here's the thing. Even if there are future changes in campaign finance law that supersede the *Citizens United* ruling, there will always be corporate and union money in politics. Yet individual American voters who select their candidate based on feeling, experience, and knowledge of the candidates will always make the choice in the voting booth. The responsibility lies with us—the American people. And the nature of our political decisions will be largely shaped by the open nature of American political discourse.

My apologies to my liberal friends, but imposing heavy restrictions on the money flowing into political races to level the playing field may be a good idea—but here is a better idea. Why not encourage more frank and open discussion and trust Americans to identify the kind of talk that actually gets us somewhere? History shows that Americans trust one another when it comes to free speech. Across political lines we stand in fierce defense of that fundamental right. Even if we banned all corporate and union money from politics, we'd still have a 24-7 political commentary machine being used by liberals and conservatives as an echo chamber to issue marching orders for their separate and narrow-minded political orthodoxies.

At the extremes of speech, most Americans are comfortable knowing that a racist can say whatever he or she wants. Most Americans disagree with racists; their constituency is marginalized. In the marketplace of ideas, they lose. So how big a threat do they pose? Yet in our current political dialogue, there is a tremendous amount of energy expended by the far ends of the political spectrum—the right wing and the left wing—in an effort to convince themselves that their ideological opponents are extremists who must be not only shunned but also silenced. For them, faith in free speech is only pure for people who agree with them.

To them, the fight over campaign finance is just another battleground where the Far Left and the Far Right are seeking advantage for themselves. It is impolitic to say this, but I am less worried about overturned campaign finance laws than I am about maintaining the vitality of our political conversations in the middle ground occupied by most Americans. In that large space—remember, there are more independent voters in America than either Democrats or Republicans—there is a hunger for a place to find rational discourse where people can agree, disagree, learn, and listen. Campaign finance laws will not help the American people to take the risk to speak honestly and openly to one another.

That is why I am not that worried about our overturned

campaign finance laws. Both sides can raise obscene amounts of money. Both sides have the support of corporations, unions, the wealthy, and manic individuals tweeting and blogging frightening messages about the other side in order to generate more money. Yes, there may be some differential in spending, with conservatives perhaps getting the better of the money wars. But the difference is not so vast that the liberal view is eclipsed in paid advertising or the number of phone banks and money paid to consultants and preachers. President Obama, a Democrat, broke all fund-raising records. More to the point, for every campaign finance law enacted there will be ingenious new ways found to get around it. That is why political consultants and lawyers get paid the big bucks. That is why so much of the conversation about campaign finance as a free-speech issue feels like a petty feud, a wheel-spinning exercise in which both sides are at their giddiest when it is their turn to demonize their opponent. On one side, the public is frightened into believing that those trying to rein in corporate spending are destroying free speech. On the other side, the public is warned that those who support the unregulated flow of money in politics are opening the door to shadowy, nefarious international groups seeking to control our national and local elections. Really?

The whole point of dissent and the American experience is that Americans are not afraid of other views. We do not run from difference of opinion. It is our national sunshine. Our greatest alarm has to come when we encounter people who are unwilling to engage and join the debate in good faith.

Unfortunately, that realization dawned on many after a terrible, violent tragedy.

Congresswoman Gabrielle Giffords was hosting a Saturday-morning open house for her constituents in a Tucson, Arizona, strip mall when a young man, Jared Lee Loughner, shot her in the head at point-blank range. She survived, but six others died as Loughner continued his shooting spree. Eighteen more were injured.

Given the vitriolic speech that characterized the political debate over immigration in Arizona at the time, there was initial speculation that Loughner had been incited by rabid right-wing rhetoric. Clarence Dupnik, the sheriff of Pima County, said the constant fury at immigrants, legal and illegal, made Tucson the capital of "the anger, the hatred and the bigotry that goes on in this country." Investigators found that Loughner regularly read a Web site with antigovernment tirades. The *New York Times* reported on its front page, "Regardless of what led to the episode, it quickly focused attention on the degree to which inflammatory language, threats and implicit instigations to violence have become a steady undercurrent in the nation's political culture."

The words and actions of conservative talk-show hosts, politicians, and Web sites came under intense scrutiny as reporters looked for evidence of their role in the attack. Analysts noted that Sarah Palin, the former vice presidential candidate, had used the symbol of a gun's crosshairs to highlight Giffords's congressional district as a target for a Republican takeover and defeat of the Democrat. Had that been a factor in Loughner's thinking?

The *New York Times* editorial board wrote a few days after the attack that it was "facile" and wrong to blame conservatives and Republicans for the violence. But the paper concluded, "It is legitimate to hold Republicans and particularly their most virulent supporters in the media responsible for the gale of anger that produced the vast majority of these threats, setting the nation on edge. Many on the Right have exploited the arguments of division, reaping political power by demonizing immigrants or welfare recipients or bureaucrats. They seem to have persuaded many Americans that the government is not just misguided, but the enemy of the people."

Further out on the Left, former MSNBC host Keith Olbermann argued that it did not matter if Loughner was found to be mentally ill and unaware that he was shooting a political leader. The crime was a product of the times. "Assume the details are coincidence. The violence is not. The rhetoric has devolved and descended past the ugly and past the threatening and past the fantastic and into the imminently murderous."

Conservative talk-show hosts, sensing they were being blamed for the shootings, responded defiantly. Their indignation rose when it became clear that there was no explicit link between Loughner and right-wing groups or subversive tracts of the kind that had inspired Oklahoma City bomber Timothy McVeigh. Rush Limbaugh castigated liberals for trying to benefit from the tragedy by using it as a reason to "regulate out of business their political opponents." Sarah Palin, who had become a leader in the strongly anti-immigrant Tea Party, issued a statement that argued against any tenuous ties being manufactured by the left wing to tie right-wing vitriol to the attack. "Acts of monstrosity stand on their own," she said. "They begin and end with the criminals who commit them, not collectively with all citizens of a state, not with those who listen to talk radio . . . not with law-abiding citizens who respectfully exercise their first amendment rights at campaign rallies."

The frightening shooting did cause a pause in the normal

tit-for-tat bickering between Republicans and Democrats in Washington. Congressmen on both sides of the aisle pledged to be more civil in their tone and language. Some members of Congress broke from the usual seating pattern for the State of the Union address, crossing party lines in a show of national unity. And President Obama, in a speech in Arizona after the tragedy, cautioned against using the tragic situation to further polarize the national debate: "But at a time when our discourse has become so sharply polarized—at a time when we are far too eager to lay the blame for all that ails the world at the feet of those who think differently than we do—it is important for us to pause for a moment and make sure that we are talking with each other in a way that heals, not a way that wounds."

The media coverage of the Tucson shooting was much more focused on possible ties to rhetoric than it was on lax gun control or inadequate treatment for people with mental illness. Somehow those relevant issues proved to be too loaded for debate, even though they are obviously at the center of the equation.

Most Americans did welcome the opportunity to reassess the nature of American political discourse, especially the extreme, circus-barker versions that attract so much attention. It was a wake-up call. As much as we might loathe an individual politician, all political parties agree that it is wrong to kill.

Yet even that kind of speech cannot be banned in America. After they bombed the federal building in Oklahoma City, the militia groups remained free to circulate their anti-Semitic, racist screeds about conspiracies. Until he starts sending actual bombs in the mail, the Unabomber is free to post his bizarre manifesto on the Internet. Free speech gives him that right. Pundits like Palin, Ed Schultz, Glenn Beck, Michael

Savage, Keith Olbermann, Rush Limbaugh, Rachel Maddow, and those writing on DailyKos and HuffPo and in publications much further to the Left or Right have the right to say and write almost anything. Their high-voltage provocations and fearmongering are a daily staple of Web sites, American talk radio, and prime-time cable news shows.

Why are such shows so shrill? Why are they so popular? Why is their language so unforgiving? Why do bellicose hosts regularly invoke military jargon about targeted opponents, political battlefields, and tactical opposition research? How can a Tea Party candidate like Nevada's Sharron Angle think that it is acceptable to suggest fixing Washington through "Second Amendment remedies"?

The Tucson shootings are a reminder of what we cannot tolerate in our society. It is not relevant what motivated Loughner. The point is that Loughner's bloody assault was a reminder that for all of the bluster and bravado of American politics, it is still based on good and decent people engaging one another in conversation and debate, not violence and demonization. What we need is more honest, genuine debate. We need to talk to one another, not at one another.

I don't blame Rush or Olbermann for the events in Tucson. But when it comes to Rush, why is it that the king of the airwaves thinks it is a wimpy idea to encourage more civil discourse? He is a leader in the media industry, and his angry, defensive posture leads his audience to react similarly, rather than reaching for some common ground. Why can't we act more responsibly? Can those who help shape public opinion not see that vitriolic talk leads us into a sea of bitterness, with no safe harbor for rational debate?

The answer is plain and simple. The media industry cannot

afford to stop and look at itself. Its members are scared. Limbaugh admitted to worrying after Tucson that there are people waiting for an excuse to "regulate out of business their political opponents." But adverse reactions are not about removing political opponents. Commentary based on envy, anger, resentful mocking, and intolerance play to our late-night cravings but give us only empty calories. The talk-show crowd fears that Americans are sick and tired of lowest-common-denominator talk that yields no upside except for the big paychecks of those who produce it.

The power of the Tucson tragedy was not that it imposed self-censorship on our ideas. It did not. Our freedom of speech remains vibrant, strong, and intact. The real power of that dark winter day in the desert was the suggestion that we must modify our behavior to increase our openness to one another, to carry on a civil conversation, and to listen respectfully to one another's ideas.

To quote President Obama in his speech in the aftermath of Tucson, a speech that was overwhelmingly heard as positive by the American people, on the Left and the Right,

> Let's remember that it is not because a simple lack of civility caused this tragedy but rather because only a more civil and honest public discourse can help us face up to our challenges as a nation. . . . We want to live up to the example of public servants like [Judge] John Roll and [Congresswoman] Gabby Giffords, who knew first and foremost that we are all Americans and that we can question each other's ideas without questioning each other's love of country. . . .
>
> I believe we can be better. . . . We may not be able to stop

all evil in the world, but I know that how we treat one an-. other is entirely up to us. I believe that for all our imperfections we are full of decency and goodness and that the forces that divide us are not as strong as those that unite us.

Amen.

EPILOGUE

I T HAPPENS ALL THE TIME.

In the middle of a political fight, I'll ask people where they get their news. What is the basis of their argument? The reply is the equivalent of brain mapping. The liberals say the *New York Times*, Jon Stewart, the Huffington Post, and NPR. The conservatives say Fox News, the *Wall Street Journal*, Rush and Sean on the radio, the Drudge Report, and Power line.com.

Left wing or right wing, they are revealing their politics by announcing the locales they gravitate toward for news. And most of the time they admit those ideologically aligned outlets are their only sources of news.

The biggest critics of Fox admit they never watch the news channel. Most of NPR's loudest critics concede they don't listen to it. I've lived on both sides of the divide. For ten years NPR and Fox simultaneously paid me to speak to their distinct audiences. When I made personal appearances for speeches in front of the different camps, I got used to people asking me,

"Why do you work for the other guys?" For conservatives it was, "Why don't you leave NPR and work full-time for Fox?" And for liberals it was, "Why do you have to work for Fox?"

When people come up to say hello to me at basketball games or airports, most introduce themselves by first telling me they are liberal or conservative. Only then do they say it is a pleasure to meet me, although a good number quickly add that they don't agree with all I have to say. All this happens before they tell me their names. When people announcing differing ideological credentials come over within seconds of each other, I find myself wondering what would happen if these people ever broke out of their tight cocoons in their respective liberal and conservative media worlds and met each other.

Would it explode their identities—some essential part of their sense of self that requires them to wear the label like an all-defining badge, "liberal" or "conservative"? Is it like fans of the Yankees and Red Sox being so locked into rooting for their team—and hating the other team—that they forget about their mutual love of baseball? Would it threaten them to hear about the stories, the passions, driving fellow Americans who think differently about the world but share the same destiny as Americans?

As this book shows, we, the American people, are not shy about speaking out and voicing our dissent. But it also shows that such disagreements are not the end of the conversation. Our debates are the *start* of the conversation.

Freedom of speech is arguably the defining aspect of the American way of life. It has been exalted by every American generation. The brightest moments in our history have come when we have gone beyond the obligation of fulfilling the constitutional grant to allow one another the right to speak and stood up to insist on it for ourselves or others who face being silenced by government or popular opinion.

America fulfills its grant of rights best when we trust that every one of us is speaking with integrity, love of country, and the best of intentions until there is contrary evidence. Even after the arguments that led to the Civil War, President Lincoln reaffirmed the Founding Fathers' dedication to the idea of free speech with the pledge that "government of the people, by the people, for the people, shall not perish from the earth."

The politically correct among us, on the Left and the Right, so self-righteous in claiming to want to protect the feelings of some minority or constituency, really want to put us all in a box to be controlled by them and their agenda. In the case of my controversial comments about Muslims dressed in religious clothes, my critics claimed to be muzzling me to protect the feelings of people wearing Muslim garb at airports. At that point all of us have to ask who benefits from insisting on this straitjacket for our thoughts and opinions. My words stand as a true expression of my feelings and a good starting point for talking about the difficult feelings many Americans have about Muslims in an era when terrorism is inextricably linked to Islam. Only corruption benefits by closing the door and shuttering the sunlight of honest dialogue among free people.

I find it endlessly interesting to openly converse with people, to get inside the minds of those who are richer, poorer, younger, older, Jewish rabbis and Christian nuns, people who live in a different part of town, have been to war, have never been enlisted, or listen to a different set of media personalities.

But apparently getting to know a varied cast of characters, even in the land of one people out of many, strikes some people as dangerous. I guess that is why NPR's president suggested that I share my feelings only with a psychiatrist.

But to my mind it is worthwhile to take the risk of saying what I am thinking and feeling, and to hear the same from other people. It is the politically correct crowd that assumes that anyone who thinks and looks different is a dork or a danger. Maybe their real fear is being open to admitting that they were wrong about "those people."

Americans on both sides of the political fence complain about how one-sided, personality-driven, and partisan the news shows have become. I tell them we get the media we deserve. The fact is the politically polarized, personality-heavy programs attract a lot of eyeballs. They consistently get high ratings, and that is why there are more and more of them. But it is also clear that on both Left and Right the viewers and listeners are in on the joke. They know it is a frivolous, guilty pleasure to sit back and get a kick out of the petty behavior, the spin doctors, the posturing, and the celebrity gossip on most of the talk news programs. But when the news is serious, like a 9/11 attack or a presidential election, Americans want more—they want hard news—real news.

They agree with Daniel Patrick Moynihan, the former senator, who said: "Everyone is entitled to his own opinion, but not his own facts." But, unfortunately, much of the time we have to deal with a climate that seems to favor people like Senator Jon Kyl, who, as reported by Slate's Dave Weigel, "made the defining Republican stumble of the [2011 spring government shutdown] debate, saying on the Senate floor that '90 percent' of Planned Parenthood's work was abortion. Within hours, his office clarified that this was not intended as a fact...." You can't make this stuff up.

Perhaps the reason Americans feel so bereft is that with careless claims thrown left and right, there's no longer the comfort (even if it was an illusion) of a single trusted news source.

The days of people across the political spectrum trusting journalists such as Edward R. Murrow, Walter Cronkite, and David Brinkley are long gone. None of those outstanding journalists, for all their credibility, could compete in the current media environment. They'd be disparaged as lacking personality and being too tied to the details of a story as opposed to debating the meaning of the story. Their successors are chosen for their personalities, their number of followers on Twitter, and their glamorous looks. Television executives now assume that the audience is coming to see a personality and not simply to get the news. The news is secondary.

The reason for that is that the nature of the news business has changed with advances in technology. At work, at home, in the car, people are listening to the radio, and they're catching a few minutes here and there from cable's twenty-four-hour coverage throughout the day. On their computers they are reading the Huffington Post and the Drudge Report, The Hill and Foxnews.com. They have links to conservative or liberal blog postings sent to their Facebook pages, which are, in turn, sent to their cell phones. If they bother to turn on the major-network evening news broadcasts, what they are getting is no longer the "news" because they've heard it already. They are really tuning in to see which stories are played at the top of the broadcast, what the network slant is on a given story. And they don't feel the need to watch regularly.

The problem of declining relevance to people also bedevils the big morning newspapers. Only a decade ago print editions paid the bills for having top reporters covering city hall and the school board. Now the Web sites for many major metropolitan newspapers get a bigger audience than the print editions. But while the Web sites have grown, the news organizations have not figured out how to get readers and advertisers to pay for the online news product. As a result, once-indispensable metropolitan dailies like the *Washington Post* have been forced to scale back their operations. Some have closed their doors entirely. If your newspaper arrives at your door by 6:00 a.m. every morning, its stories have been on the paper's Web site for at least a few hours. The stories are no longer news. Jay Leno, the late-night comedian, said in a monologue a few years ago that the *New York Times* had won seven Pulitzer Prizes that day, but he read about it on Google News.

What people do want is to make sense of the news. Most people don't have the time or energy to make sense of the complex and often frustrating political problems of our times. They are busy holding down a job, driving the kids to soccer, and paying the bills. They don't have enough time to get a good night's sleep, much less dedicate time to understanding the news when it requires context, history, and assessment of the motivations of the key players involved.

As a result, most people look for simple answers, uncomplicated interpretations, infotainment and satire, good guys and bad guys. More and more people look for one-stop shopping—news coverage they can trust to digest the news for them and help them reach a conclusion. And it has to be fun to watch, read, or listen to. However, polls show people don't feel they are getting the trustworthy part. What they get is predictable political spin, along with big doses of fear, fright, and fury. Which is why many Americans have lost trust in the news media. A surprising number of people, mostly young people and especially young women, report in surveys that they have become disengaged from the news—even as the media is swimming in news programs.

In moments of crisis, people yearn for media that have the guts to provide honest and open accounts of events, fair debates that show a willingness to consistently cross the lines of political dialogue in search of the truth, not close the door on it. And too often they don't find it. Amid the sideshow of commentary and canned news, they realize that an ever-increasing number of media outlets pretend to honor open dialogue, a symphony of ideas and opinions, but only offer a one-note performance: their niche brand. That leaves us with a lot of free speech, but free speech at the fringes. And the fringes do not promote sincere debate between Left and Right. At best, they give us shouting matches.

The honest middle, where much of the nation lives, can't find a place to hear a genuine discussion. And this bothers people all over the political spectrum, including the Far Right and Far Left. Smart people, including those on the political extremes, consistently tell me they want to know what the other side is thinking, even if only to be certain they are right and everyone else is wrong.

I believe there is an audience for honest, credible, intelligent coverage of the changing political, social, and economic landscape. And there is so much seismic change taking place in the world. The budget deficit is going over the cliff; racial and ethnic population shifts are altering the cultural DNA of the country; global economics are unsettling the structural base of manufacturing and service-industry jobs in the United States.

Those big storms are creating winds of change of hurricane force. In the last dozen years the American public has seen a president impeached, a controversial presidential election settled by the Supreme Court, and a massive terror attack on the United States. They have watched the country enter two long-running wars overseas. They have participated in three straight elections in which political power has shifted between the parties in the legislative or executive branches.

These gales are blowing through every town in America.

The nation's racial and ethnic makeup is shifting daily. About 92 percent of the increase in the nation's population in the last decade resulted from the increased number of minorities, mostly Hispanics and Asians. For the first time in our nation's history, minorities are a third of the population.

The role of women in American life is also changing fast, as is the structure of the American family.

Women are now the majority of the nation's high-school and college graduates. They are the majority of the workforce. The number of single, divorced, and widowed women has never been higher, especially among minorities. Women vote in higher numbers than men, and their influence on politics, including as officeholders, continues to grow. A record number of women sit on the Supreme Court, and in recent years a record number of women have held seats in Congress, led states as governors, and run major corporations.

Immigrants, both legal and illegal, are transforming our neighborhoods and states, as they arrive from Mexico, Asia, and Central America. The number of Muslims in the United States has also increased. Christian, Western European countries historically provided the bulk of America's immigrants. But it is a new day. The need for honest conversations across racial as well as ethnic and religious lines has never been greater.

The magnitude of the shift in the nation's population is most obvious in looking at the surge in people of Hispanic origin. Their numbers grew by more than 40 percent between 2000 and 2010. Hispanics are now the nation's largest minority, making up 16 percent of the population (Asians are 5 percent of the population). In Texas, the state whose population grew the most in the first decade of the century, 95 percent of the growth in people under eighteen was among Hispanics. Nationwide the birthrate among Hispanics and Asians is far higher than that among whites, meaning more diversity is on the way. The Census Bureau estimates that most American children will be minorities by 2023 and that there will be no racial majority in the country in about thirty years.

Blacks held steady at 12 percent of the population. This is bumping up the growth of the black middle class, blacks living in the suburbs, and blacks in political power, including as president. All of this signals the dawning of a new face of America.

While baby boomers over fifty now make up about 30 percent of the population, that demographic is close to the quarter of the population younger than eighteen. Americans in both these demographic groups say the economy is their top priority, but each has very different concerns. Seniors over sixty-five are focused on the immediate cost of living—on retaining their Social Security and Medicare programs—while younger people are worried about education and the tight job market.

Seniors, overwhelmingly white, are pessimistic about the nation's future. The young are overwhelmingly diverse and, while cynical, are not as pessimistic as the seniors. The young vote heavily for Democrats, while the seniors cast their votes for Republicans. When it comes to tough issues like budget cuts, the need for honest debate between these generations is greater than ever. Today's Americans are confronting bigger divisions of age and race and class than ever before.

"Politically, an age-race divide could create even sharper divisions between candidates and parties that espouse more or less government support for measures benefitting the young, like education or affordable housing, and those benefitting the old, like Social Security and Medicare," says William Frey, a demographer for the Brookings Institution, a Washington think tank.

What this all suggests is that the nation is going through significant realignment, something that happens every few generations. These hurricane forces are social, political, and economic. And when they occur, people get frightened, and— to paraphrase President Obama—they cling to what they know, what is familiar and comforting, and sometimes to the loudest, most commanding voice present, including bombastic media personalities. But it is harder to have an honest debate when the starting point is anxiety laced with resentment and the biggest TV and radio personalities are playing to our fears.

To my mind, the only way to confront these fears is to face them head-on. That means talking to one another. It means telling one another how we feel, including those we don't see eye to eye with. We have to acknowledge that none of us knows everything. We have to accommodate ourselves to new circumstances and facts and seek peace, compromise, and progress. I am not saying that any of us should throw principle out the window. But my career as a professional reporter, columnist, and commentator has taught me that no one has a monopoly on the answers.

Not all media is about fright, fury, and fear. There are still first-rate, trustworthy professional journalists making contributions to the great American conversation. Putting aside their editorial pages and simply focusing on their news coverage, that includes the *Wall Street Journal,* the *New York Times,* the *Washington Post,* the *Los Angeles Times, USA Today,* and many other publications that provide real journalism with integrity.

And then there is National Public Radio. Despite the circumstances under which their organization threw me out, I continue to have tremendous respect for many of the news reporters at NPR who do excellent work every day. My problem remains with NPR's management, its holier-than-thou culture, its editorial bias, and the corruption in its fund-raising from nonprofit foundations that are pushing one agenda or another while claiming not to be advertisers.

Let me end this book by going back to where I started. One question I get asked a lot, even to the point of being pressured by friends who are liberals, is where I stand on government funding of NPR. Republicans in Congress, citing my unjust firing as evidence of NPR's bias, voted to defund NPR in early 2011. Many of my longtime colleagues in journalism called on me to rise above any vindictive instinct and declare my support for NPR.

Despite the way I was treated by NPR's CEO, I did not call for defunding NPR. I am first and foremost a journalist, and NPR is an important platform for journalism in an era when quality journalism is in decline.

Nonetheless, I have come to the conclusion that it is time to defund NPR. And despite what some may think, this is not the small-minded spite of a vindictive mind.

There is something far bigger than my feelings at stake here. NPR journalism has come to embody elitism, arrogance, and the resentments of its highly educated, upper-income managers and funders. Any approach to journalism that is at variance with NPR management's ideas is considered justification for banishment.

The personal attacks on my work and my integrity revealed to me that NPR's leadership has lost sight of the fact that good journalism is the essential product of NPR. People like Vivian Schiller and Ellen Weiss came to think of themselves as smarter than anyone else in the room and were self-righteous in their pursuit of funding from the federal government and nonprofit groups. That hunger for money led NPR's former top fund-raiser to be caught in a videotape sting operation engaged in a grubby attempt to get money from the Muslim Brotherhood, a group with links to terrorists.

The NPR fund-raising exec heard on that tape felt free to pander to the Muslim Brotherhood by disparaging Jews, calling the entire Tea Party racist, and announcing his pride in NPR's decision to fire me because "NPR stood for ... nonracist, nonbigoted, straightforward telling of the news ... and [Williams] lost all credibility, and that breaks your basic ethics as a journalist."

He opined that "liberals today might be more educated, fair, and balanced than conservatives."

His comments opened a window on the mind-set of top NPR managers, who had lost sight of the importance of journalism as a basis for the honest debate so essential in a democratic society. They could not see their own corruption in angling for donations from a group of terrorists.

And their values infected the NPR news operation. NPR editors and journalists found themselves caught in a game of trying to please a leadership team who did not want to hear stories on the air about conservatives, the poor, or anyone who didn't fit their profitable design of NPR as the official voice of college-educated, white, liberal-leaning, upper-income America.

In the middle of the congressional debate over NPR funding, a Democratic New York congressman, Steve Israel, sent out a fund-raising letter that included an appeal to liberals to send donations to the Democratic Congressional Campaign Committee so it could protect NPR as a counter to Republicans who wanted "the likes of Glenn Beck, Limbaugh and Sarah Palin to dominate the airwaves."

The congressman made the case better than any conservative critic that NPR had become news by and for liberal Democrats.

The *New York Times* and other journalism outlets may have budget struggles, but they do fine journalism without accepting government support. NPR has a valuable news product that is prized by many listeners. I believe it can attract the financial support it needs from advertisers, sponsors, and its audience without compromising the work of its journalists. It doesn't need government funding.

House majority leader Eric Cantor later said: "Why should we allow taxpayer dollars to be used [by NPR] to advocate one ideology?" Cantor is right. NPR's troubled management team turned its fund-raising efforts into a weapon against its essential product: top-quality, balanced reporting and analysis. They lost sight of journalism in their obsession with funding.

Ultimately, the idea of government-funded media does not fit the United States. No matter the good intentions behind the funding of public radio and the excesses of conservative talk radio, journalists should not be doing news to please any single constituency or any elected official out of fear of losing that funding. The tremendous variety of sources for news— in print, broadcast, on the radio, and on the Internet—also argues against the U.S. government making a priority of giving financial support to NPR while cutting funding for school breakfast programs, college scholarships, and health care.

I am still an NPR fan. I find that most NPR stations providing local and state news coverage are often singular pillars of information for their communities. But I am no fan of the self-serving, self-righteous thinking that has dominated the management of the NPR news operation in Washington for too long and has tainted a once-great journalistic brand. I am still hoping that the NPR board can right the ship and put better managers in place. Part of that transition will be to reaffirm the idea of journalistic independence by ending NPR's reliance on federal funding. It will be a step toward good health for NPR and the end of the travesty of journalists doing news with an eye to pleasing donors, whether they are political parties, foundations, government officials, or wealthy private citizens.

My recent experience at NPR is a timely reminder for all of us. What is at stake is the cherished principle of free speech and its extensions in free press, freedom of individual thought, and freedom of individual expression.

At the White House Christmas party in 2010, David Westin, the former president of ABC News, came up to me and said he'd been in the New York newsroom when he noticed my face on several monitors simultaneously and asked what had happened. When he was told I had been fired and why, he turned to his top editors and said: "I didn't know we'd reached that point in this country . . . where you can't say what's on your mind, you can't say you are afraid."

Free speech imposes a responsibility on all of us, when it comes to matters of national importance and consequence, to speak seriously and honestly and to allow others to do the same.

In order to do that we need to listen to one another. We must respect facts; facts do matter. When our fellow citizens or institutions, public or private, renege on the good faith needed to recognize facts in service to our most vital national exchanges—critical debates about security, economics, and politics—that is when we should be most on guard and concerned. The identity game—the game of politicians and political and media personalities—encourages most of us to be blind to any fact or point of data that puts a crack in our ideological shield, the thinking that supposedly "defines" our group.

Avoiding that end is the heart of Orwell's *1984*. In the novel the nation has one political party. It controls the nation's history and carefully monitors what is said to limit any unapproved, rebellious line of thought. Every contrary word is banned. The purpose of controlling language in the fictional tale is, in the words of one character, "to narrow the range of thought [until] . . . there will be no thought, as we understand it. . . . Orthodoxy means not thinking—not needing to think—orthodoxy is unconsciousness."

That is the danger of limiting honest debate. That is the danger of letting ourselves be muzzled. No journalistic organization should place itself in the role of the thought police. No Americans who embrace democracy and respect free speech should be willing to put fixed ideological positions ahead of honest exchanges.

Such cowardice is the essence of putting ourselves before our country. If we can't, as individual Americans, sacrifice our egos for the greater good, then "E Pluribus Unum" is only a phrase from a dead language.

And that we cannot accept.

ACKNOWLEDGMENTS

It is easy to find out who your friends are when you are publicly lambasted and fired. They are the ones standing by you. The hard part is being that friend.

To those friends who reached out to me in the middle of my crisis to offer strength and resolve—thank you.

Thank you to the skilled editors and researchers who helped me tell this story. That begins with Eric Lupfer at William Morris Endeavor Entertainment, who helped me pull together research, schedules, and ideas. Roger Scholl, a terrific editor, at Crown has been the guiding, caring hand throughout the project. Molly Stern, the publisher, gave life to this book with her strong conviction that the story had to be told. Through the compressed writing and publishing schedule for creating this book, Eric and Roger stayed with me all the way. Gentlemen, thank you.

Joe Sangiorgio helped me collect my thoughts and draft bright concepts. Michael Santorelli, Andrew Carter, and Kevin Golen worked fast and effectively as passionate researchers who went way beyond the call of duty to put themselves into this book. I am grateful to each of you.

My agents at William Morris Endeavor Entertainment, Henry Reisch and Suzanne Gluck, are masters of their craft. They are even better people. Henry, I am lucky to have you on my team. You play best when the game is on the line.

The Crown team behind this book includes Penny Simon, Annsley Rosner, Julie Cepler, Mark Birkey, and Logan Balestrino. This is an all-star team of book publishing.

In the first furies of this storm, when I was stunned by what was happening, Bill Shine, executive vice president of Fox News, and Sean Hannity displayed grace, friendship, and strength. Michael

Clemente, vice president for news, took charge of masterfully guiding me through the first days of telling my side of the story and keeping me on track despite the big stakes and all the pressures at play. Irena Brigante and Stephanie Kelly led me through the media blitz. Lynne Jordal Martin's energy and smarts made me look good at FoxNews.com.

People always ask me—*What is Bill O'Reilly really like?* As the old saying goes, actions speak louder than words. Bill is the real deal in standing with an embattled friend.

Roger Ailes, the president and CEO of Fox News, cares about people and the news business, and he loves his country. I am a big fan, a loyal friend, and honored to work with a living legend.

Hugo Gurdon, editor in chief of The Hill, reached out to me from the first days of the whirlwind to offer me the chance to write for him. Jim Finkelstein, chairman, gave the go-ahead to bring me on board, and I deeply appreciate that show of faith at a critical moment. Keith White and Emmanuel Touhey are good editors who have made the column work. A. B. Stoddard, my colleague at The Hill and Fox, is the epitome of a good reporter and trusted guide.

My Fox friends kept me going during the whirlwind and after. Thanks to Arthur Aidala, David Asman, Bret Baier, Ann Banker, Dan Banker, Peter Barnes, Porter Berry, Eric Bolling, Brian Boughton, Diane Brandi, John Cuneo, Lana Britt, Betsy Burkhard, Juan Casanas, Dana Cash, Caitlin Clark, Shannon Bream, Andrea DeVito, Brian Doherty, Alex Finland, John Finley, Nate Fredman, Lauren Fritts, Victor Garcia, Jenna Gibson, Don Grannum, Jennifer Griffin, Cherie Grzech, Kata Hall, Mary Katharine Ham, Stephen Hayes, Bill Hemmer, Cory Howard, Brit Hume, Rhonda Jenkins, Eliana Johnson, Mae Joo, Megyn Kelly, Stephanie Kelly, Dana Klinghoffer, Charles Krauthammer, Mary Kreinbihl, Bill Kristol, Judy Laterza, Mara Liasson, Jennie Lubart, Stacia Lynds, Lori Martin, Gwen Marder, Chris

Mills, Ron Mitchell, Andrew Napolitano, Clay Rawson, Cristina Robbins, Doug Rohrbeck, James Rosen, Marty Ryan, Bill Sammon, Shep Smith, Amy Sohnen, Seneca Stevens, Chris Stirewalt, David Tabacoff, Mary-Ellen Tasillo, Lauren Tate, Nicole Tripodi, Lamonte Tyler, Claire Villaverde, Chris Wallace, Jesse Watters, Makeda Wubneh, and Eldad Yaron.

Thanks to my friends at American Program Bureau, beginning with its leaders, Perry Steinberg and Robert Walker.

My personal friends know I love them, but here is a public thank-you: Thank you Charles Cobb, Bill and Cynthianna Lightfoot, James Loadholt, Courtland Milloy, Barrett and Judy Nnoka, Sec. Alphonso Jackson and Marcia Jackson, Diane Thomson, Lucille Blair, Bess Rothenberg, Michael Hicks, Donna Brazile, Robert Traynham, David Brand, Cheryl Gibert, Dante James, Armstrong Williams, Gabe Mehretaab, Fritz and Diane Bech, Dean Elliott, Bob Wilson, Catherine Cook-Holmes, Jerralynn Ness, Cathleen O'Brian, Scott Simon, Alex Chadwick, Richard Strauss, Paul Thaler, Bill Burton, Elizabeth Burch, Serena Jones, Chris Cowan, Bill and Gail Herald, and my trusted minister, Father John Harmon.

My brother and sister, Roger and Elena, are lifelong treasures. My in-laws are always surrounding me with love: Scooter and Leathia West, Ginger Macomber, and Beat Jenny. Thanks to my cousins, Ligia, Gracie, Haroldo, Ricardo, Calito, Rilda, Armonia, Ruby, Linda. And much love to the next generation, Jonathan, Jonathan, Alexandria, Marisa, Ashely, Christopher, Paul, Chip, Omar, and Nadia.

And I am eternally grateful for my core—beginning with my loving wife, Delise. You put up with a lot and I know it.

Thanks to my children for being so loving—Antonio, Regan, Raffi, son-in-law Patrick, and the joyful one—my grandson, Elias West Herald. God Bless.

INDEX